I0812999

IMAGES
of America

OKLAHOMA CITY REDISCOVERED

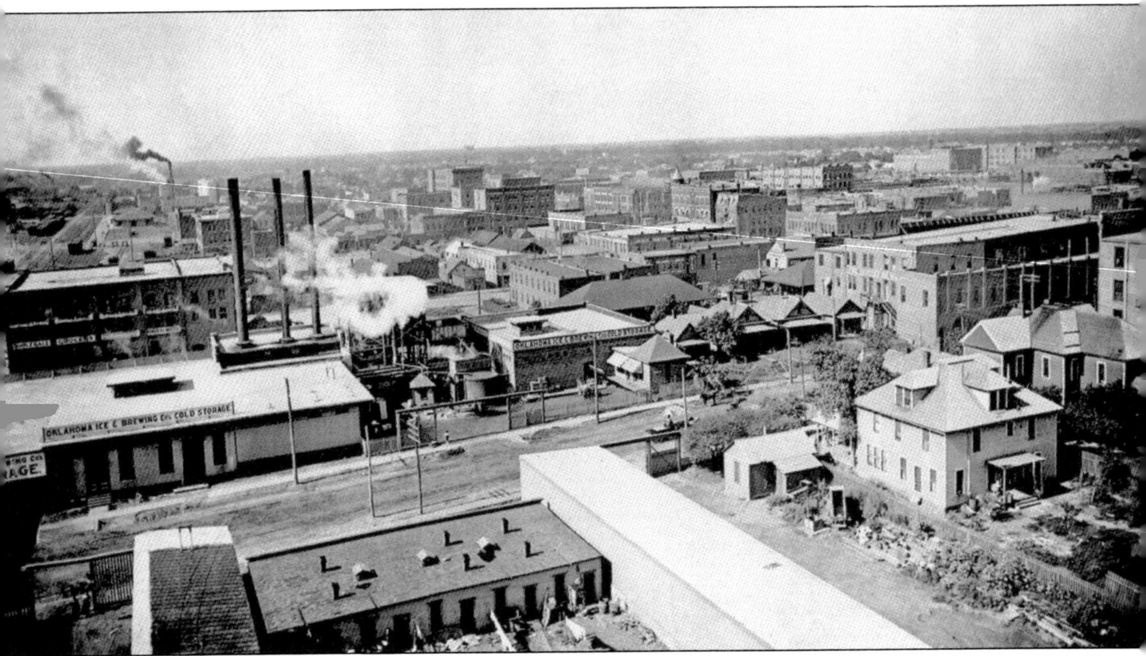

This view of the warehouse district taken in 1905 is one of the earliest known photographs of what would later become Bricktown. Just beyond the three smokestacks is the central business district of Oklahoma City. This image was taken by journalist Fred Barde, a reporter for the *Kansas City Star* who was assigned to cover the emerging new territory of Oklahoma on the verge of statehood. (Courtesy Oklahoma Historical Society.)

On the cover: By the late 1920s, Oklahoma City was booming largely due to oil production in the state and the newly discovered field just south of Capitol Hill. Downtown Oklahoma City was awash with newfound wealth, bringing with it a robust economy. At the intersection of West Main Street and Broadway, seen here, is the Bassett Block Building. Note the latest model of Buick automobile on the billboard on top. This image was photographed by Zenias P. Meyers, who was one of Oklahoma City's premier photographers for over 45 years. (Courtesy Oklahoma Historical Society.)

IMAGES
of America

OKLAHOMA CITY REDISCOVERED

William D. Welge

ARCADIA
PUBLISHING

Copyright © 2007 by William D. Welge
ISBN 978-0-7385-5149-4

Published by Arcadia Publishing
Charleston, South Carolina

Printed in the United States of America

Library of Congress Catalog Card Number: 2007921381

For all general information contact Arcadia Publishing at:
Telephone 843-853-2070
Fax 843-853-0044
E-mail sales@arcadiapublishing.com
For customer service and orders:
Toll-Free 1-888-313-2665

Visit us on the Internet at www.arcadiapublishing.com

To Martha Royce Blaine and Mary Moran,
I shall always be grateful for your friendship.

Contents

ACKNOWLEDGMENTS

There are several individuals who I would like to thank for the many contributions of photographs, time, and talent without which this work would not be possible. I am in debt to Anita Arnold, executive director of Black Liberated Arts Center for providing important images and history of Deep Deuce and the contacts that she pointed me to that enabled me to locate a rich array of persons to include within these pages. David Sellers, editor and publisher of the *Capitol Hill Beacon*, opened his files of photographs and early history that vividly depicted the development of south Oklahoma City. Ann Amme, owner of the Red Stone Inn Bed and Breakfast, allowed access to unpublished photographs and family history of Dr. Wyatt Slaughter for which I am grateful. I also wish to thank Leroy Parks for his memories of Deep Deuce and Gerald Harris for his information regarding his grandfather William T. Vivette. The folks at Nonna's, Avis, and Darla were very helpful with providing key information about their historic building, also Rand Elliott of Elliott and Associates for vital documentation about the Heierding Building. I wish to thank Larry and Beth Schwartz for providing personal family photographs; Dr. Bob L. Blackburn, executive director of the Oklahoma Historical Society; Laura Martin, Jennifer Towry, and Francie Helm of the Oklahoma Historical Society Research Library for their efforts toward this project; and Jim Gabbert of the state historic preservation office for providing access to important records relating to Deep Deuce, Bricktown, and Automobile Alley. I sincerely appreciate Chester Cowen, photographic archivist of the Oklahoma Historical Society, relying on his vast institutional memory of the collections to make available many photographs not published before and his extremely helpful assistant Kathy Gibbs who made countless searches for images located in obscure collections. I deeply appreciate Jaymie Lang for perusing the multitude of images, seeking out examples that would engage the reader, and providing a rich scenic pictorial history. And lastly, I want to thank Rachel Mosman for her passion for the project, her willingness to go the extra mile to bring out the richness of the images as the photographer had intended, for without her the project would not be possible.

INTRODUCTION

Oklahoma City quite literally was created in one day. On Monday at high noon April 22, 1889, with the roar of cannon and pistol fire, home seekers from all over the United States and beyond made a mad dash to stake a claim in the hard packed virgin prairie soil that would become home. They made the "Run of 1889" by foot, speedy horse, by buggy or bicycle, if you can imagine, and by railroad, all for the chance for a new life in what would one day become Oklahoma.

Oklahoma City is located on what is known as the Osage Plains, which is an extension of the central lowlands region of the United States. The topography of the area can be described as level, fertile land with sufficient rainfall to aid in crop production, and at an elevation of 1,214 feet above sea level it was considered by the Santa Fe railroad as suitable for town site development.

Almost in the center of the unassigned lands was a rail stop known as Oklahoma Station. There the Santa Fe railroad had built a station along with water tank and a few outbuildings in 1887. Within minutes after the signal had created this surge of humanity, workers from the Santa Fe, most notably William L. Couch, stepped off the station platform and staked a claim, a claim that would be contested for several years.

By nightfall, some 5,000 to 7,000 persons occupied land near the Santa Fe depot. A tent city stretching as far as the eye could see. Within days of the opening, wooden structures were replacing canvas and all manner of business enterprise began to take root as well as houses of worship. Another aspect of the new town was the lack of authorization to organize a municipal government. These enterprising pioneers did not let that hinder their efforts, so a provisional government was formed with Couch elected as the first mayor.

Within its first year as a town, brick structures were appearing. The rival city of Guthrie, the territorial capital, was losing citizens to the more progressive Oklahoma City, and according to the *Daily Times-Journal* published in Oklahoma City, "brick frontage was double that of Guthrie." By 1894, Guthrie had a slight edge in population, but Oklahoma City had far more business structures and material wealth. By the mid-1890s, Oklahoma City was becoming a metropolitan wholesale and manufacturing center. With the addition of the Choctaw, Oklahoma and Gulf Railroad (later the Rock Island) in 1895, the city now had an east–west route to the Santa Fe's north–south system. Although initially the additional railway caused a recession, certain city leaders pushed forward to the point that within a decade the city would have six railroads bisecting the community, making it the distribution center of Oklahoma Territory.

Two sectors of the growing city would trace their roots to the end of the 19th century, first the manufacturing district (later to be dubbed Bricktown) and second the suburb of Capitol Hill would be founded a mile south of the main business district of Oklahoma City.

Deep Deuce would come of age with the rise of blues and jazz music during the 1920s, developing a central business district east of downtown for the growing African American population of Oklahoma City.

With the advent of the horseless carriage a new mode of transportation was created. By 1910, several commercial automobile dealers set up business along Broadway, north of Fifth Street. Broadway, with a 100-foot right-of-way, was platted as the widest north–south street in the original 1889 town site plat.

Each of these sectors of the vibrant community has had a unique development and positive contribution to the history of Oklahoma City.

One

Oklahoma City on the Rise

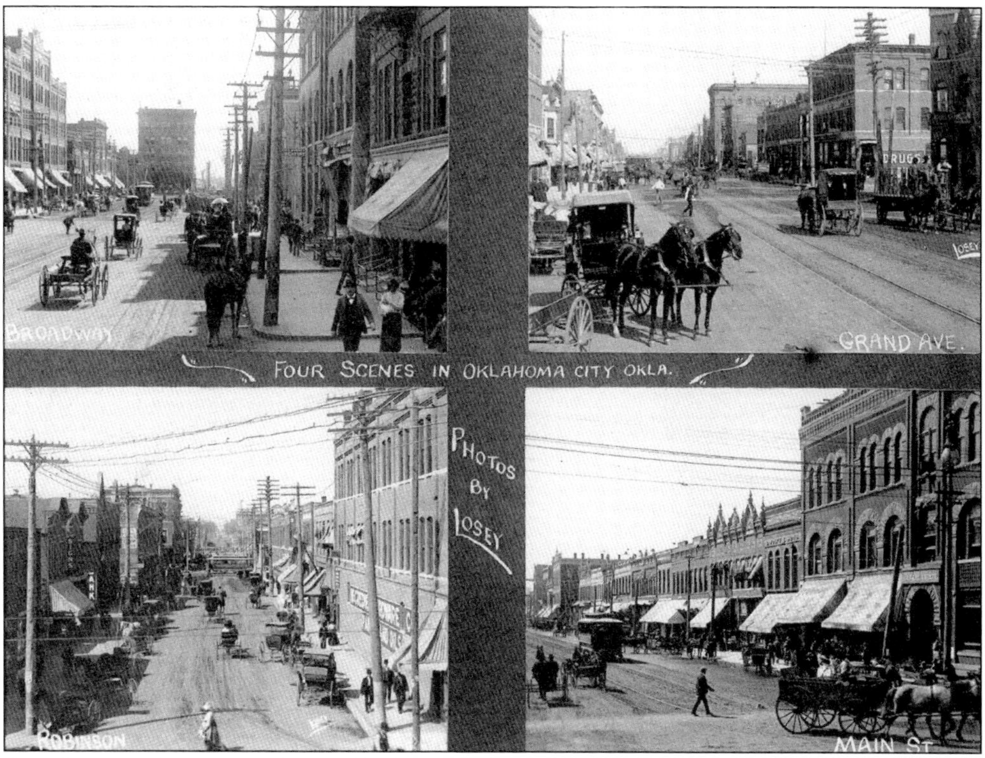

Seen here are four views of early Oklahoma City showing Broadway, Grand Avenue, Robinson Street, and Main Street as they appeared in 1898. Taken by portrait photographer North Losey, one gets a sense of the energy of a rapidly growing city that one day will become the capital of a great state. Each photograph displays rich architecture and a diverse community as they enter into the 20th century. (Courtesy Oklahoma Historical Society.)

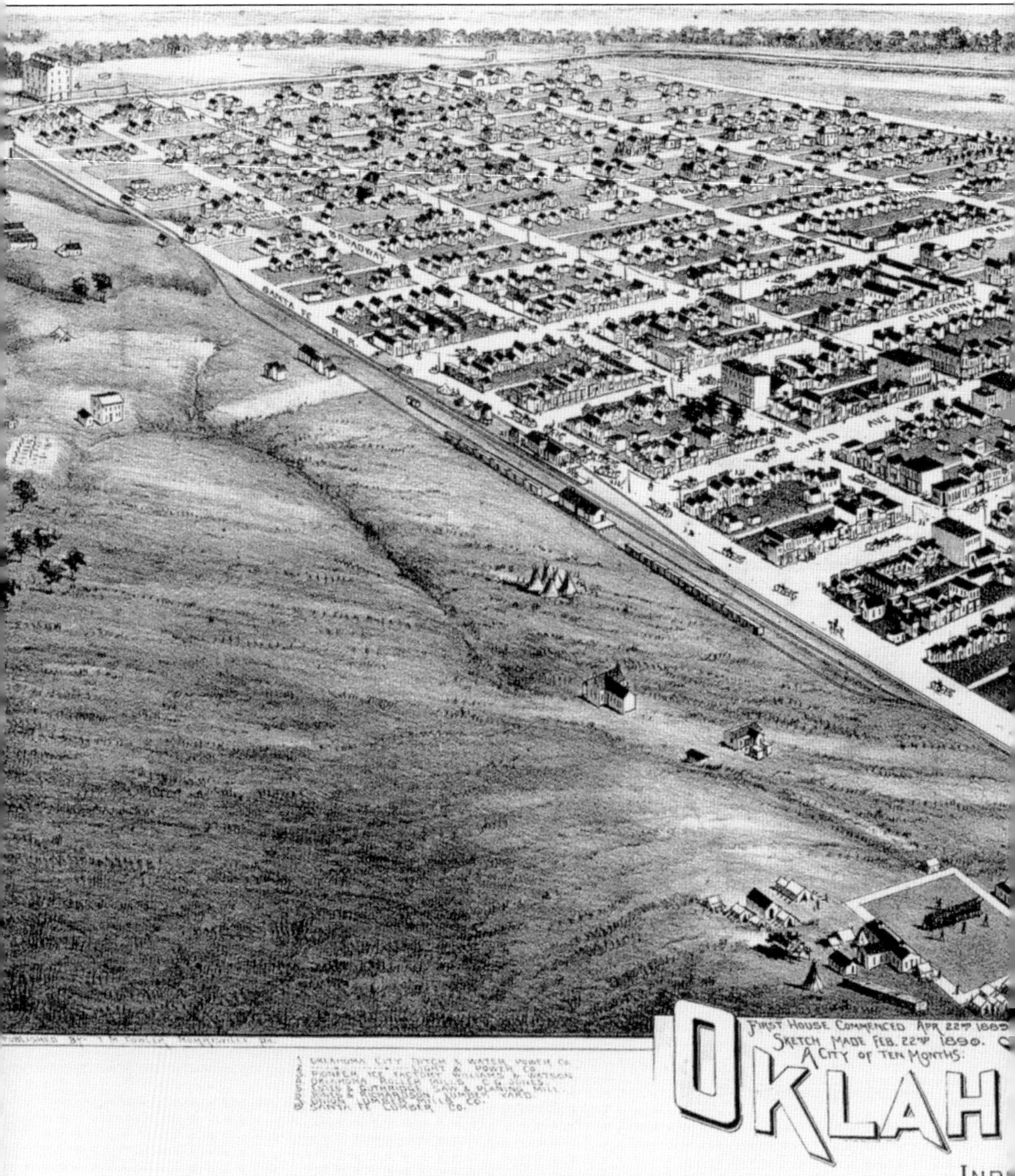

This bird's-eye view of Oklahoma City is looking to the west–southwest and dates from February 1890. Sketched some 10 months after the land run, this view incorporates all the sectors that will develop in or near the city. If one looks closely in the distance, beyond the tree line along the North Canadian River, one can see a slight rise on the horizon. That rise is where Capitol Hill will be located soon after 1900. At the top left is a two-story structure near the Santa Fe tracks. That building begins the nucleus of the warehouse district that will play a very prominent role in the city during the last decade of the 20th century. East of the railroad depot is the future

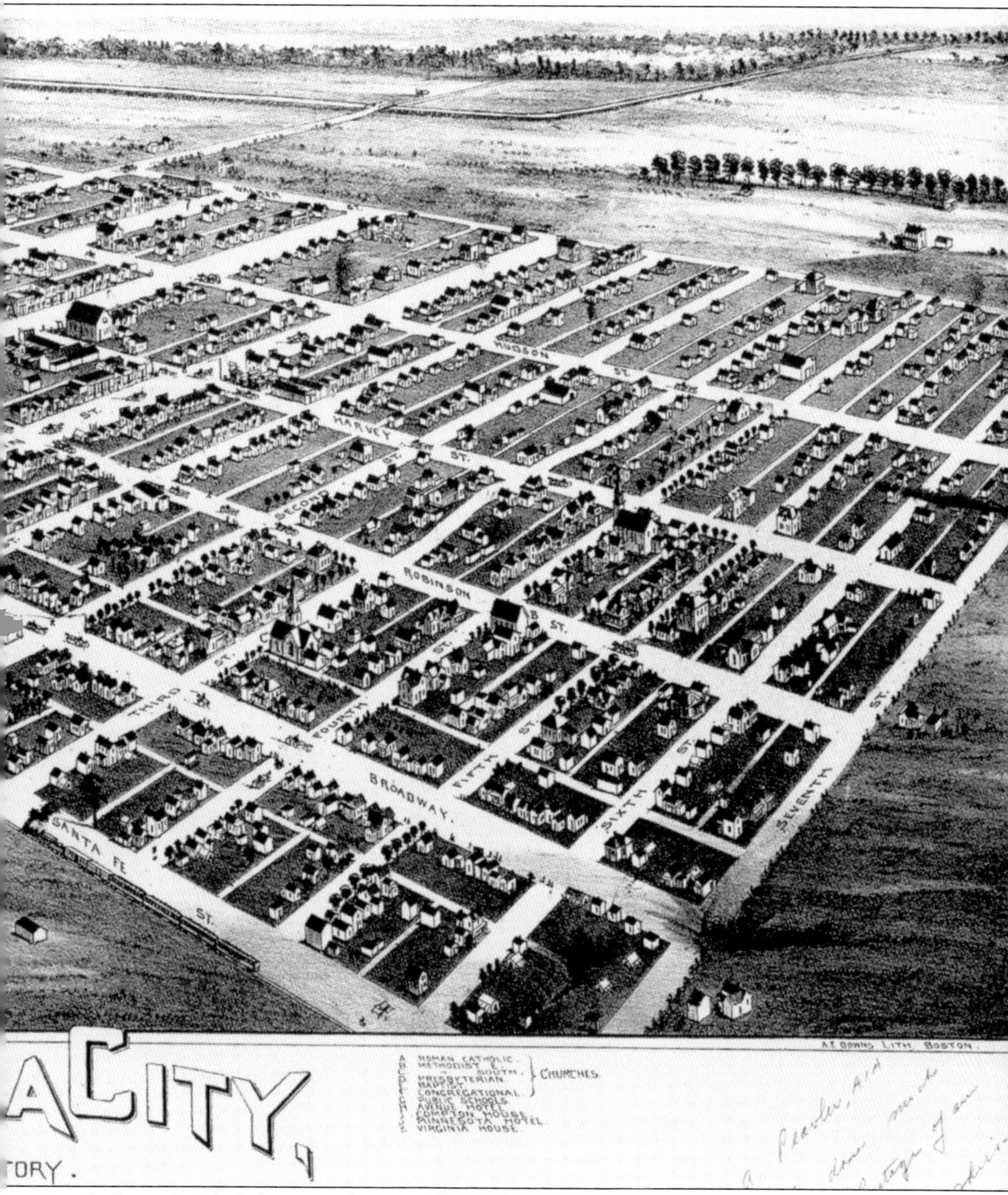

site of where the black business district will develop. In 1890, most African Americans lived at the south edge of town near the North Canadian River. It would be 20-plus years before African Americans would be able to settle in the Deep Deuce area. Broadway in 1890 extended as far north as Seventh Street. It would be another 15 or 20 years before businesses related to the automobile industry would begin to locate on this busy thoroughfare. (Courtesy Oklahoma Historical Society.)

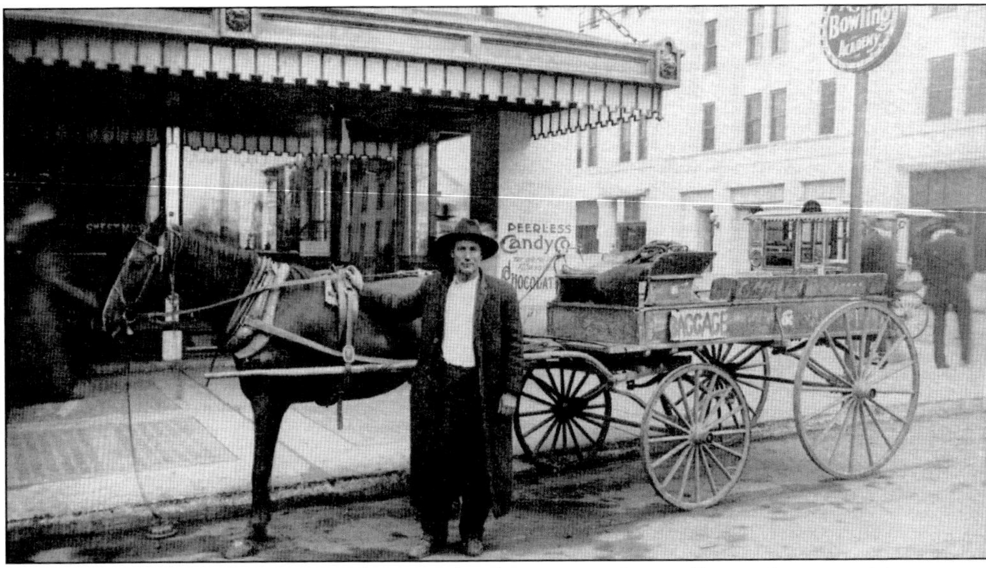

Statehood brought many new residents to the future capital city. One such enterprising person was James Avery Holton. Holton, a native of Texas, was born in 1868 and migrated to Oklahoma in 1906. He started the Oklahoma Baggage Company in 1908 with a horse and wagon. Seen here parked across the street from the Pioneer Telephone Company, located at Third Street and North Broadway, Holton did a lively business transporting telephone workers with their heavy tools to wherever they needed to perform repair and maintenance jobs. Three generations operated the Holton Transport Company until it was sold in 1981. The founder, seen in this photograph, passed away in 1936. Holton's grandson Jack donated this image to the Oklahoma Historical Society in 2000. (Courtesy Oklahoma Historical Society.)

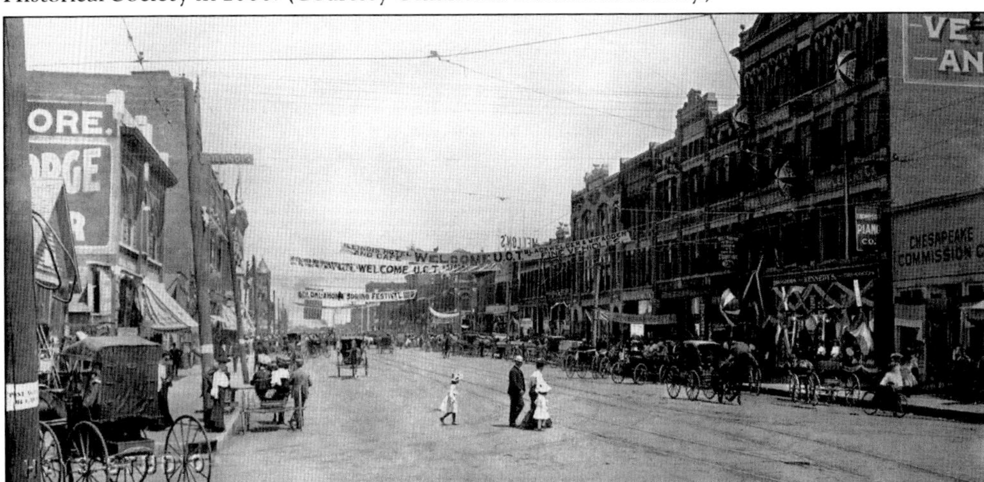

This early image of downtown was taken around 1908 by the Hays Studio of Shamrock, Texas, showing Main Street looking east toward the warehouse district. Many of these buildings survived until urban renewal demolished all but one of the structures in the early 1970s. The last pre-statehood building, dating from 1906, was located at 34 West Main Street. It was torn down to make room for the Renaissance Hotel in early 2000. This image was reproduced by freelance photographer Bob Duncan, whose career spanned from 1954 to 1985. (Courtesy Oklahoma Historical Society.)

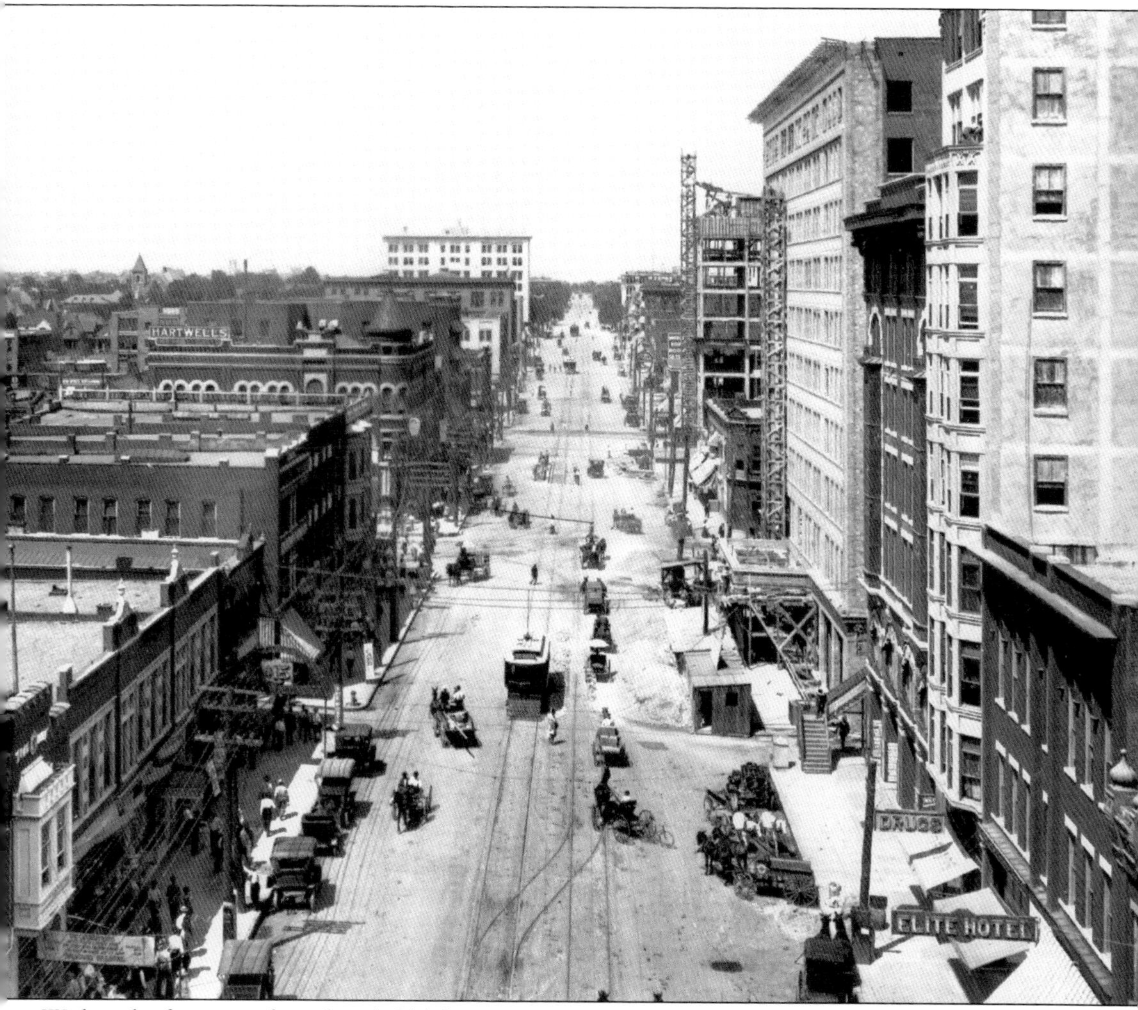

Within the first year of statehood, Oklahoma City was rapidly growing. In 1907, the population of the city that included Capitol Hill and outlying suburbs exceeded 45,000 persons. Building permits for the first six months of 1907 included 462 residences and some 57 businesses totaling more than $1,669,930. In 1908, the construction boom continued. This image of Broadway, looking north from Grand Avenue, shows the final stages of the Huckins Hotel under construction. Located at 20 North Broadway, the Lee-Huckins would serve a historic role in early statehood politics once Oklahoma City became the state capital in 1910. (Courtesy Oklahoma Historical Society.)

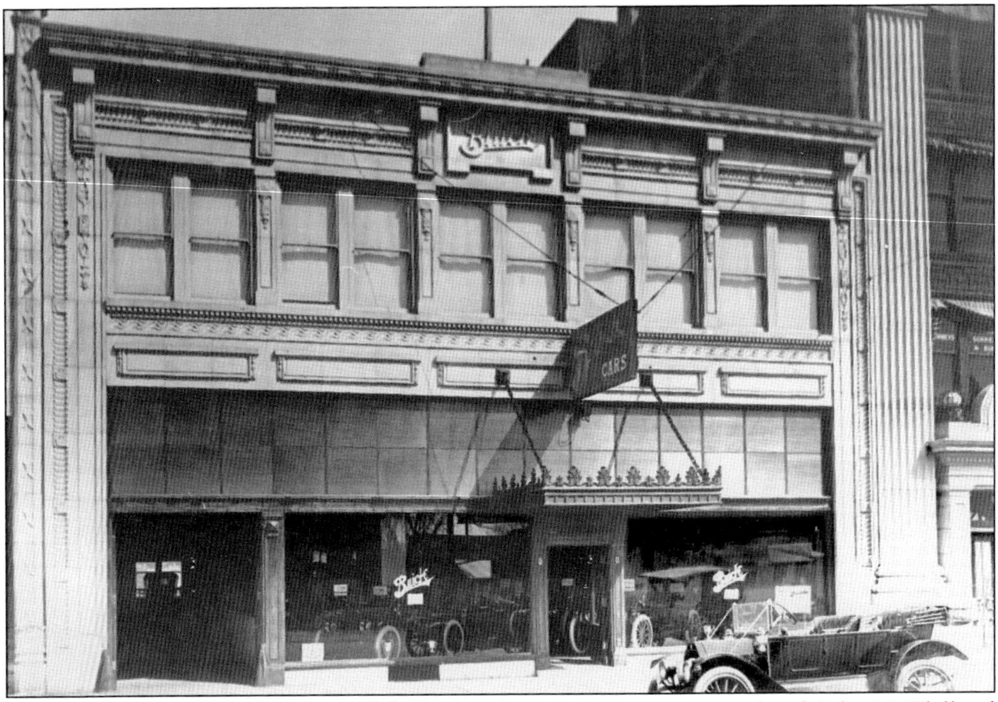

In 1910, the first Oklahoma Automobile Dealers Association was organized with John McClelland as president. One such dealership was Buick, located at 504 North Broadway. The building is a two-story stone classical revival–style structure. At the time Z. P. Meyers took this photograph, W. H. Vesper was the treasurer of the dealership. The Buick building is one of the principle structures that comprises the Automobile Alley Historic District found on the National Register of Historic Places. (Courtesy Oklahoma Historical Society.)

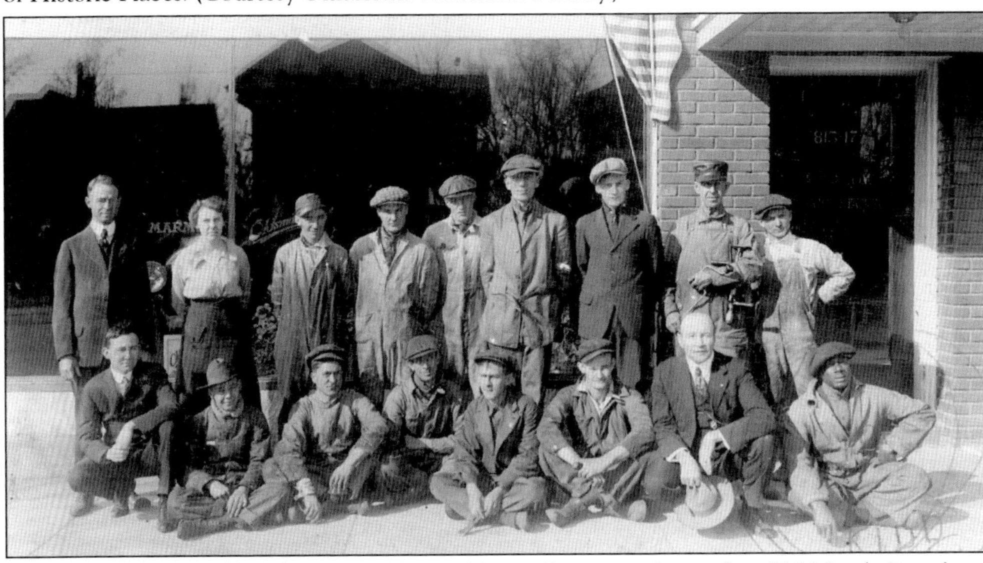

Sales and service staff of the W. C. Norris Motor Company, located at 815 North Broadway, posed for this photograph in 1918. The company was the state distributor for Oldsmobile and Marmon automobiles plus "Judge" Gary and Diamond T trucks. Bert Estes (perhaps standing far left) was manager of the company. (Courtesy Oklahoma Historical Society.)

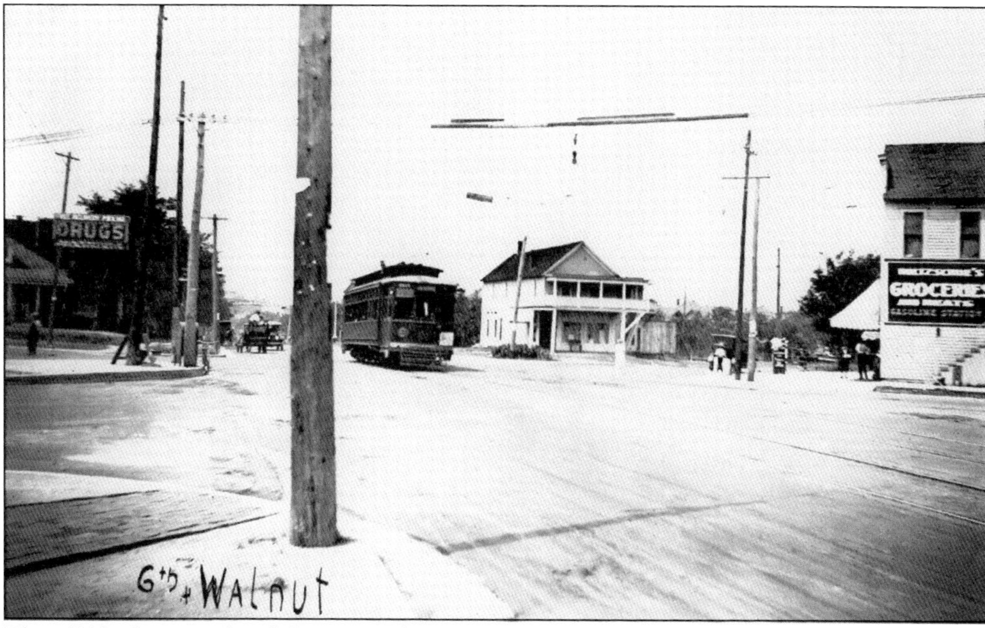

This 1915 photograph of the interurban coursing its way from Northeast Sixth Street and Walnut Avenue was a common scene. As the city grew, more urban dwellers would use this means of transportation. In 1906, the electric rail system carried over three and a half million passengers, in a time before the automobile began to dominate as a means of travel. (Courtesy Oklahoma Historical Society.)

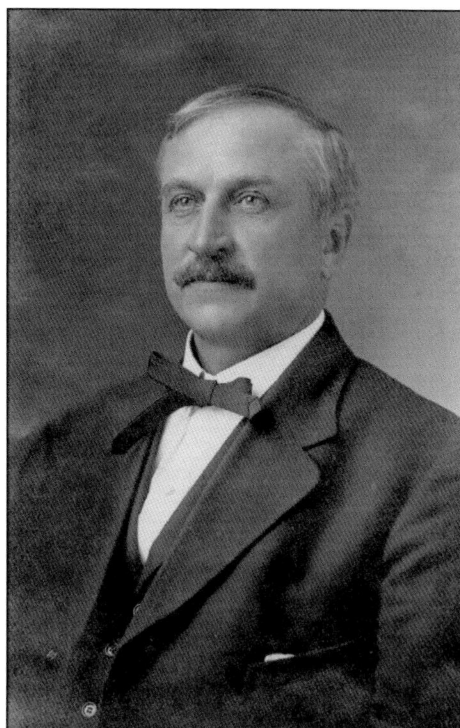

Businessman Anton Classen, along with entrepreneur John Shartel, was the principle promoter of a mass transit system in Oklahoma City. Classen, who was also involved with real estate interests, determined where the interurban routes would run, much to the advantage of his real estate ventures. Classen is seen here around 1915, as featured in *Sturm's Oklahoma Magazine*. (Courtesy Oklahoma Historical Society.)

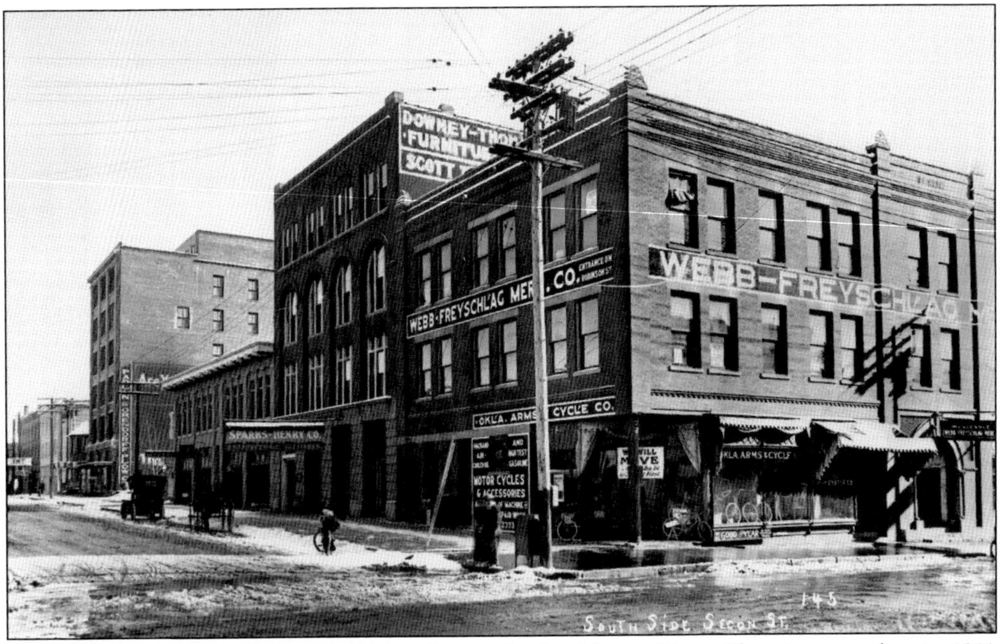

One block west of Broadway is Robinson Street. In this Meyers Photo Shop image, taken in 1911 at the corner of Robinson and Second Streets, is the Oklahoma Arms and Cycle Company at 224 North Robinson Street. It specialized in motorcycles, bicycles, and related supplies. Bert and H. L. Strough were the owners of the company. (Courtesy Oklahoma Historical Society.)

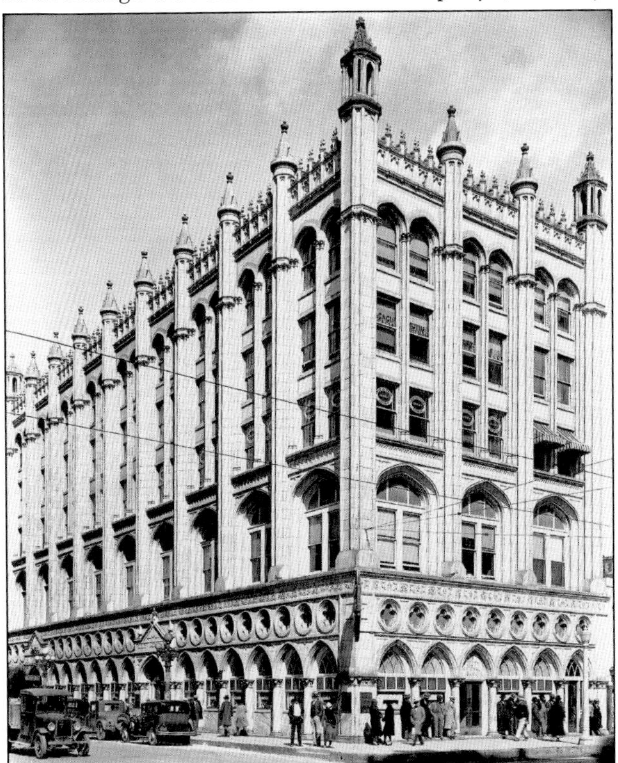

One block south on Robinson Street was the ornate Baum Building on the northeast corner of Grand Avenue and Robinson Street. Built in 1909 and completed by 1910, it was patterned after the Doges Palace in Venice, Italy. It symbolized the growing economic boom after Oklahoma became a state. However, by the late 1960s, its fate was sealed with urban renewal as it was destroyed. Two of the cupolas have been preserved, one by the State Historical Society, the other by the Oklahoma City/County Historical Society. (Courtesy Oklahoma Historical Society.)

Two

Broadway Before World War II

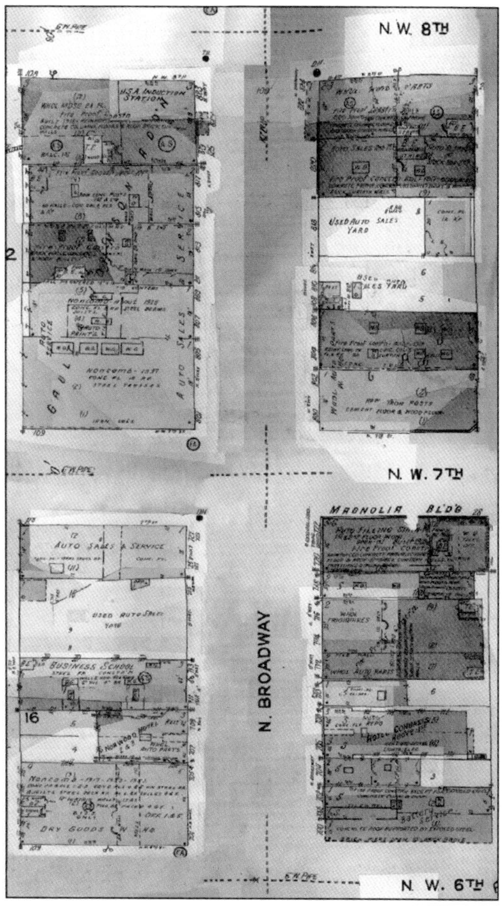

This map between Northwest Fifth Street and Northwest Eighth Street and Broadway amplifies the designation of Automobile Alley. Taken from a 1922 Sanborn Map, one can see the many related businesses tied to the automobile industry besides dealerships. Included will be battery sales, wholesale parts stores, service stations, and automobile repair shops. (Courtesy Oklahoma Historical Society.)

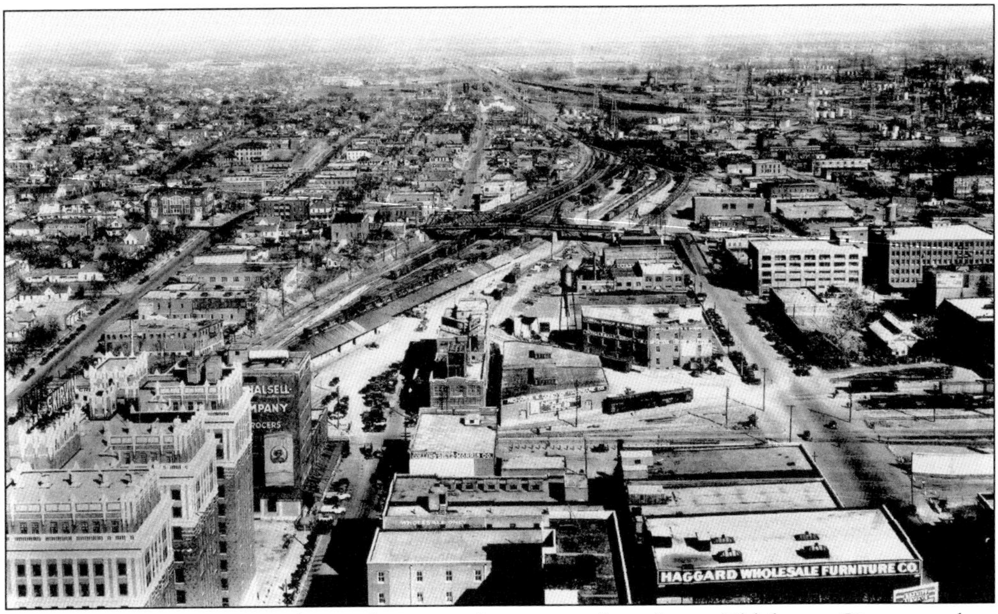

This aerial view of the warehouse district and portions of northeast Oklahoma City was taken around 1913. The Skirvin Hotel is seen in the lower left-hand corner at 200 North Broadway. In the middle of the image is the Walnut Avenue Viaduct crossing over the Rock Island Railroad tracks. Just left of the viaduct is the Canton Hotel and Calvary Baptist Church. It was at Calvary that the peaceful marches would start in the late 1950s to end segregation in Oklahoma City. (Courtesy Oklahoma Historical Society.)

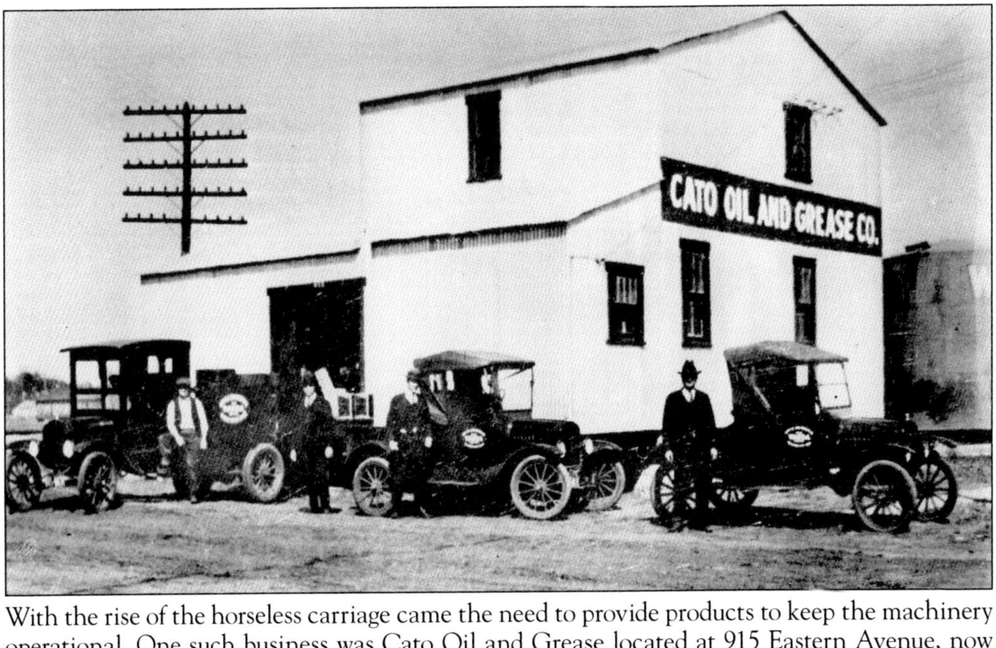

With the rise of the horseless carriage came the need to provide products to keep the machinery operational. One such business was Cato Oil and Grease located at 915 Eastern Avenue, now Martin Luther King Boulevard. The company was a subsidiary of Kerr McGee Corporation. Seen here are four members of the staff as photographed by Z. P. Meyers in the mid-1920s. (Courtesy Oklahoma Historical Society.)

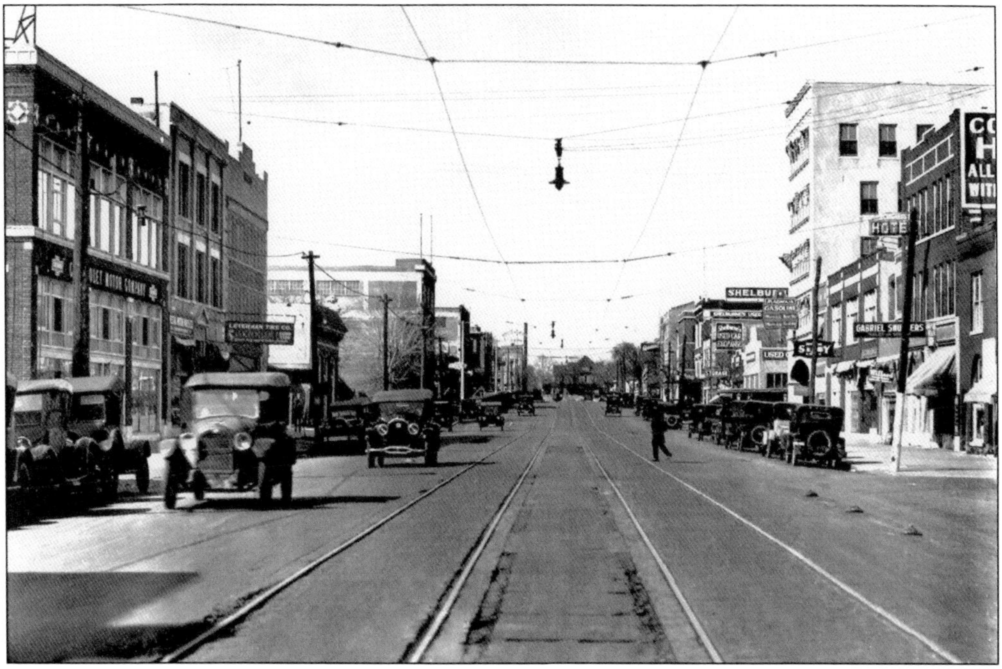

These two images depict both north and south views of Broadway taken by Meyers Photo Shop around the middle to late part of the second decade of the 20th century. The influence of the automobile is quite evident in this view looking north. Note the Chevrolet dealership on the left while on the right of the Magnolia Petroleum Building is Shelburne's Used Car lot. Although not taken from precisely the same spot, Meyers shot Broadway looking south with the Magnolia building on the left and the Pioneer Telephone Building located where the interurban is seen coming north. Note the rise of a new industry with the Atwater Kent Radio sign. Oklahoma City had the third licensed radio station in the United States, WKY in 1920. (Courtesy Oklahoma Historical Society.)

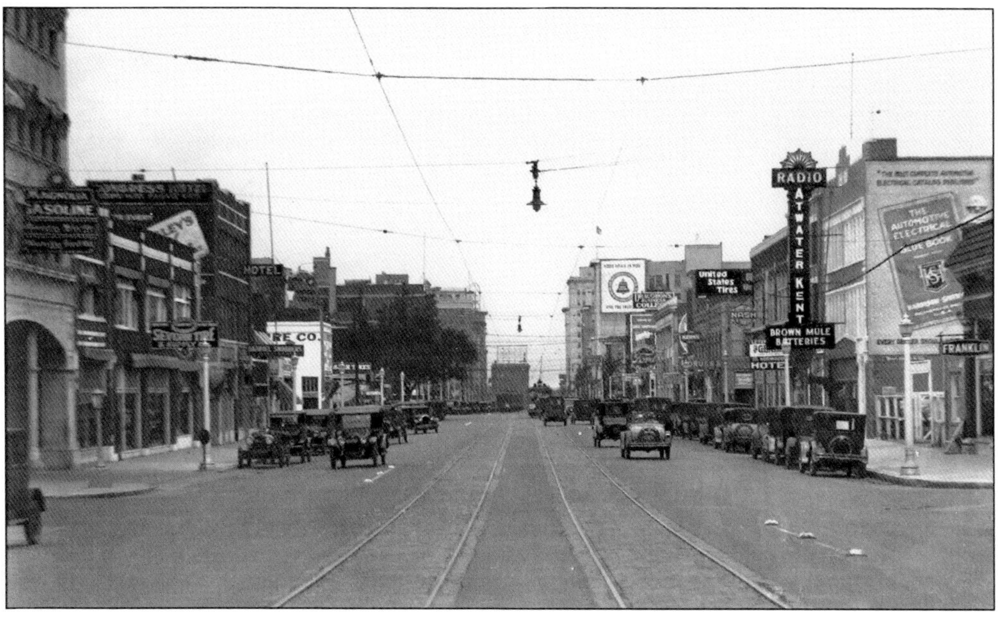

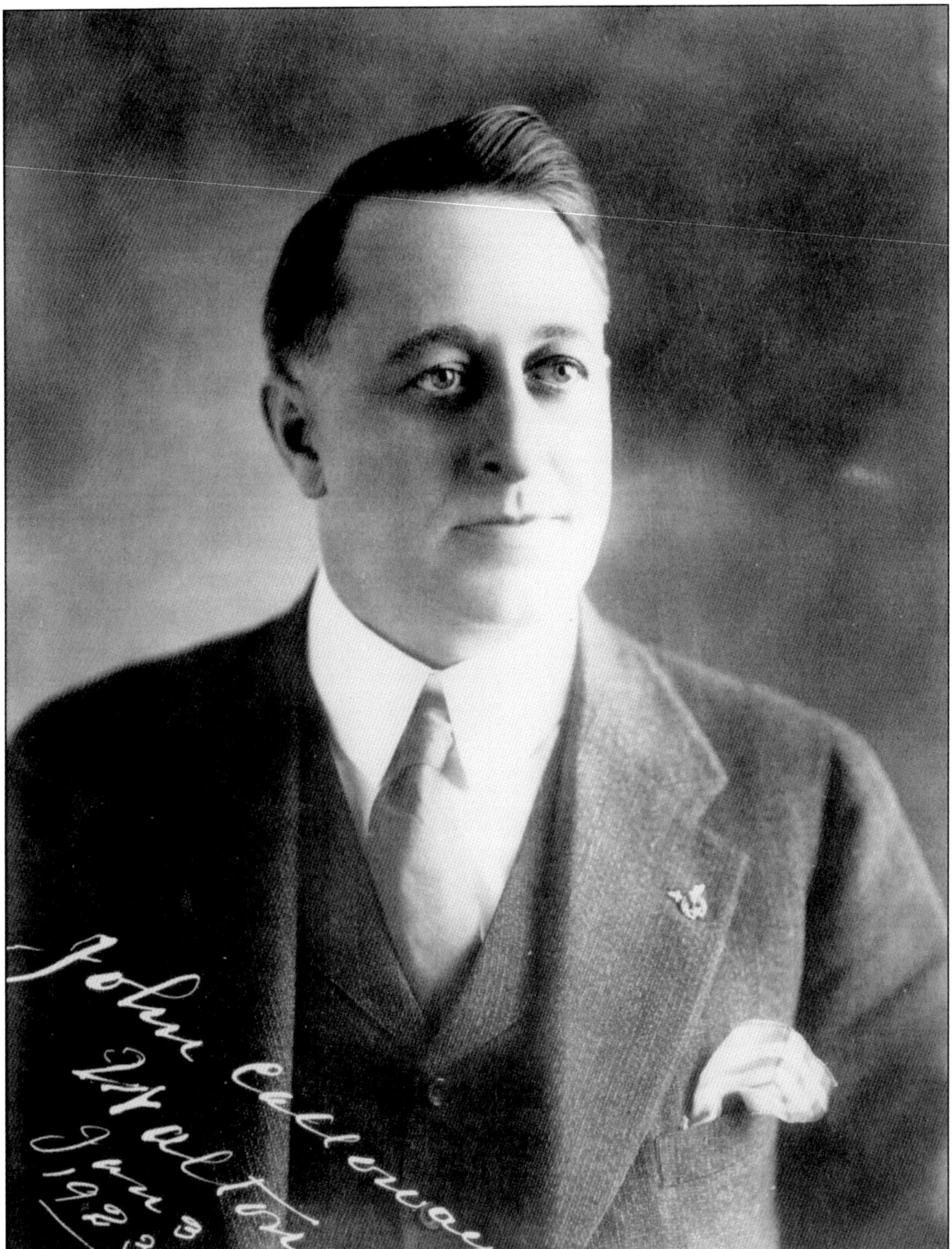

Oklahoma, and Oklahoma City in particular, felt the impact of the Great War. The boom experienced after statehood slowed as attention was redirected toward the war effort. After the armistice was concluded in 1918, the city saw rising prices on goods and services that further dampened economic prosperity. This depression continued through 1919. In April 1919, John C. Walton was elected mayor. One of the first measures he helped push through was to create a welfare board as unemployment reached acute levels. Walton later was elected governor of the state in 1921 only to be impeached in 1923. (Courtesy Oklahoma Historical Society.)

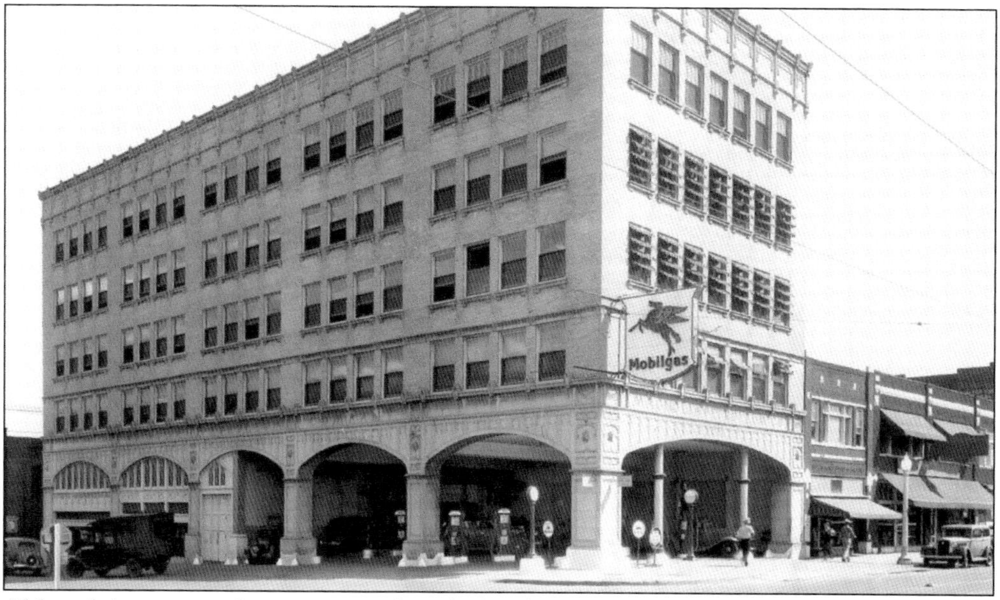

Although business and construction slowed after the war, it did not come to a complete halt. In 1919, the Magnolia Petroleum Building was built. Located at 722 North Broadway, this five-story structure was designed by the architects of Hawk and Parr using the Sullivanesque style of the late-19th- and early-20th-century American movement. Magnolia Petroleum was a major retail oil pipeline company from 1911 to 1925, when it was purchased by Mobil, now Exxon-Mobil. One of its unique features was the open drive-through service station on the ground level that continued to operate in that fashion until 1960. It was added to the National Register of Historic Places in 1979. (Courtesy of Oklahoma Historical Society.)

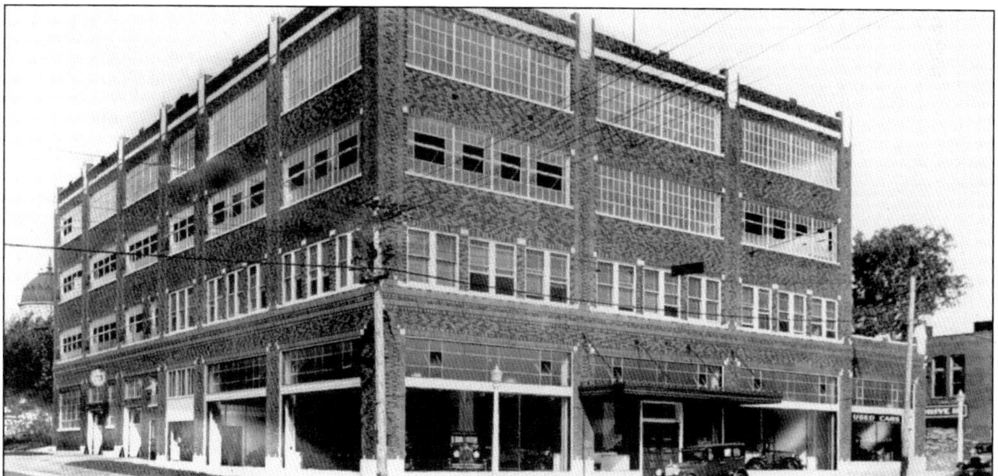

Eventually the economic malaise of late in the second decade of the 20th century and early 1920s gave way to the Roaring 20s. By 1926, the city was once again showing considerable increases in population, manufacturing, retail, and banking. In 1919, the city had some 117,963 persons compared to 149,616 in 1926. Seen here is the new Buick Motor Company building that was built in 1926. Located at 1101 North Broadway, it is typical of the brick commercial style with a flat roof and a parapet. This photograph was taken by Mitchell-Byfield Studios of Oklahoma City. (Courtesy Oklahoma Historical Society.)

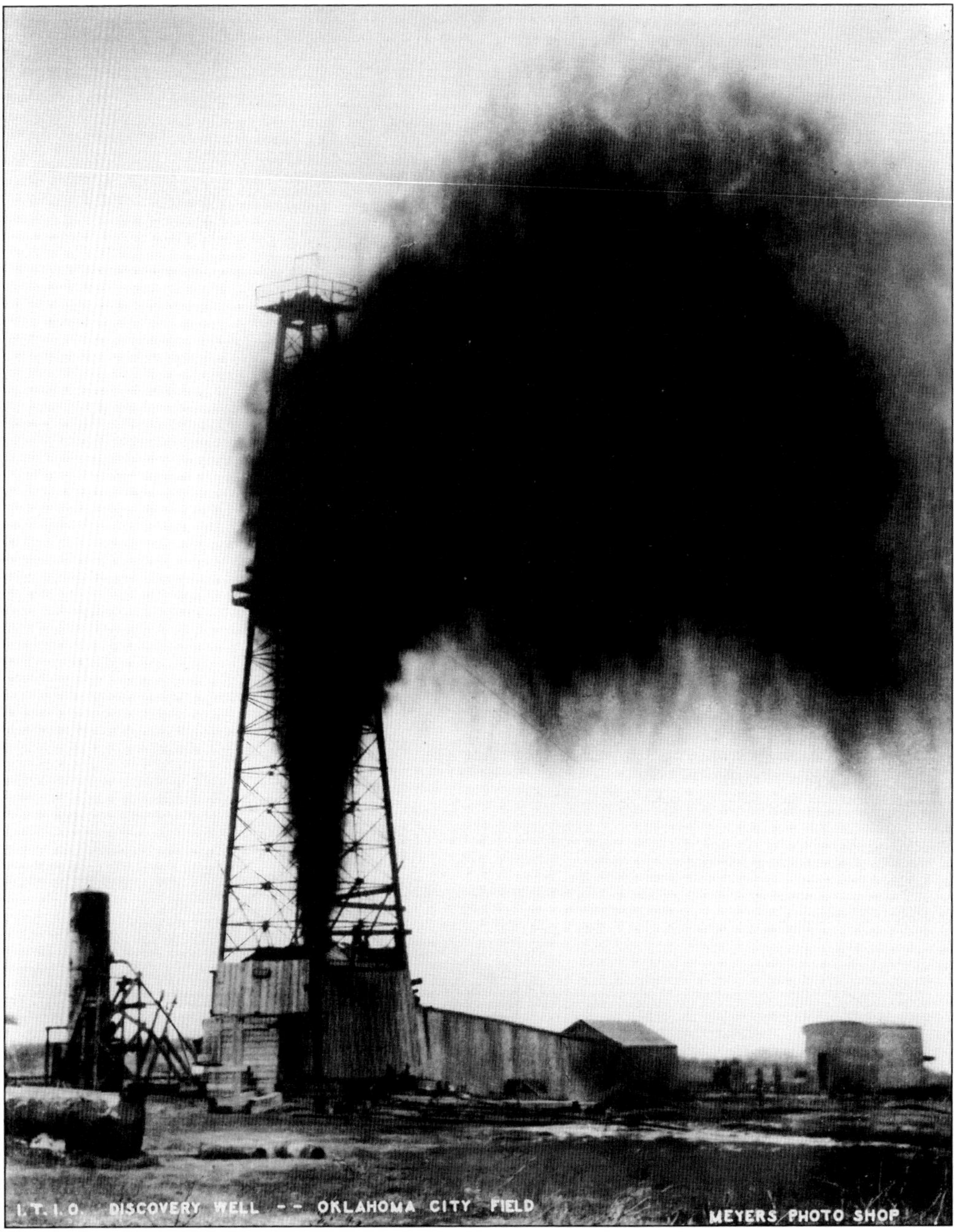

In December 1928, the economy of Oklahoma City would take a dramatic upward turn. The opening of the Oklahoma City field came "with a roar like thunder . . . black gold flowed," as it was reported in a local newspaper. The discovery well was owned by the Indian Territory Illuminating Oil Company with the site near present-day Southeast Fifty-ninth Street and Bryant Avenue. However, the euphoria over the new discovery would soon disappear as the Great Depression gripped the country and staggered the local economy. By 1932, the impact of the Depression caused oil consumption to slow just when production was at its peak. Prices tumbled below 15¢ a barrel. By 1935, production began to recover from the slump and the search for new discoveries began. (Courtesy Oklahoma Historical Society.)

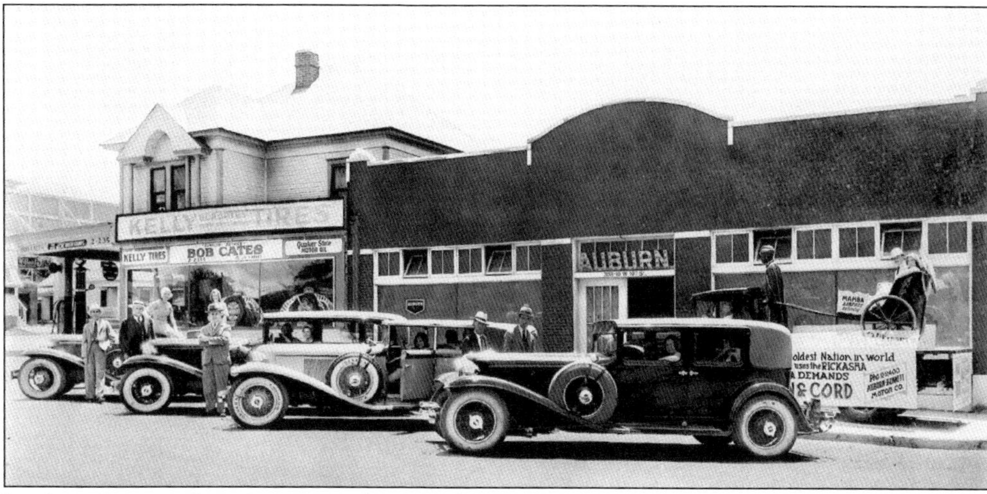

In this photograph, taken around 1930, the Great Depression had not hit Oklahoma City hard—yet. Here the Auburn dealership located at 308 West Tenth Street sold high-end automobiles to those individuals accustomed to luxury. This image is a Waterhouse print of Oklahoma City. (Courtesy Oklahoma Historical Society.)

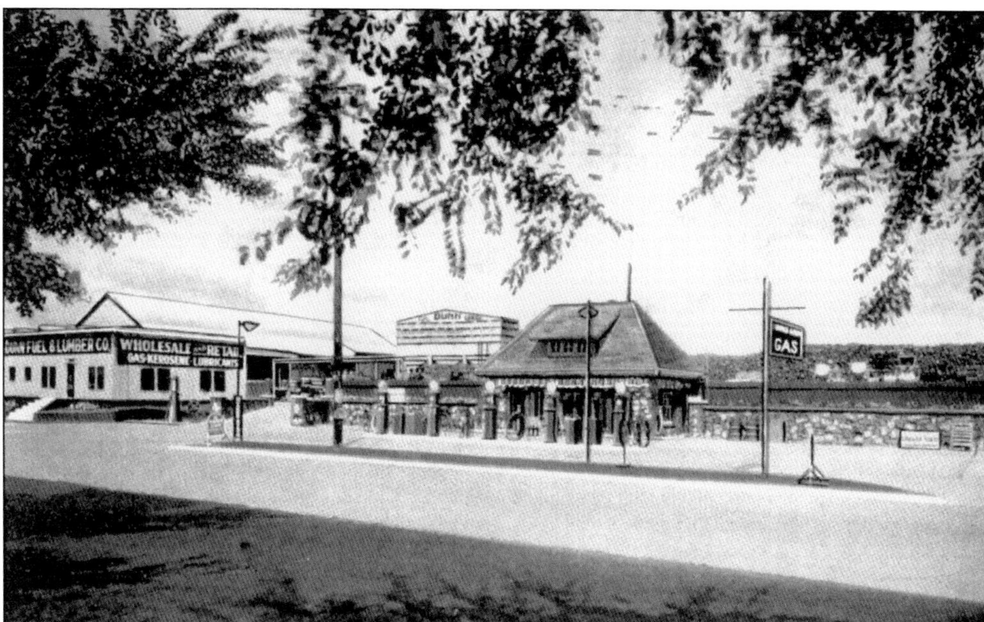

At the far north end of what would become Automobile Alley near Northwest Twenty-second Street and Broadway was Dunn's Service Station. With five pumps, it handled several grades of gasoline to meet customers' needs. Although no garage is evident, nonetheless, the customer could expect the service station attendant to fill the tank, wash the windows, and check the oil, radiator, and tire pressure. Haskell Pruett, a native of Mangum and professor at Oklahoma A. and M. College at Stillwater, took this image in October 1933. (Courtesy Oklahoma Historical Society.)

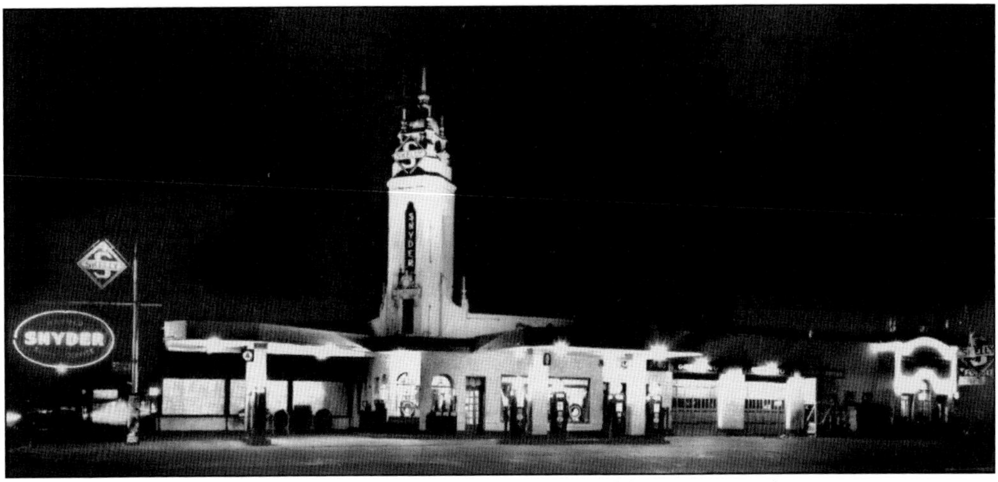

This full-service station could provide repair work in addition to regular customer service. Snyder's Super Service Station at 1325 North Broadway was owned by Harold H. Snyder. The Skelly brand of gasoline is native to Oklahoma as W. G. Skelly of Tulsa franchised his company across the state. This night view of the station was taken by photographer Ray Jacoby around 1937. (Courtesy Oklahoma Historical Society.)

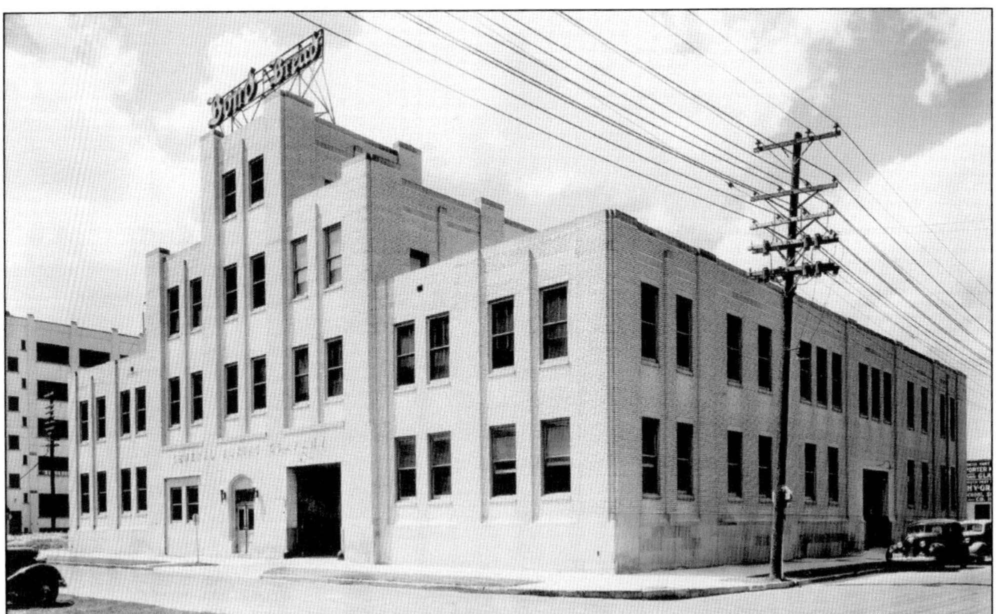

Just east off Broadway and Northeast Twelfth Street was the General Baking Company that produced the Bond Bread line of products. Within a mile north of this facility was the Rainbo Bread Company. Between the two bread manufacturers, not a sweeter aromatic scent could be found. This building still stands and now is a company that stores business records. This image is by commercial photographer Z. P. Meyers of Oklahoma City. (Courtesy of Oklahoma Historical Society.)

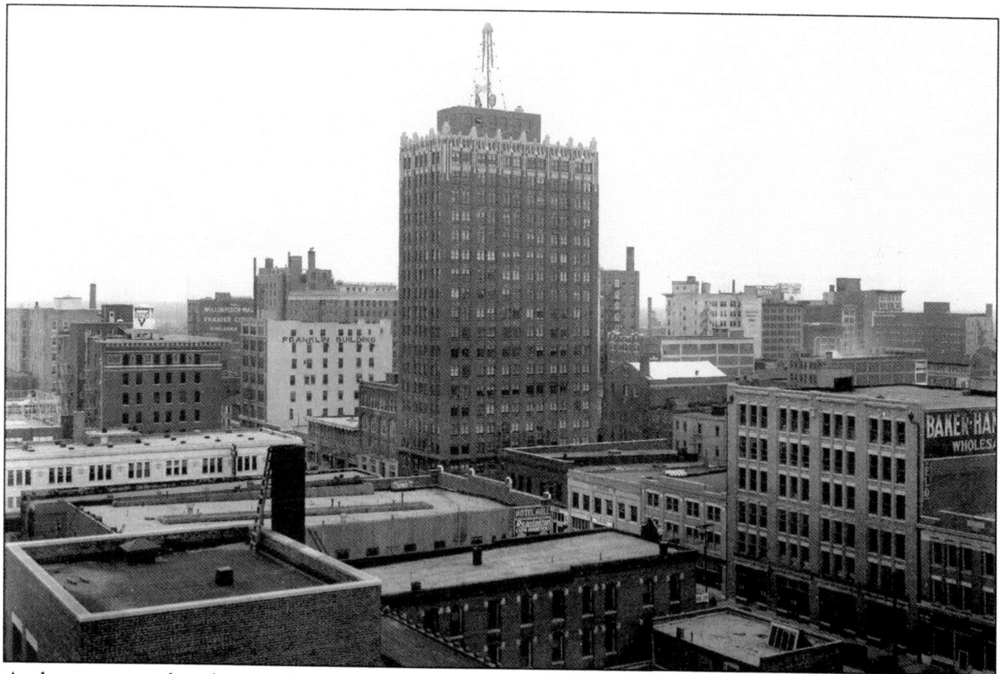

As business and industry slowly emerged from the depressed economic state, building permits began to increase. In 1937, some 2,169 permits were issued. The skyline of the city took on new heights with taller structures, such as the Ramsey Tower and the First National Bank. This image taken by Meyers Photo Shop is looking southeast from the 200 block of Northwest Second Street. (Courtesy Oklahoma Historical Society.)

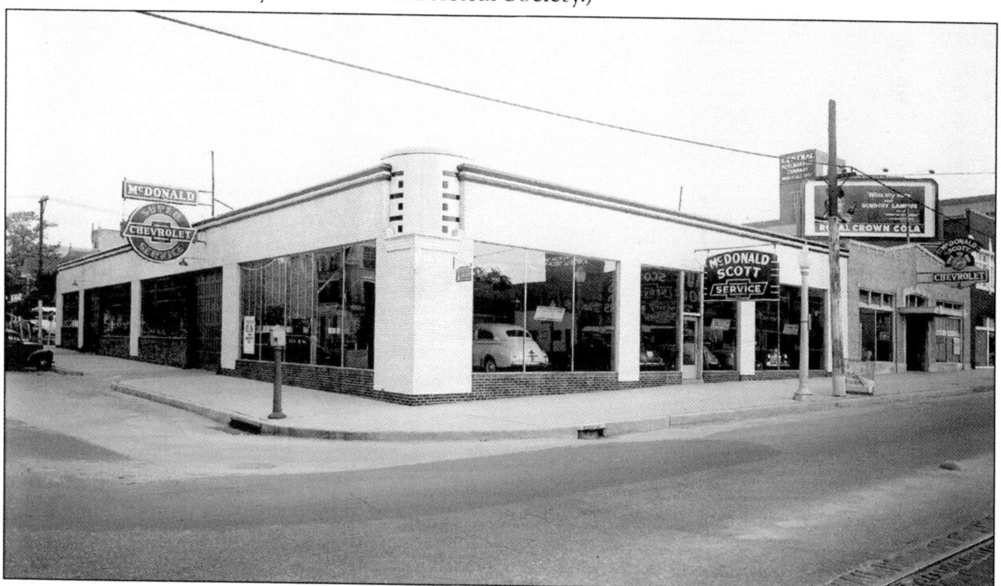

A longtime fixture in downtown Oklahoma City was McDonald Scott Chevrolet. Located at Northwest Seventh Street and Broadway, it remained in the downtown area long after other dealerships had moved to the outskirts of town. When Scott bought out McDonald, Scott's Chevrolet continued in the same location for many years. This 1940s image was taken by Z. P. Meyers of Oklahoma City. (Courtesy Oklahoma Historical Society.)

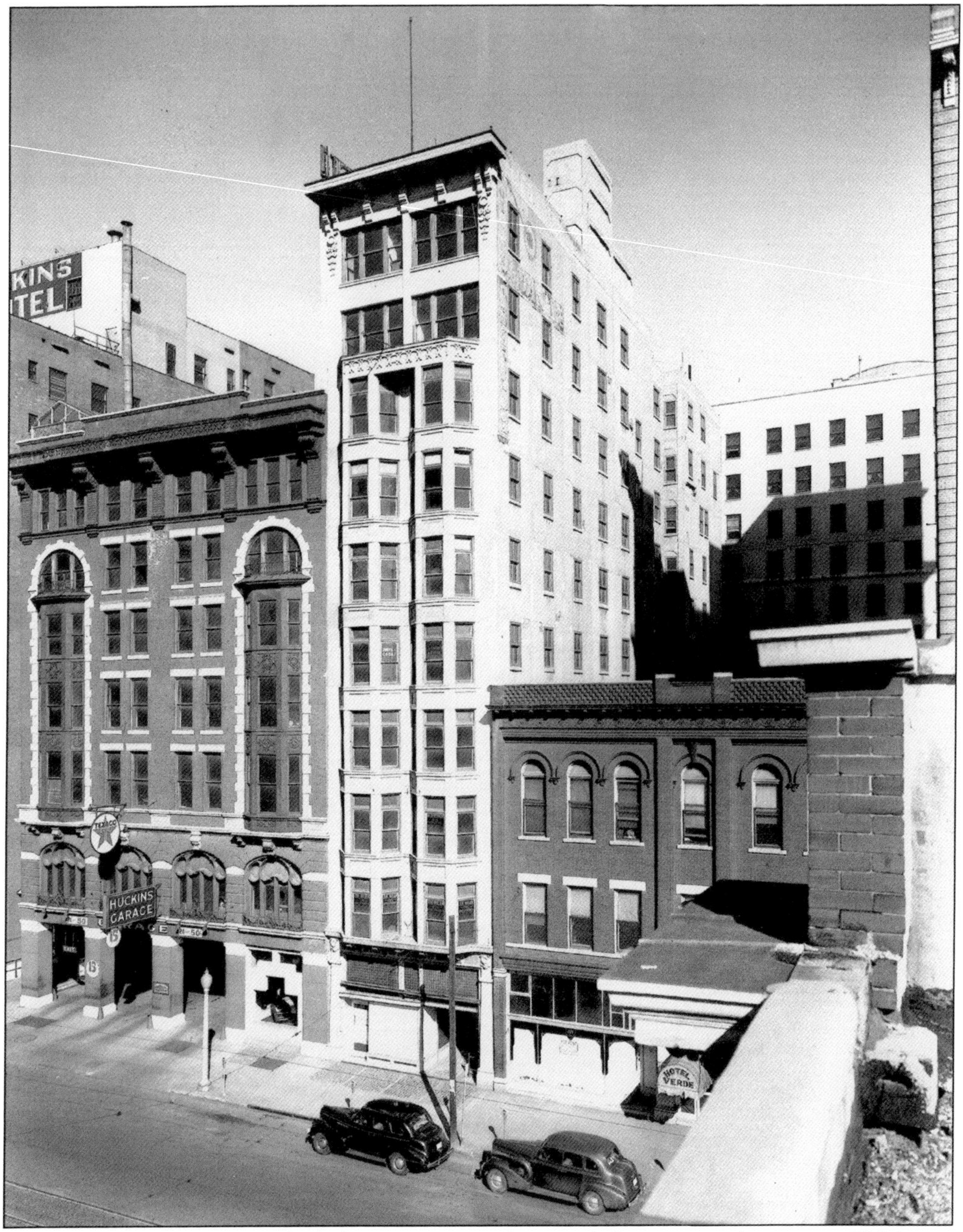

With more and more individuals buying cars, working and shopping in downtown Oklahoma City may have been more convenient, however, there were only so many parking spaces that could accommodate the growing number of automobiles. The innovation of parking garages solved at least part of the problem. The Huckins Garage, located adjacent to the hotel at 12 North Broadway, was photographed by Z. P. Meyers around the 1940s. (Courtesy Oklahoma Historical Society.)

Three

THE FOUNDING OF CAPITOL HILL

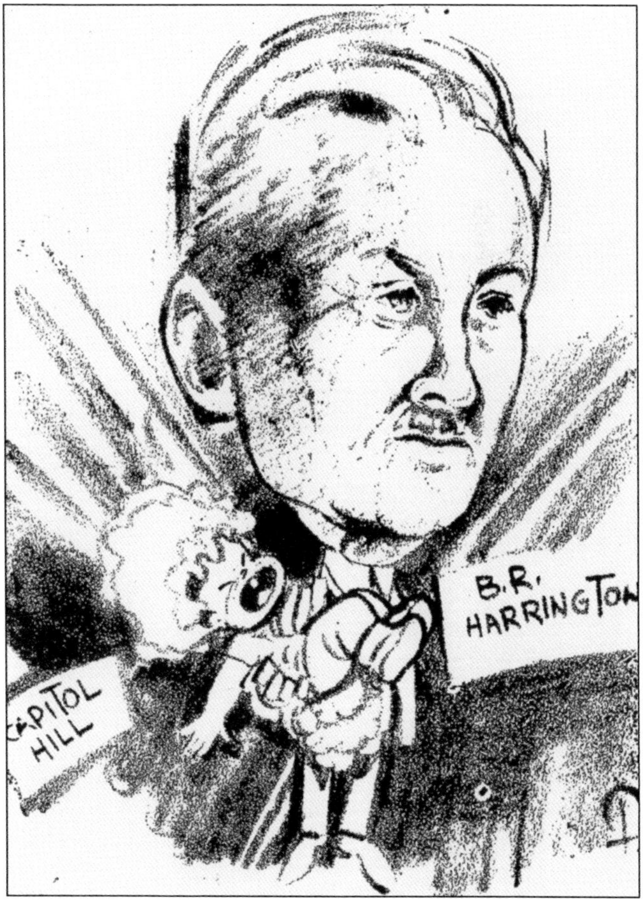

The history of Capitol Hill cannot be found in any of the standard histories of Oklahoma City or County. Yet its history is dynamic and has contributed to the overall growth of south Oklahoma City, as it would be eventually called. Capitol Hill was founded in 1905 but can trace its beginnings to Benoni R. Harrington, who purchased the land for the purpose of "giving sober and industrious mechanics an opportunity to secure homes." Harrington was a correspondent for the *Wichita Beacon* when he traveled through the Unassigned Lands in 1887. Harrington made the "Run of 1889" purchasing lots on California Avenue. Just three-quarters of a mile south of downtown Oklahoma City, Harrington purchased land that he saw as a possible future site for the seat of state government. This sketch is by Francis Noonan. (Courtesy Capitol Hill Beacon.)

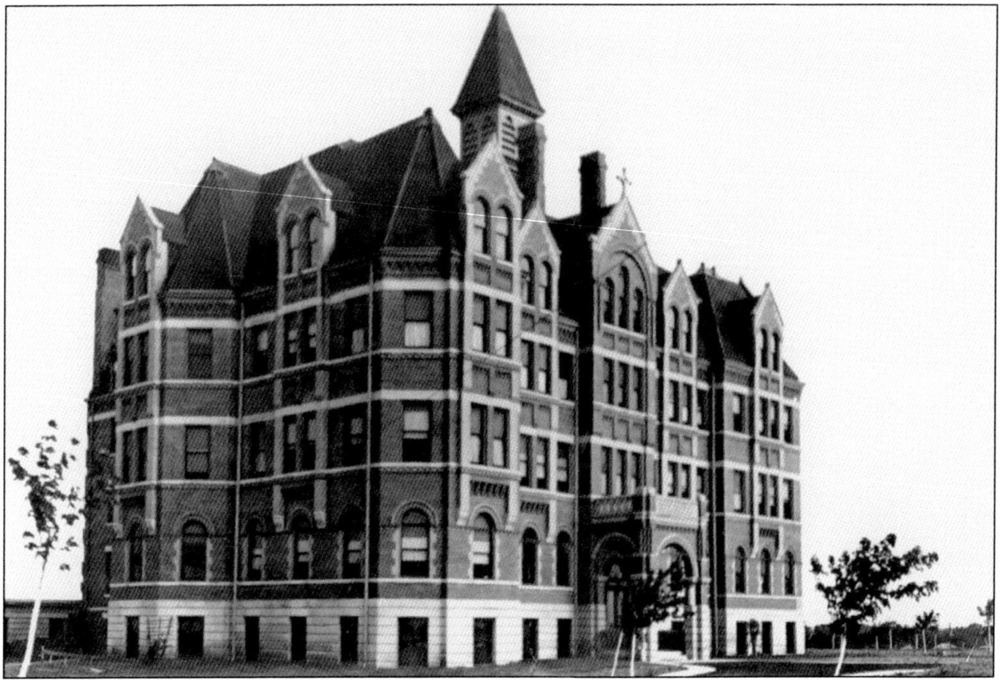

Capitol Hill was incorporated on May 3, 1904. It was about the same time that Mount St. Mary's Academy was built. Built perhaps on the highest point on the hill, the school is operated by Catholic sisters. Its first class graduated in 1906. Located at 2801 South Shartel Avenue, the facility is a private high school for girls. (Courtesy Oklahoma Historical Society.)

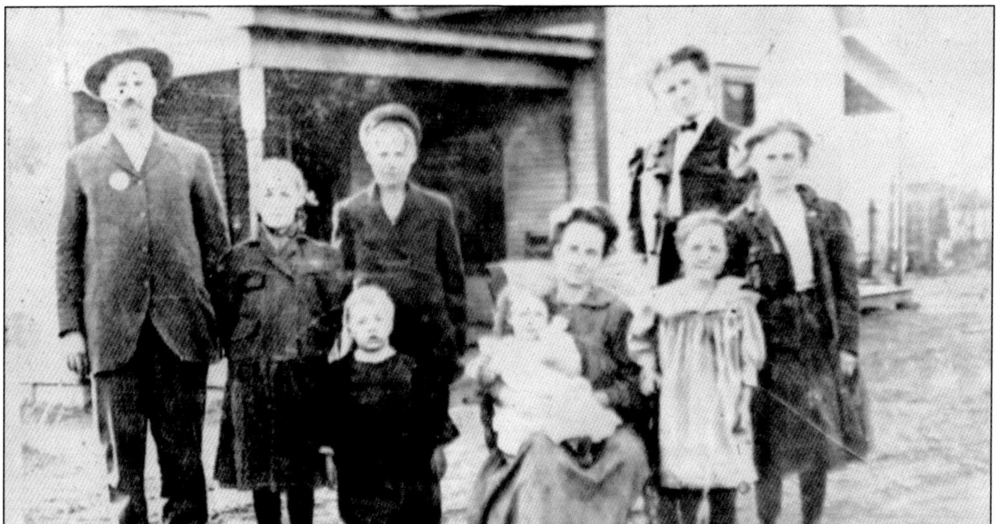

Frank Bodine and family were early residents of Capitol Hill. In 1905, Bodine had a blacksmith shop and was reputed to be one of the finest in the area. By 1906, when this photograph was taken, Bodine was city marshal. From left to right are marshal Frank Bodine, daughter Wynette, Lon Donnelly a small neighbor boy, son James, Ida Manning Bodine with baby Grace, Margueritte in front, Florence in back, and Helen. The photographer is unknown. (Courtesy Capitol Hill Beacon.)

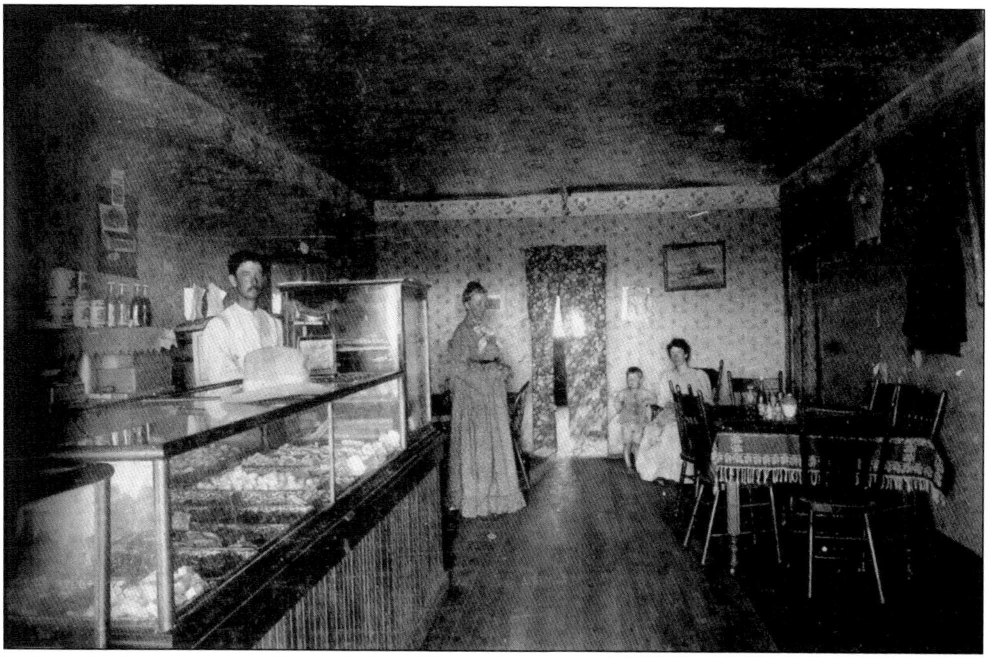

This early photograph is of Lewis Oliver Whitnah, owner of the Capitol Hill Restaurant in 1906. He is seen here with (from left to right) his mother, his son Chester who later became the owner of Capitol Hill Florist, and Ida Whitnah. Single meals, as advertised in the *Capitol Hill News* as it was called then, went for 20¢ or $3.50 board for a week. (Courtesy Capitol Hill Beacon.)

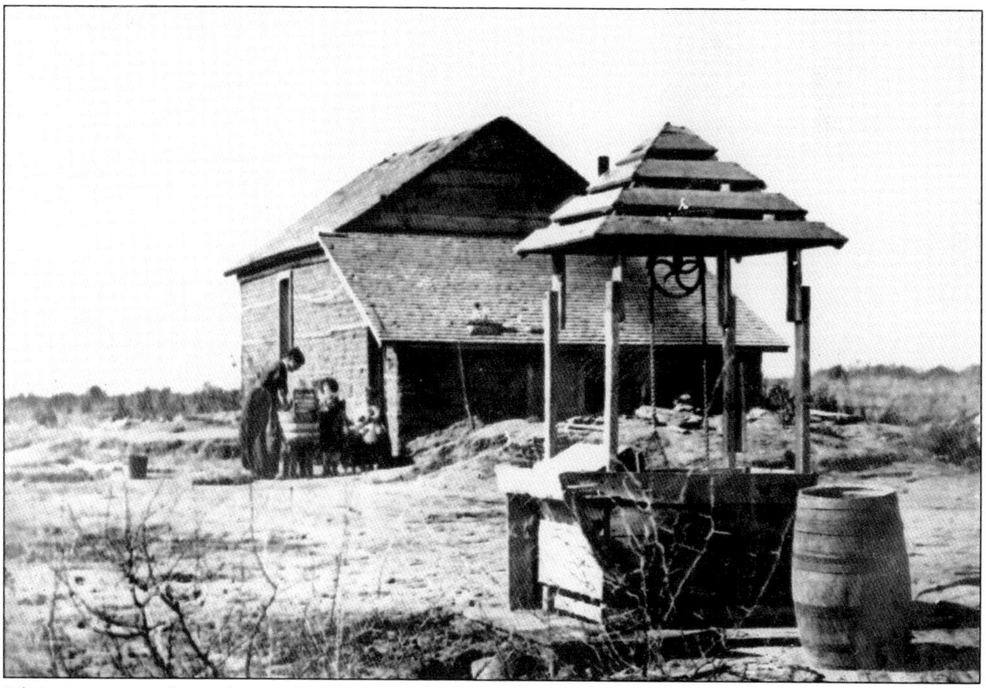

This is a typical residence found in early Capitol Hill around 1906 or 1907. Well water was found at a depth of 60 feet in a bed of gravel and no doubt was fed by the North Canadian River located not far away. The photographer is unknown. (Courtesy Capitol Hill Beacon.)

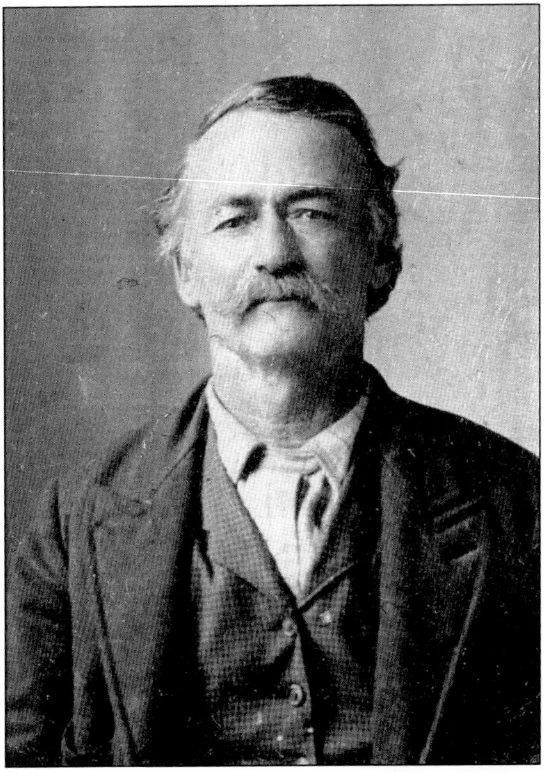

The first publisher of the *Capitol Hill News* was Sewell M. Jackson, a native of Nebraska and most recently of Agra. He had nursed the idea of establishing a newspaper in the community and purchased four lots in Capitol Hill before returning to Agra. He returned in 1905, and on September 15, produced the first issue of the paper that has continued for over 100 years as the source for news on the Hill. (Courtesy Capitol Hill Beacon.)

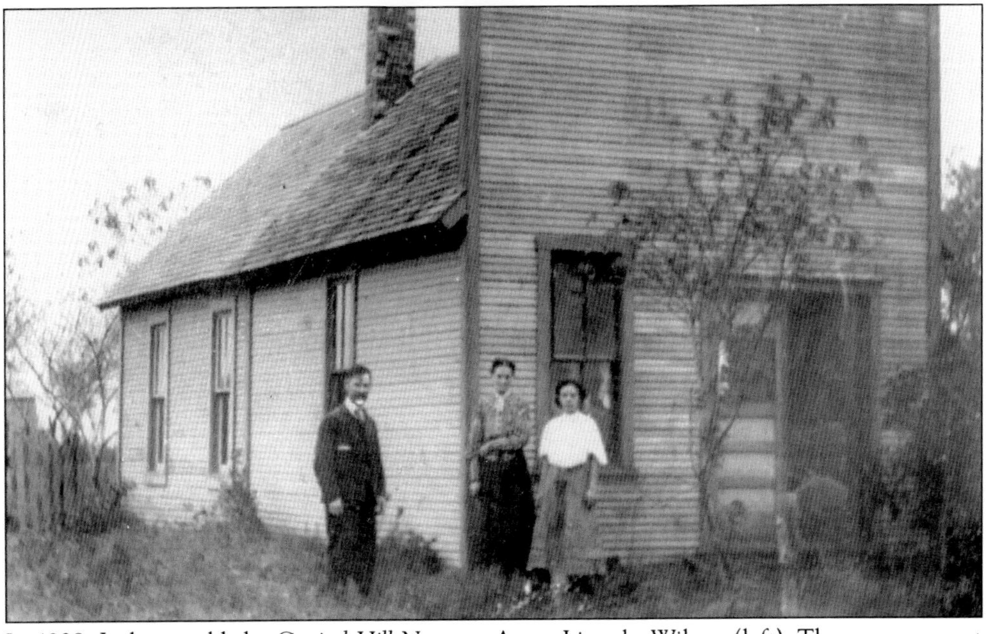

In 1908, Jackson sold the *Capitol Hill News* to Amos Lincoln Wilson (left). The newspaper at the time of the sale was located at 212–216 Southwest Twenty-fourth Street. Seen here is Wilson and Ella E. Rugan (center), who contributed local news, kept the books, and proofread the copy, as well as solicited additional work for the publishing firm to generate. Also pictured is Mazie Salladay (right), who would set type. (Courtesy Capitol Hill Beacon.)

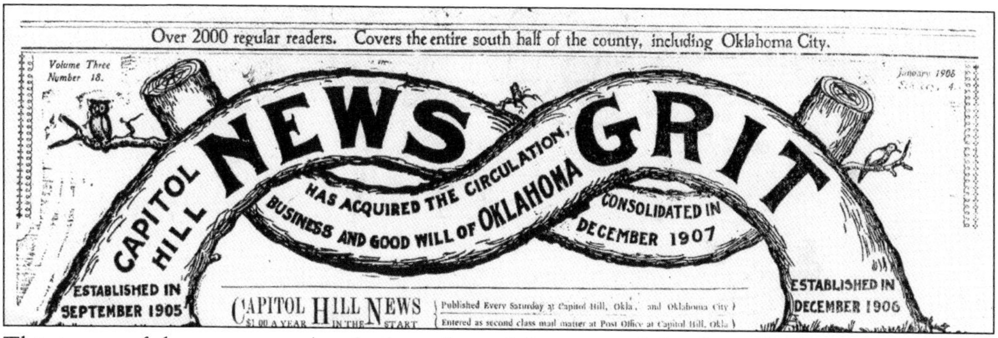

This is one of the many mastheads that adorned the pages of the *Capitol Hill News*, from 1907. The newspaper had acquired the *Oklahoma Grit* that had been founded in 1906. It remained as the masthead until 1910 when Amos Wilson, the publisher, changed it again. Through his ownership of 17 years, several different mastheads were used. In the mid-1920s, the final change occurred renaming the newspaper the *Capitol Hill Beacon*. (Courtesy Capitol Hill Beacon.)

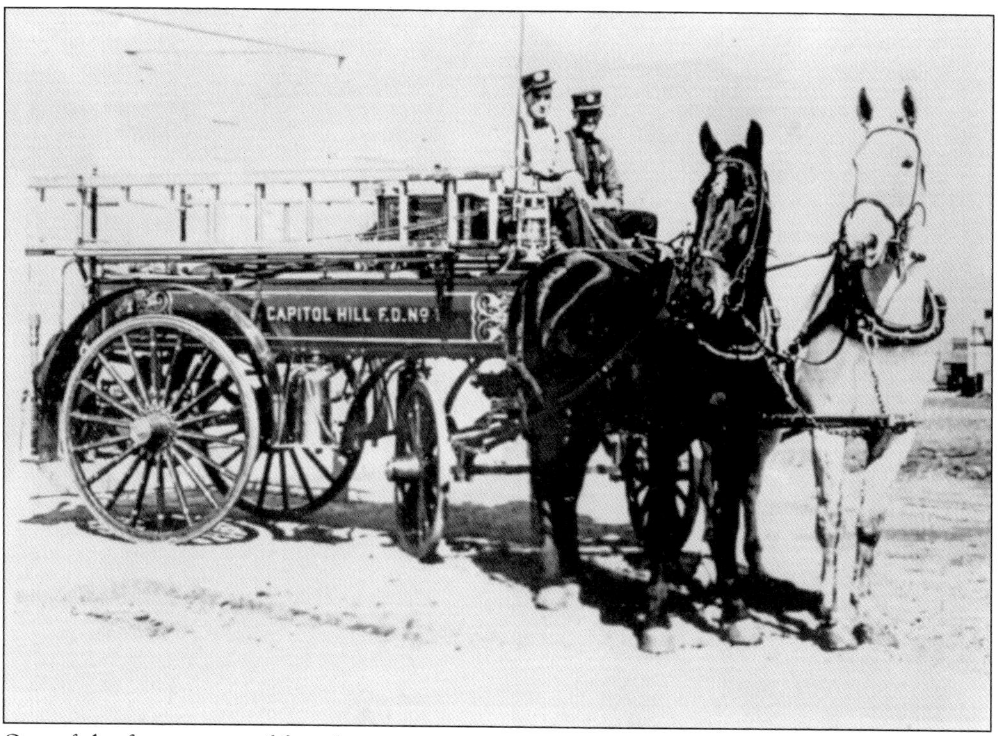

One of the first aspects of founding a new community is establishing essential services such as police and fire departments. This early image from around 1906 shows the horse-drawn vehicle used to fight any fire. The photograph was loaned to the Beacon by Fire Chief Ben Dancy. (Courtesy Capitol Hill Beacon.)

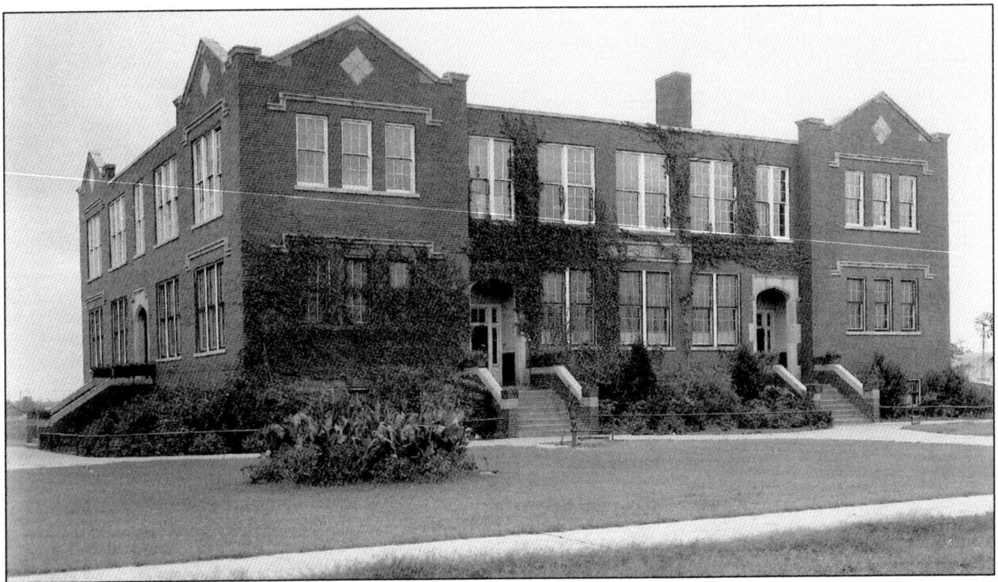

Police and fire protection is of primary importance. However, the establishment of educational institutions plays a vital role in the development of any community. Capitol Hill was no different. One of the foremost activists to encourage educational advances was Arthur H. Parmelee. To quote the *Capitol Hill Beacon*, "it is to him . . . that Capitol Hill owes many of its finest achievements." One such achievement was the building of Lee Elementary School, named for Robert E. Lee. Built in 1910, it was located at Hudson and G Streets, now Southwest Twenty-ninth Street. This image was photographed by Fred Stone, who went by the moniker, "That Man Stone." (Courtesy Oklahoma Historical Society.)

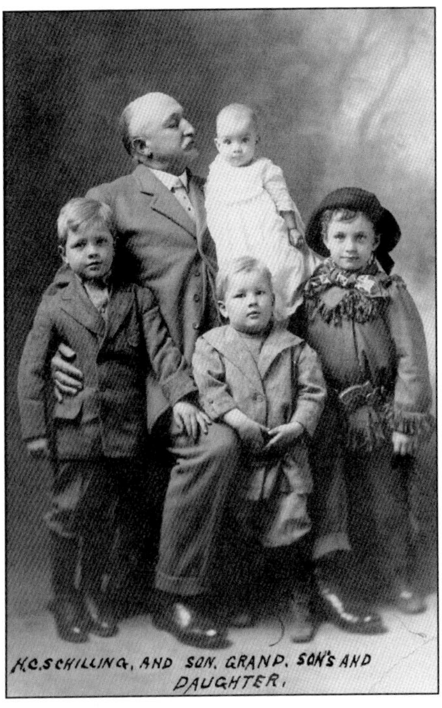

Another prominent individual in the life of the new town of Capitol Hill was H. C. Schilling. Schilling, who was a businessman and early civic and political figure, sought a franchise of a telephone exchange for the community in 1906. He also served as mayor for a period of time. Here Schilling is seen with his son, grandsons, and daughter. (Courtesy Oklahoma Historical Society.)

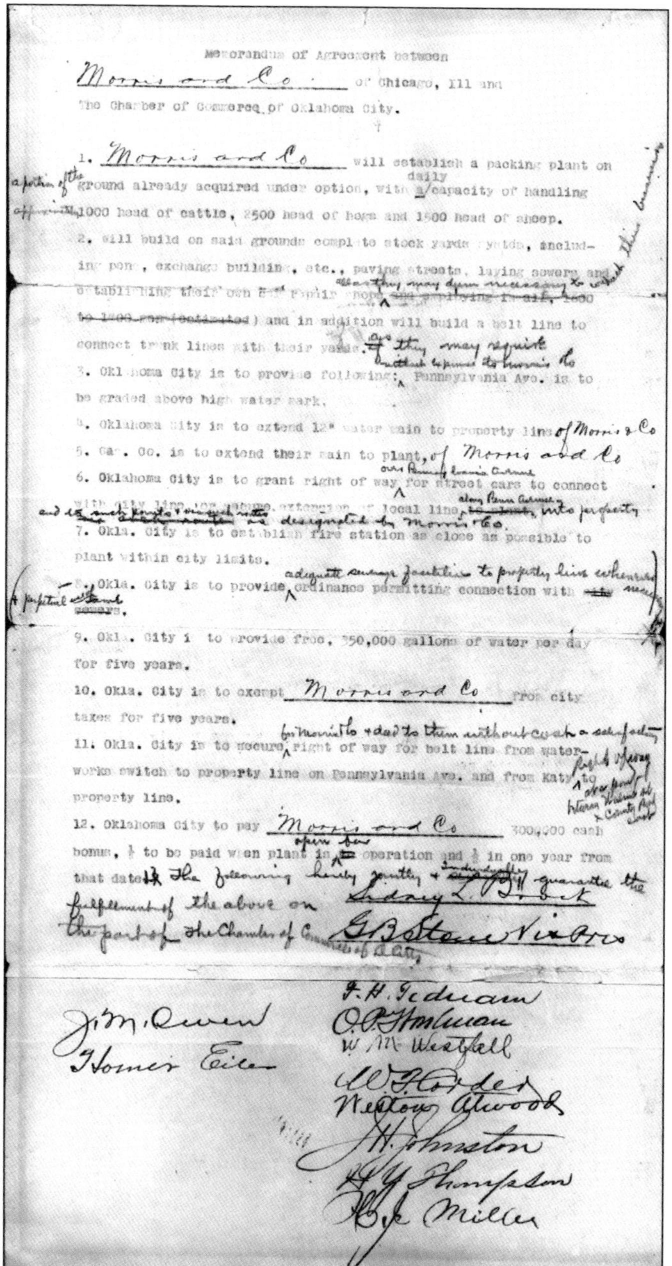

Memorandum of Agreement between
Morris and Co of Chicago, Ill and
The Chamber of Commerce of Oklahoma City.

1. Morris and Co will establish a packing plant on a portion of the ground already acquired under option, with a daily capacity of handling 1000 head of cattle, 2500 head of hogs and 1500 head of sheep.
2. Will build on said grounds complete stock yards, including pens, exchange building, etc., paving streets, laying sewers and establishing their own [illegible] and in addition will build a belt line to connect trunk lines with their yards as they may require without expense to Morris Co
3. Oklahoma City is to provide following; Pennsylvania Ave. is to be graded above high water mark.
4. Oklahoma City is to extend 12" water main to property line of Morris & Co
5. Gas Co. is to extend their main to plant of Morris and Co
6. Oklahoma City is to grant right of way over Pennsylvania Avenue for street cars to connect with city line [illegible] local line, along Penn Avenue into property [illegible] designated by Morris Co.
7. Okla. City is to establish fire station as close as possible to plant within city limits.
8. Okla. City is to provide adequate sewage facilities to property line [illegible] ordinance permitting connection with [illegible] sewers.
9. Okla. City is to provide free, 350,000 gallons of water per day for five years.
10. Okla. City is to exempt Morris and Co from city taxes for five years.
11. Okla. City is to secure for Morris Co + deed to them without cost [illegible] right of way for belt line from waterworks switch to property line on Pennsylvania Ave. and from Katy to property line.
12. Oklahoma City to pay Morris and Co 300,000 cash bonus, ½ to be paid when plant is open for operation and ½ in one year from that date. The following hereby jointly + individually guarantee the fulfillment of the above on the part of the Chamber of Commerce of Okla City

Sidney L. Brock
G. B. Stone Vice Pres

W. M. Westfall
Newton Atwood
J. H. Johnston

The most significant event to take place early in Capitol Hill's history was the securing of the Morris packing plant west of town. In May 1909, members of the Oklahoma City Commercial Club (forerunner to the chamber of commerce), invited representatives of the Nelson Morris and Company, a Chicago packing firm, to visit Oklahoma City as a possible site to locate a meatpacking plant. The representative was impressed with the central location of the metropolis and therefore offered to locate the plant if the company was given a cash bonus of $300,000. Within a very short period, the money was raised by city business leaders and the agreement seen here consummated the deal to bring Nelson Morris and Company to Oklahoma. (Courtesy Oklahoma Historical Society.)

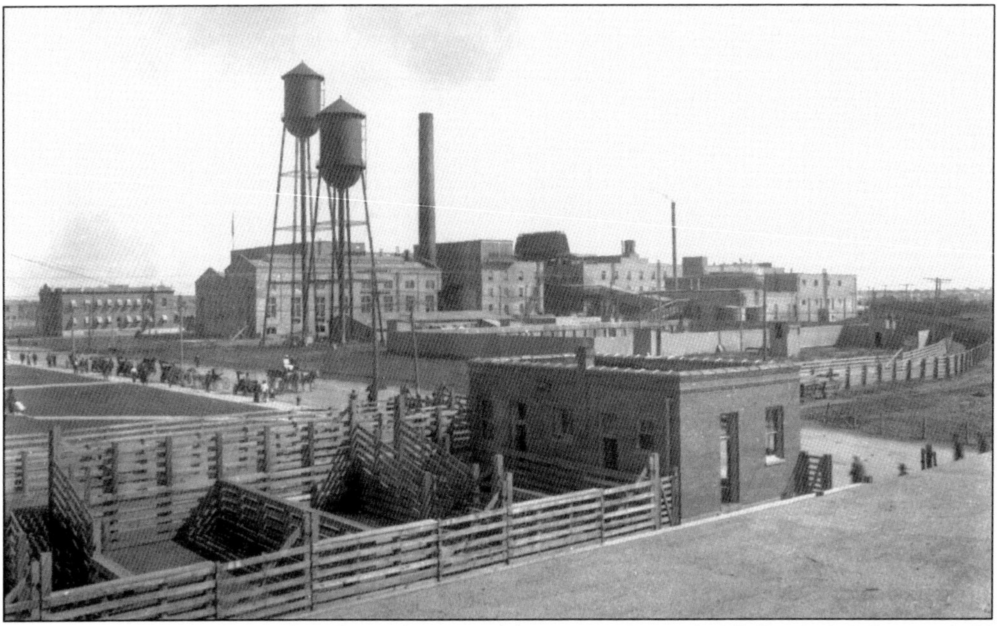

This view is of the packing plant five miles west of downtown Capitol Hill. By 1910, Schwarzschild and Sulzberger Packing Company of Chicago had also built a plant near the Morris facility that lead to the area being designated Packingtown. This infusion of industry and new residents boosted the business district of Capitol Hill in a variety of ways. (Courtesy Oklahoma Historical Society.)

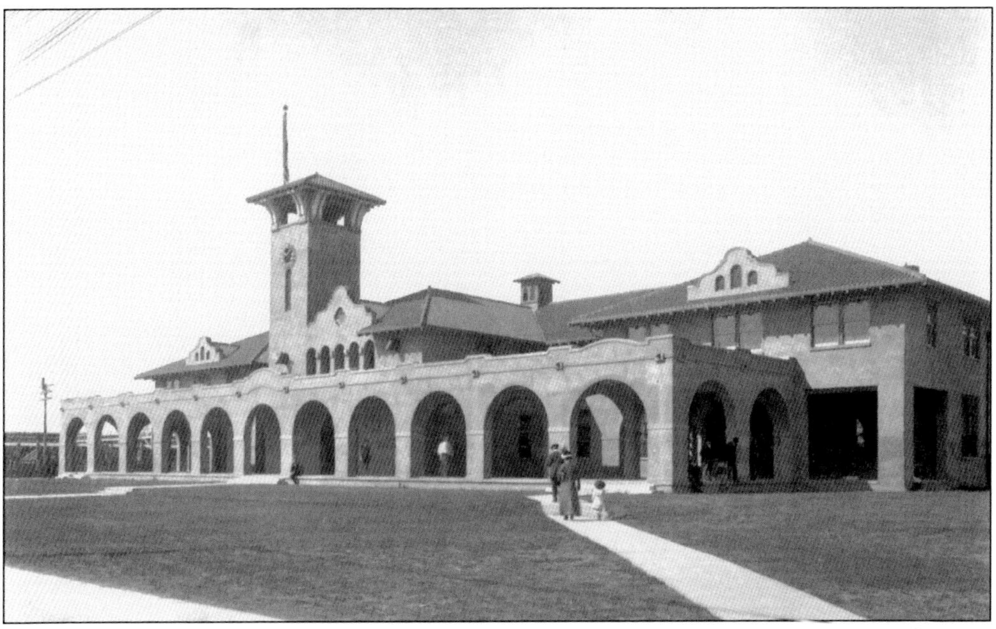

Livestock Exchange Building was built sometime after 1910 to serve as the central offices of the Stockyards Company. The building is of masonry construction covered with stucco and red clay tile roof. This building was listed with others as a historic structure for nomination to the National Register of Historic Places as a historic district. On June 7, 1980, fire destroyed the building. The fire was believed to be by arson. (Courtesy Oklahoma Historical Society.)

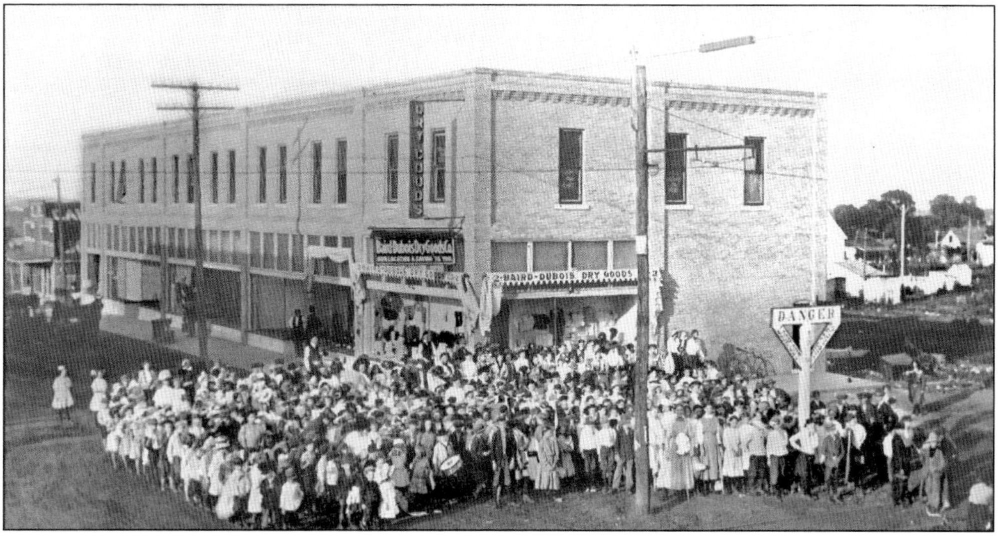

In 1908, the Baird-Dubois Dry Goods building started construction at the corner of Commerce (Southwest Twenty-fifth) and Robinson Streets. In 1910, a group photograph of students, teachers, and Prof. Arthur Parmelee pose in front of the store in support of an upcoming bond election to build additional educational facilities. (Courtesy Capitol Hill Beacon.)

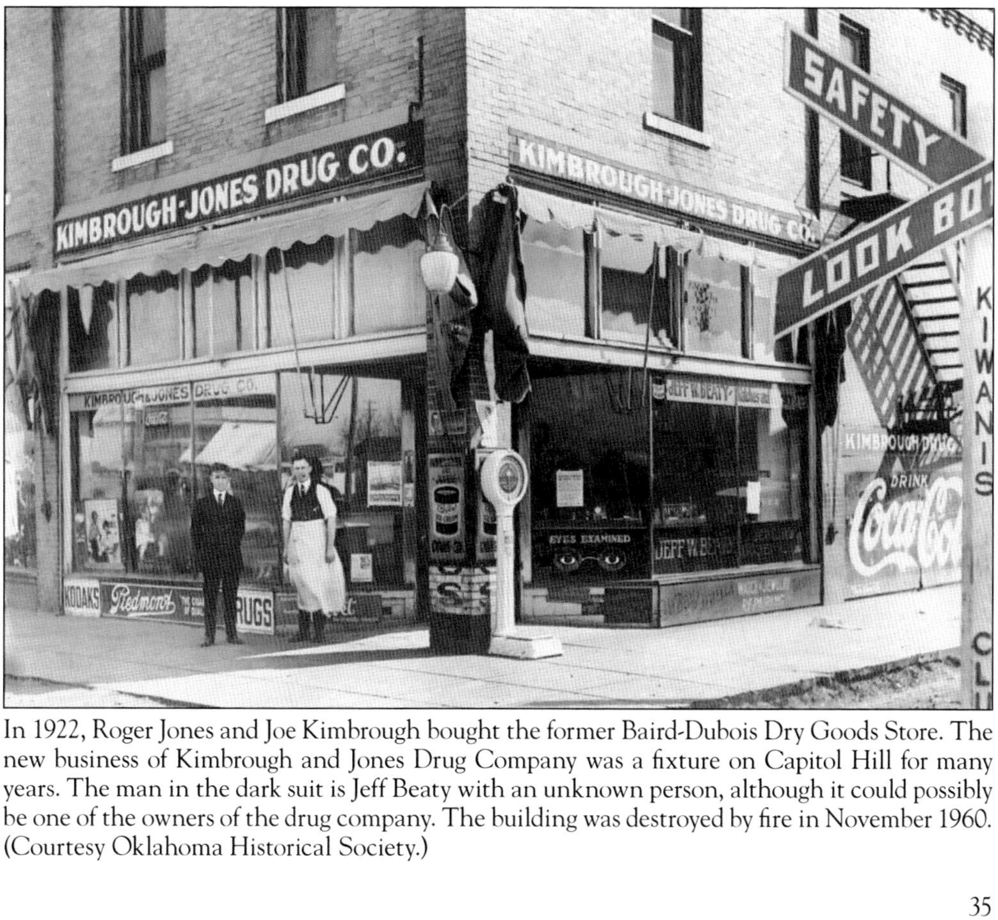

In 1922, Roger Jones and Joe Kimbrough bought the former Baird-Dubois Dry Goods Store. The new business of Kimbrough and Jones Drug Company was a fixture on Capitol Hill for many years. The man in the dark suit is Jeff Beaty with an unknown person, although it could possibly be one of the owners of the drug company. The building was destroyed by fire in November 1960. (Courtesy Oklahoma Historical Society.)

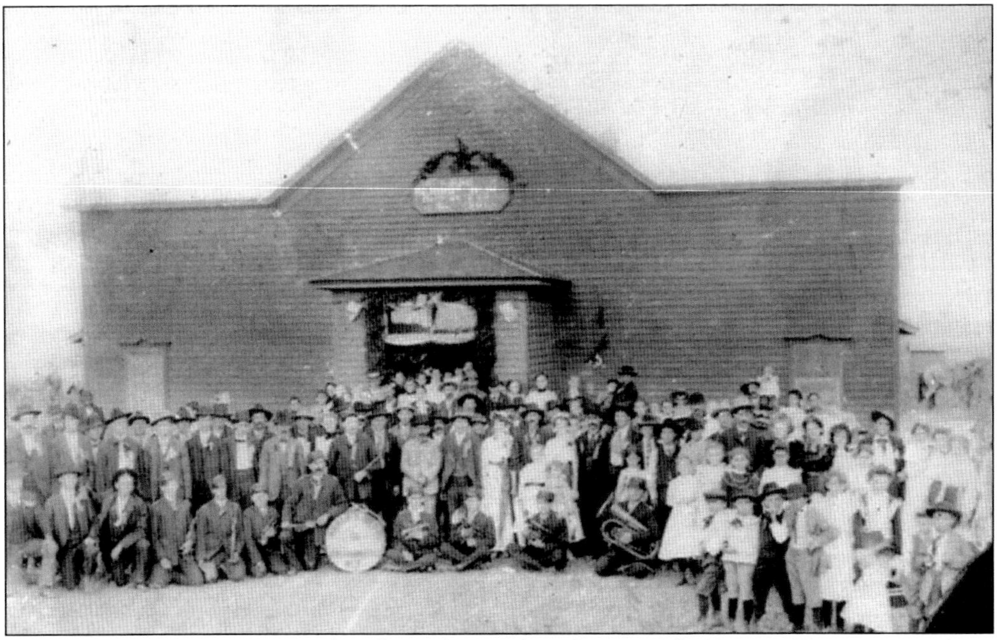

About the same time as Capitol Hill was being platted in 1900 by Benoni Harrington, a large group of Czechs who had made the Run of 1889 organized the Oklahomsky Rolnik, a lodge near 3800 South Portland Avenue. This *rad*, or "lodge," translated meant "Oklahoma Farmer." The lodge building was completed in the fall of 1901, and more than 500 persons attended to witness the dedication. (Courtesy Capitol Hill Beacon.)

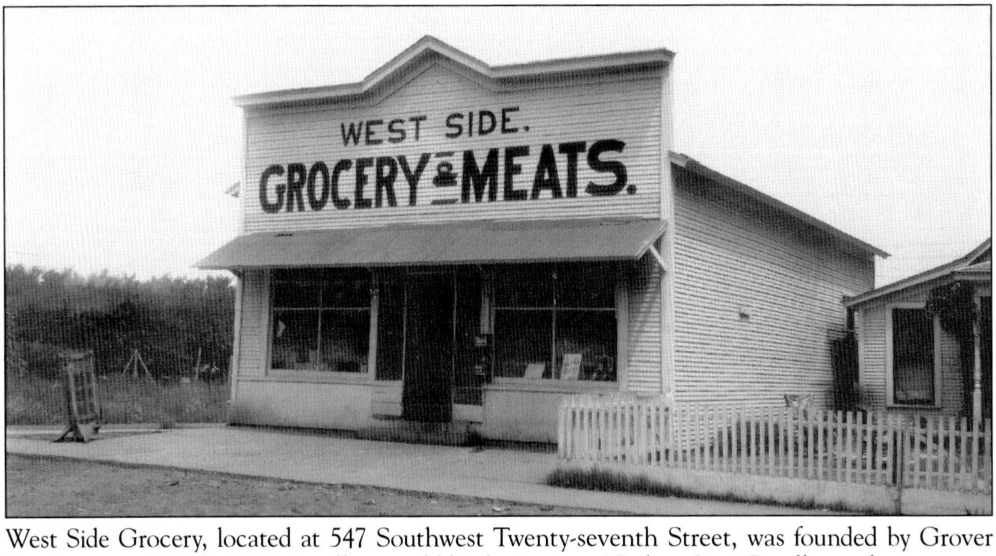

West Side Grocery, located at 547 Southwest Twenty-seventh Street, was founded by Grover Pendleton in 1912. In 1922, Pendleton sold his business to Harlow Gers. Pendleton then went to manage the Certified Groceries Association. In the early 1930s, Pendleton ran for public office and was successful as a city councilman and later county commissioner. (Courtesy Oklahoma Historical Society.)

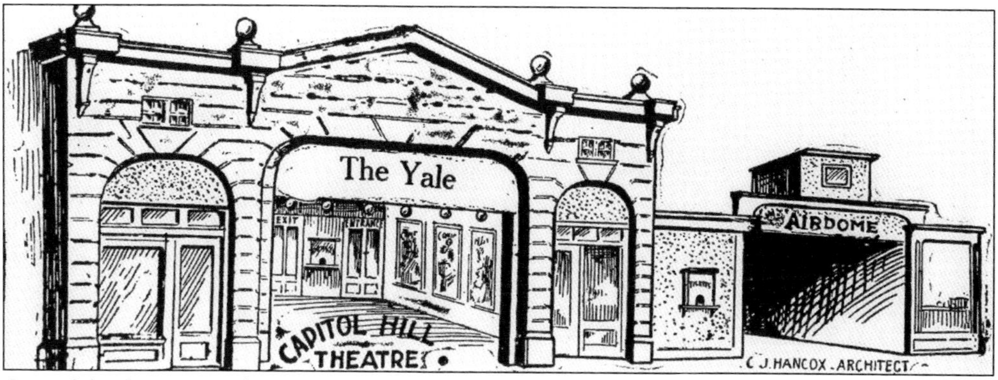

One of the first movie theaters in Capitol Hill was the Capitol Hill Theatre located on C Street, what became Commerce Street. In 1921, the name was changed to the Yale Theatre, which was operated by Pete and Sam Caporal, local businessmen. (Courtesy Capitol Hill Beacon.)

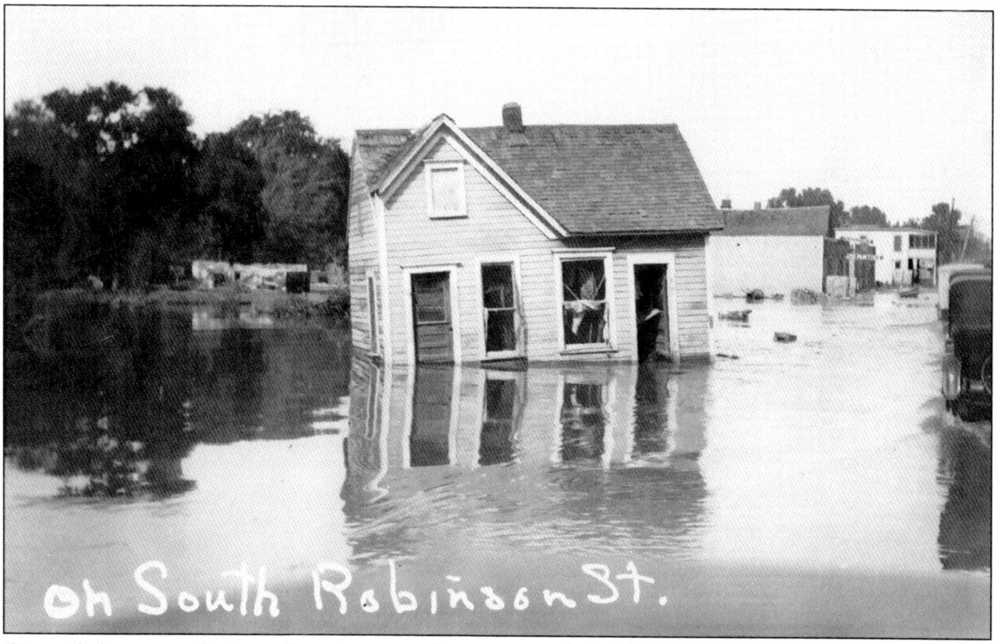

One of the annual rites of spring was the continual flooding problems that inflicted much damage and financial hardship on the people of Capitol Hill. In the spring of 1923, because of heavy rains, both the North Canadian River and Lightening Creek overflowed their banks to cause considerable damage to homes and businesses. Here on South Robinson Street a residence underwater from flooding in June 1923 can be seen. This photograph was taken by the MacArthur Company of Oklahoma City. (Courtesy Oklahoma Historical Society.)

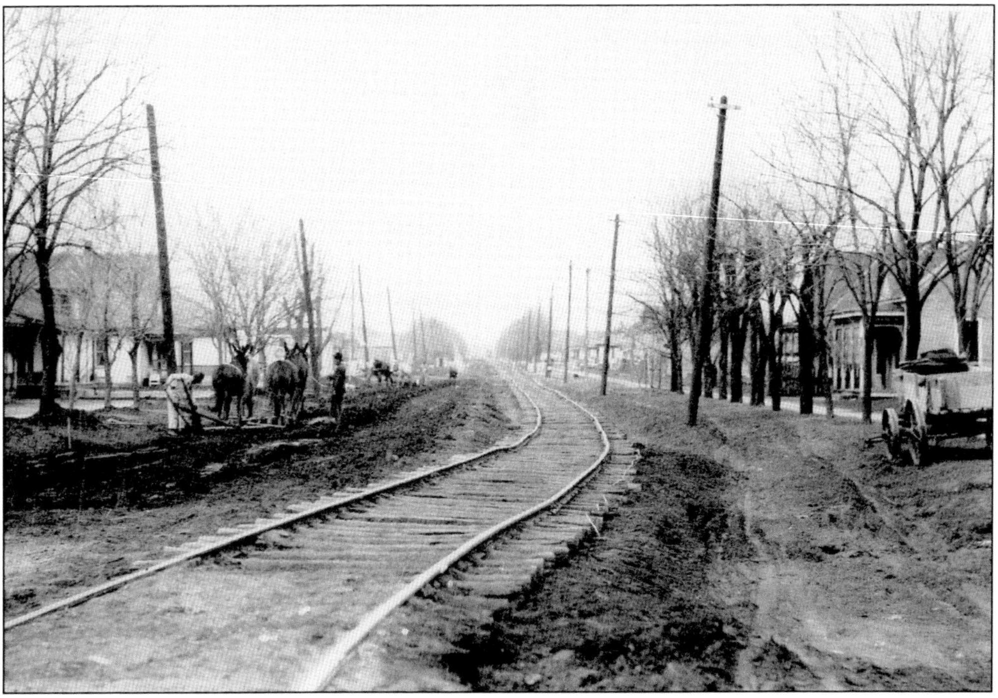

In this photograph, taken after floodwaters from June 1923 had receded, demonstrates how the railroad bed was warped due to the flooding. This scene is near South Central, just east of the main business district of Capitol Hill. (Courtesy Capitol Hill Beacon.)

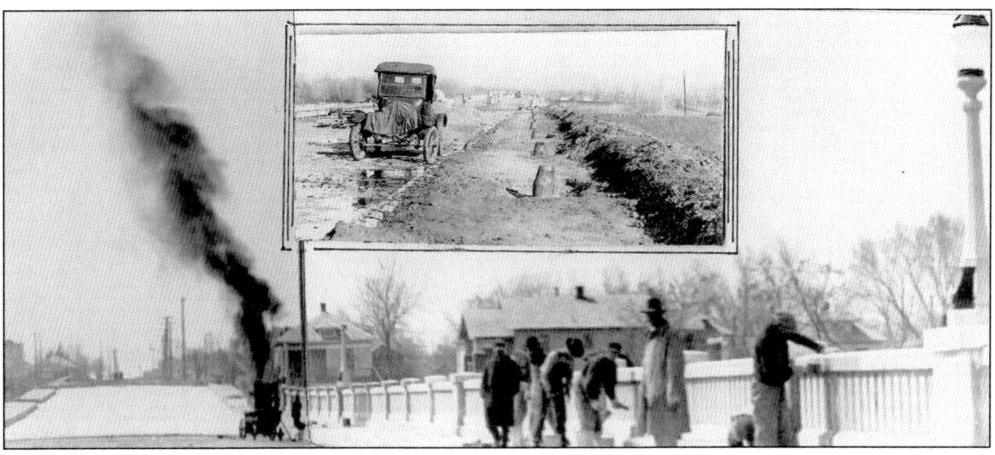

One of the principal barriers between Capitol Hill and Oklahoma City was the North Canadian River (now known as the Oklahoma River). The earliest avenues were railroad bridges. Having reliable crossings was a must. In 1923, a more substantial concrete bridge was built to span the Canadian thus allowing for greater ease of movement for the people living in Capitol Hill. (Courtesy Capitol Hill Beacon.)

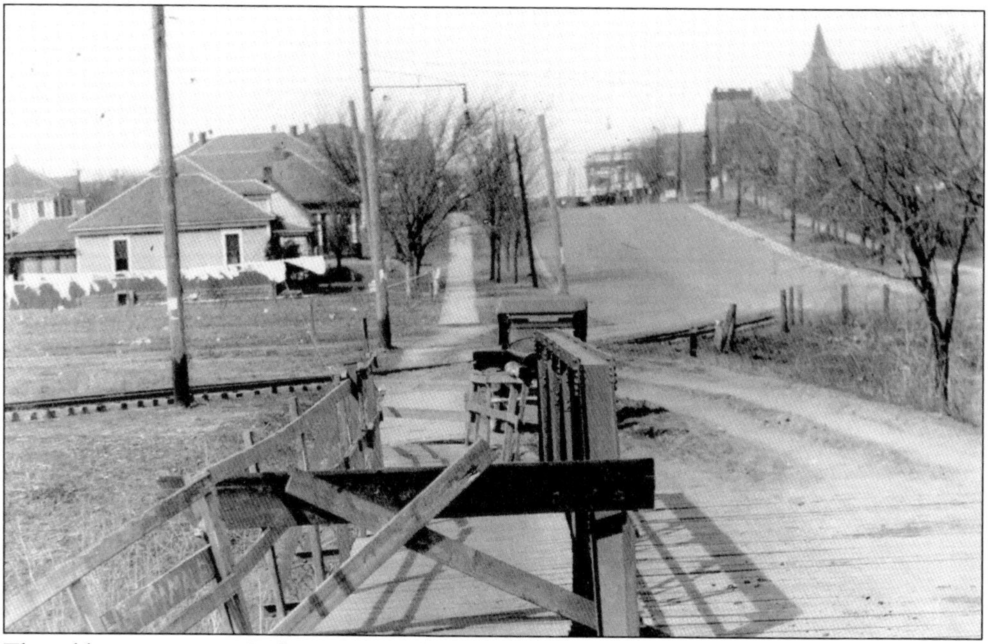

This old crossing over Lightening Creek, just east of Commerce Street, was replaced in the summer of 1924. Note how the road jogs from the dirt to the paved section of road nearing the central business district. The photograph was produced by the Capitol Hill Beacon. (Courtesy Capitol Hill Beacon.)

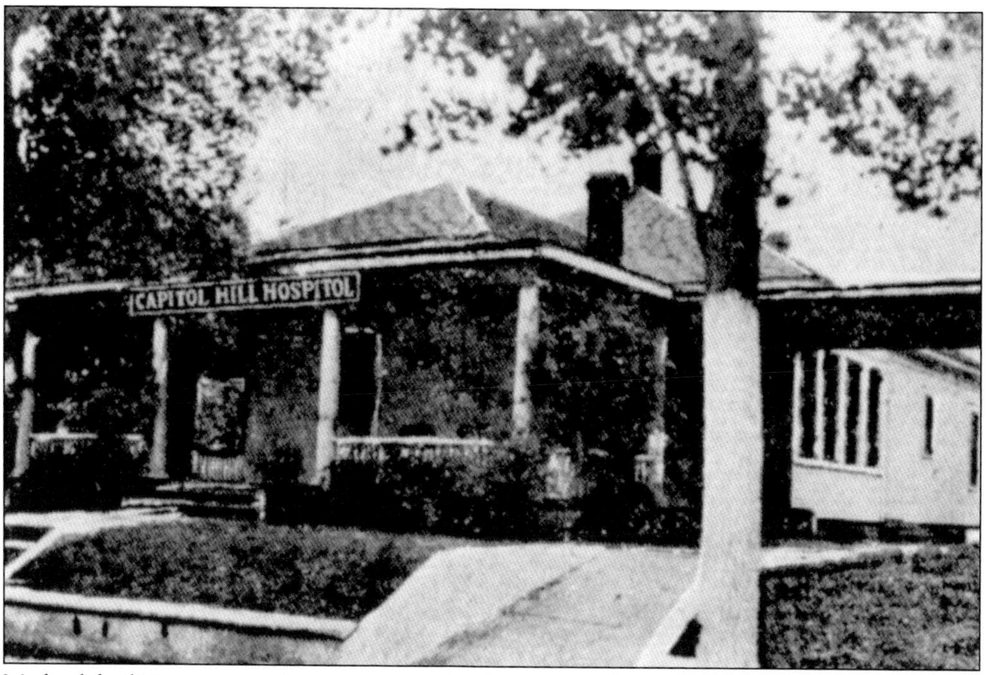

Medical facilities were another important development in the growth of Capitol Hill. The first hospital was the Hottle Hospital named for Dr. W. C. Hottle. Hottle's home, located at the southwest corner of Broadway and C Street (now Commerce Street), was the only hospital south of the river. This image was taken in 1912. (Courtesy Capitol Hill Beacon.)

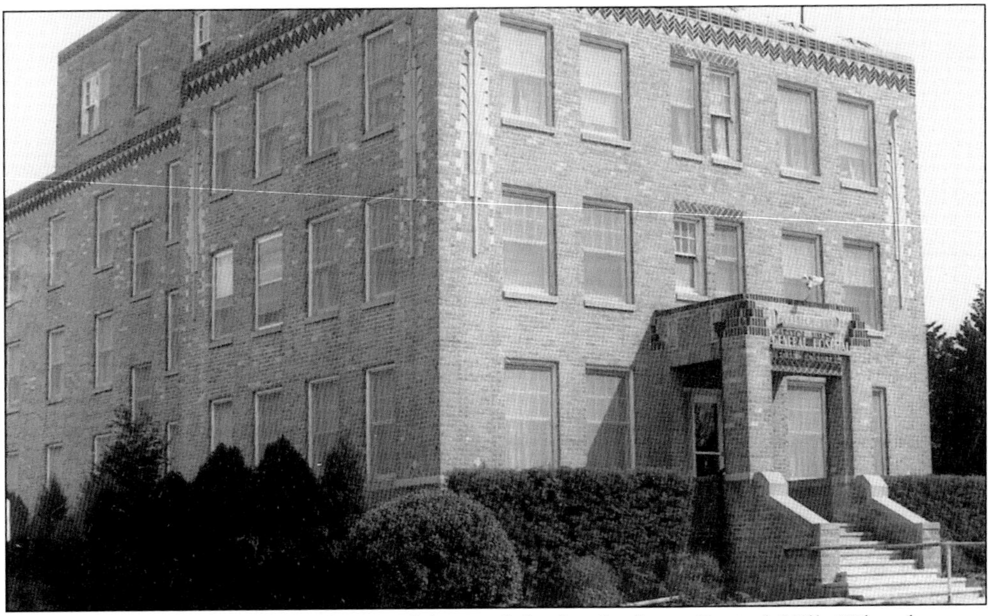

Not until 1929 was a more substantial hospital facility built in Capitol Hill. What became Capitol Hill General Hospital was to be built at South Harvey Avenue and A Street (Southwest Twenty-third). The cost of construction was $100,000 with a capacity of 50 beds, with offices and three operating rooms. The hospital would include medical and dental professions. The hospital continued to serve the community until a much more advanced facility was built in the mid-1960s that became South Community Hospital at Southwest Forty-fourth Street and Western Avenue. (Courtesy Capitol Hill Beacon.)

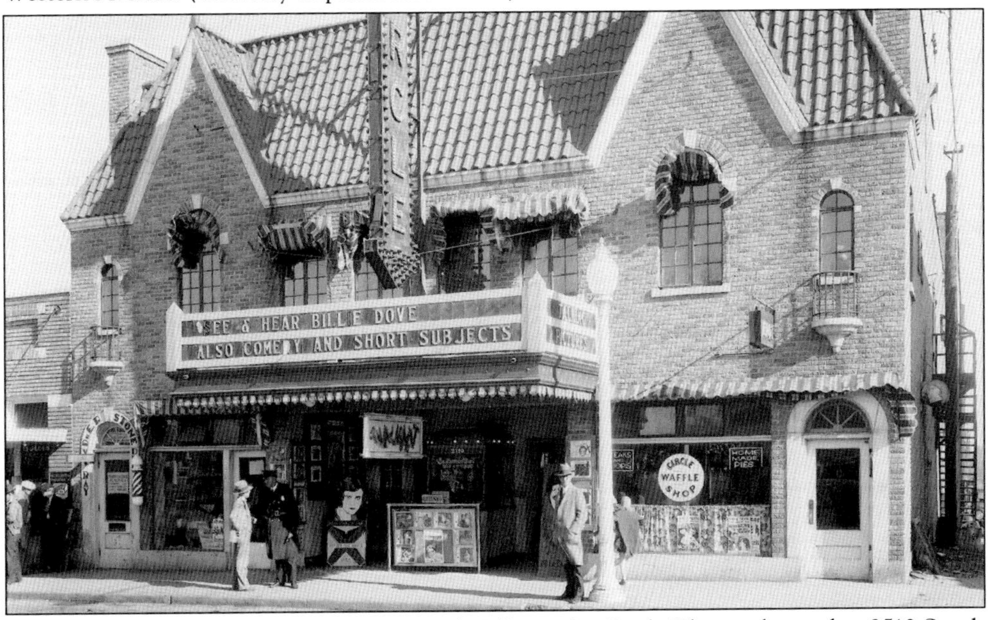

One of the more ornate buildings in Capitol Hill was the Circle Theatre located at 2510 South Robinson Street. The building, in addition to the theater, included a barbershop and café. Photographed by Z. P. Meyers in 1929, the theater ran silent films at the time this image was taken. (Courtesy Oklahoma Historical Society.)

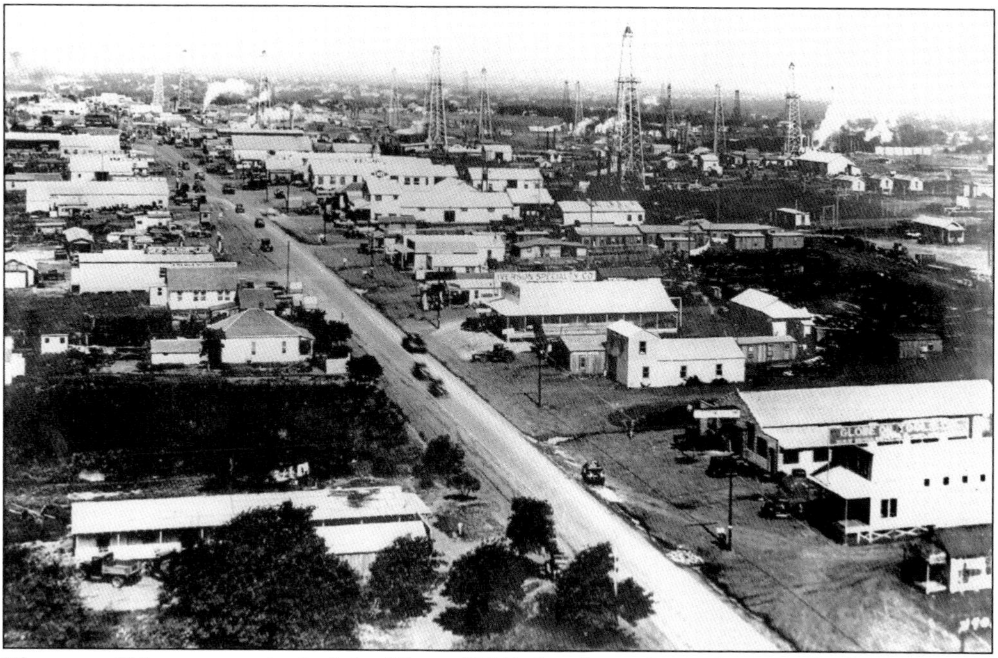

The second-biggest event in the life of Capitol Hill after the packing plant was the discovery of oil just southeast of the main business district. In December 1928, the Indian Territory Illuminating Oil Company (ITIO), struck a massive reserve of petroleum near Southeast Fifty-ninth Street and Bryant Avenue. It first hit gas at a depth of 4,816 feet then after several setbacks, with the machinery choked, an earth-ripping roar tore through the derrick floor and a flood of black crude hit the sky. This image reveals the many oil-related businesses that developed to service the newfound field in far south Oklahoma City. (Courtesy Capitol Hill Beacon.)

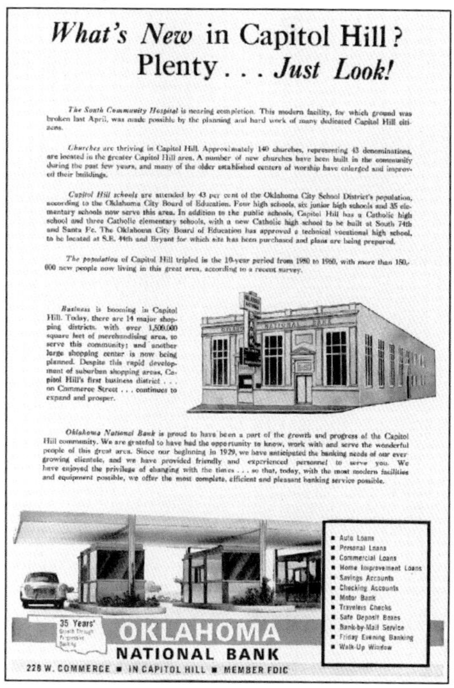

The Depression affected every facet of life in America in the 1930s. In 1928, the area economy was booming. Construction saw over 1,400 permits issued, most likely due to the new oil field. Banking institutions had deposits of more than $88,067,134. By 1932 however, those deposits shrank to just under $71 million. One of the mainstays in Capitol Hill was Oklahoma National Bank, located at 228 West Commerce Street, it weathered the stormy financial sea of the Great Depression, especially since it was founded in 1929, the year of the great stock market crash. (Courtesy Capitol Hill Beacon.)

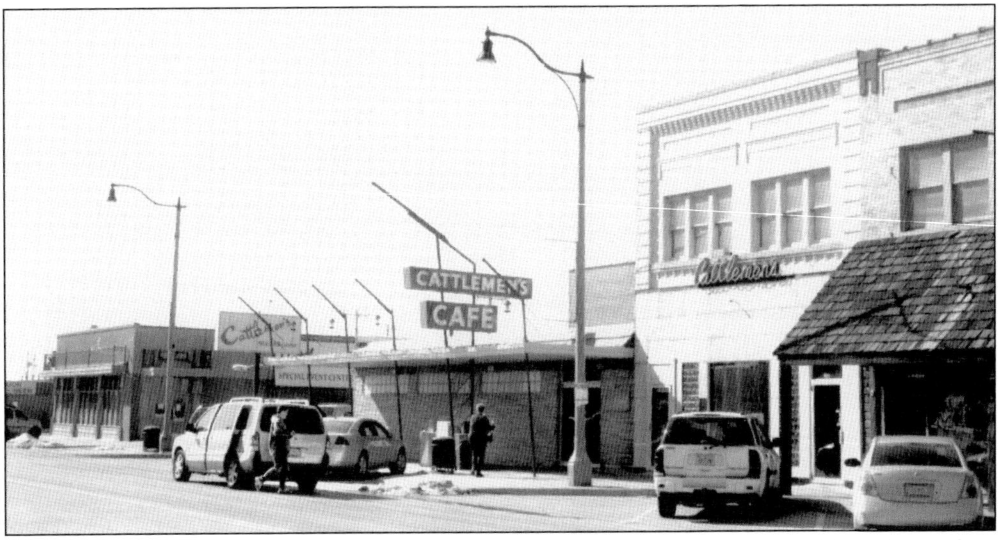

Cattlemen's Café is an institution in Stockyards City. The original building located at 1309 South Agnew Avenue was built in 1910. The local legend is that Gene Wade, longtime owner of the restaurant, won it in a poker game. It too survived the dirty 1930s, catering to ranchers and tenderfeet alike. It is known for its steaks and is the restaurant of choice in Stockyards City. (Courtesy William D. Welge.)

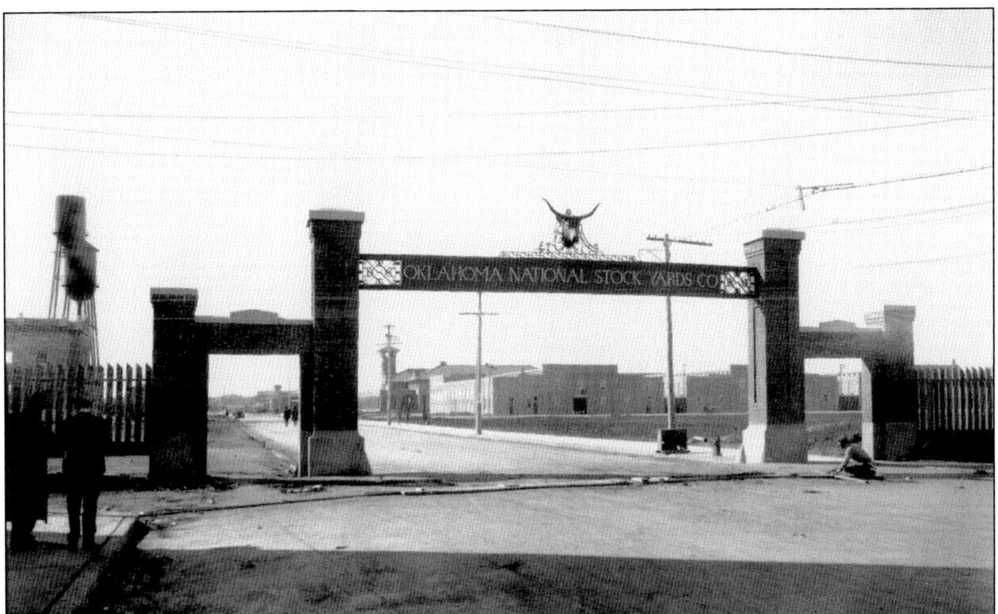

Another iconic image of Stockyard City is the main entrance to the Oklahoma National Stockyards on Exchange Avenue. It was built of masonry construction with ornamental ironwork spanning the width of the street passing below, and no date of the construction is known. The earliest image of the entrance dates from a 1914 postcard. Seen in the background is the Livestock Exchange Building. (Courtesy Oklahoma Historical Society.)

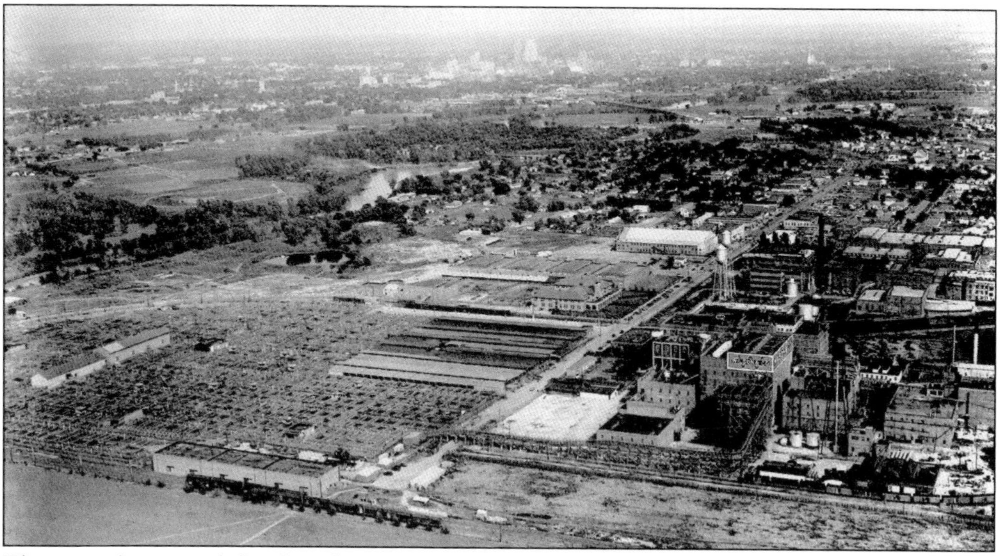

This aerial view of Stockyards City was produced for the Oklahoma City Chamber of Commerce. In the lower right is the former Morris plant, now Wilson and Company Packing Plant. Immediately to the left of the plant will be the Oklahoma National Stockyards. Also seen in the center of the image, near the top, is Oklahoma City. This view is looking northeast and was probably taken in the mid-1940s. (Courtesy Oklahoma Historical Society.)

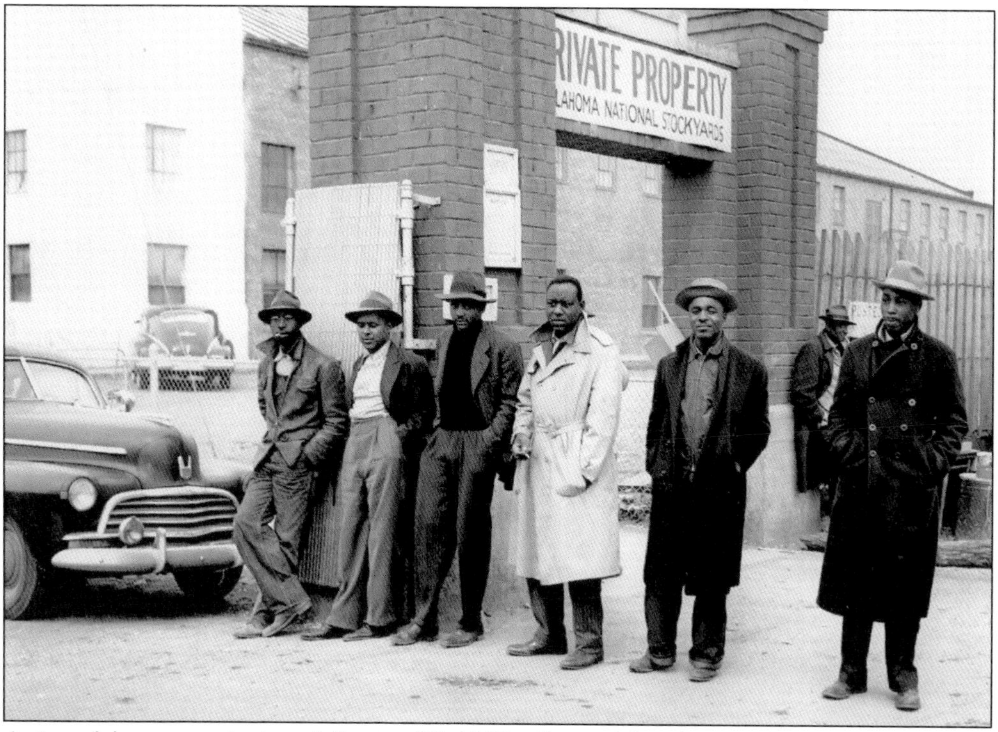

A sign of the economic times following World War II were labor disputes for higher wages. Seen here are several workers on strike in the spring of 1948 just outside the property of the Oklahoma National Stockyards. This photograph was taken by Robert V. Mitchell of the firm Mitchell-Byfield Studio of Oklahoma City. (Courtesy Oklahoma Historical Society.)

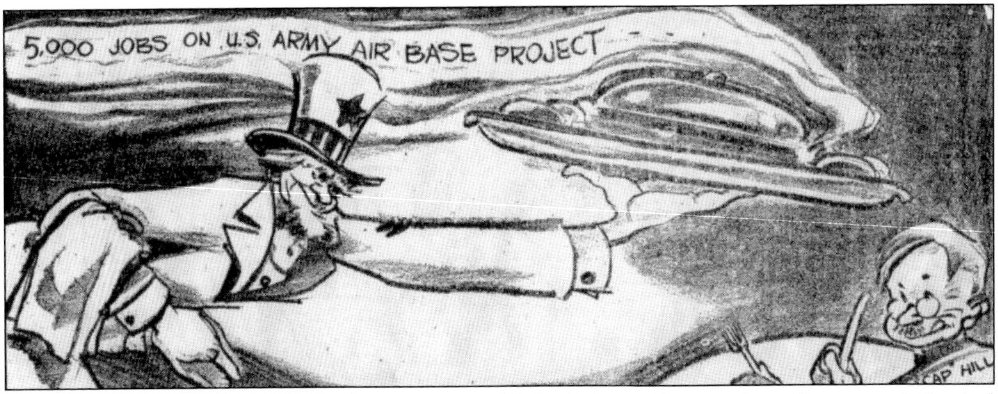

During World War II, a supply depot was established about five to six miles east of Capitol Hill. That depot was renamed Tinker Field in 1942 honoring native Oklahoman and Osage Indian Gen. Clarence Tinker, who was killed during the war. This illustration, which appeared in the *Capitol Hill Beacon* in the early 1940s, would have a direct benefit to the growth of the community and a major economic impact. (Courtesy Capitol Hill Beacon.)

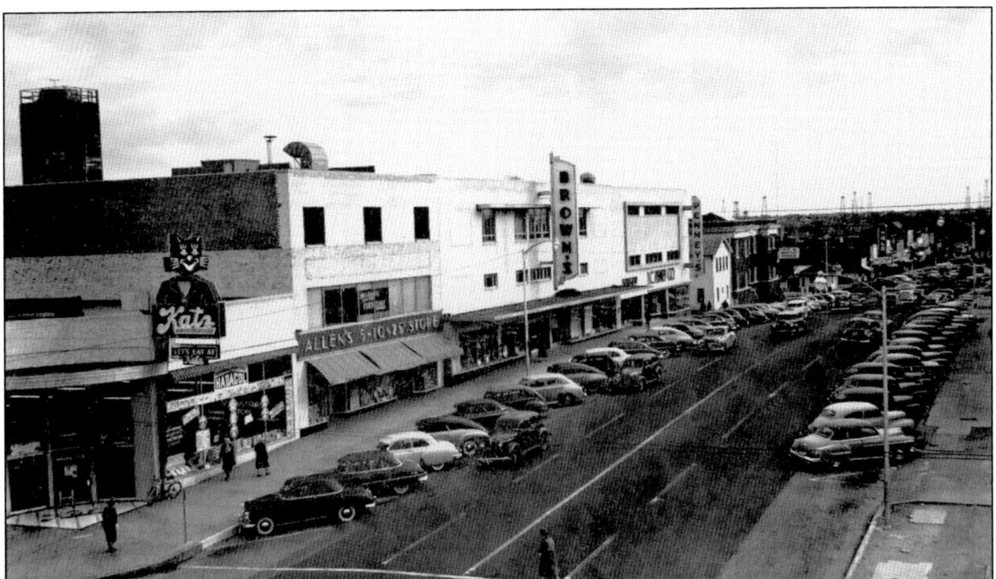

The core business block of Capitol Hill was the 300 block of Commerce Street or Southwest Twenty-fifth Street. In its heyday, one could find department, drug, and specialty stores; cafés; and banking all within walking distance from one another. This vintage view includes, from left to right, Katz Drug, Langston Department Store, John A. Brown Company, and J. C. Penney Company. This image dates from 1947 or 1948 and shows vibrant ongoing business. In the early 1970s, when the United States post office moved, it signaled the start of the decline of Capitol Hill. (Courtesy Oklahoma Historical Society.)

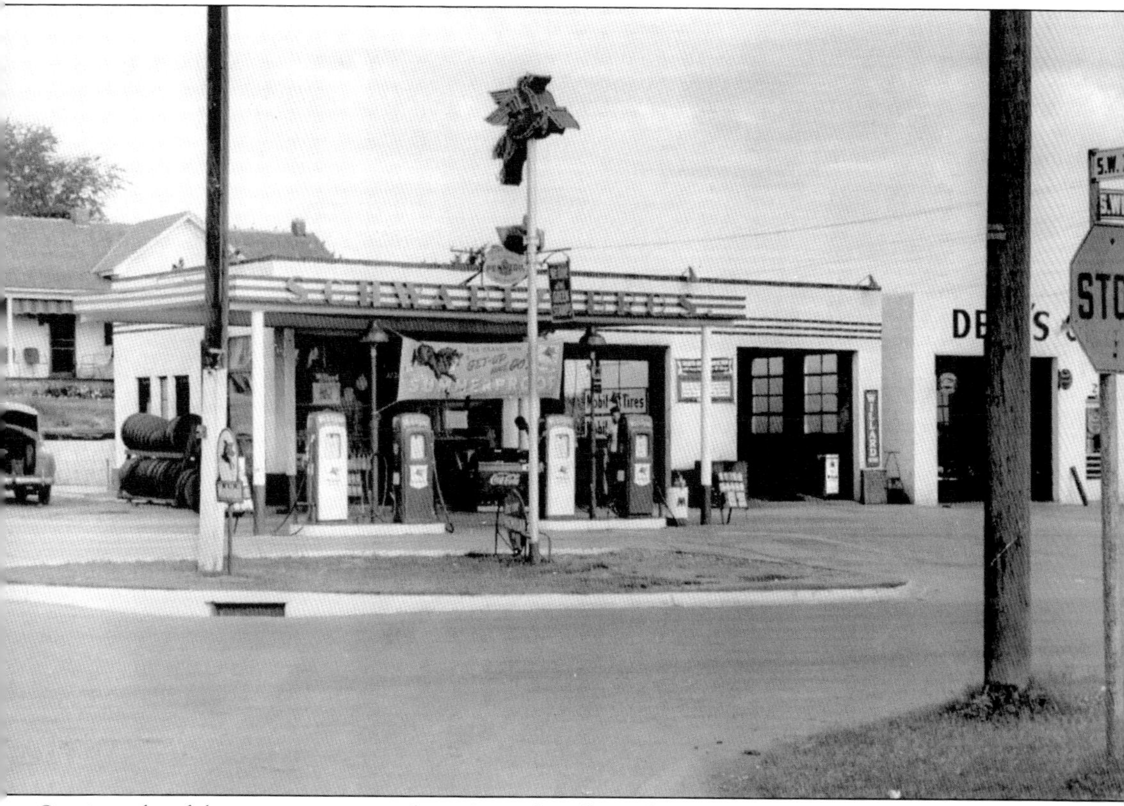

Service-related businesses prospered in Capitol Hill as the community continued to grow, especially after World War II. One such business was Schwartz Brothers Service Station at 2721 South Western Avenue. Louis and Henry Schwartz were native-born Oklahomans. and their station carried Magnolia gas and oil products, later Mobil Oil. By the 1960s, they had expanded their business to include automobile repair and wrecker service. (Courtesy Larry and Beth Schwartz.)

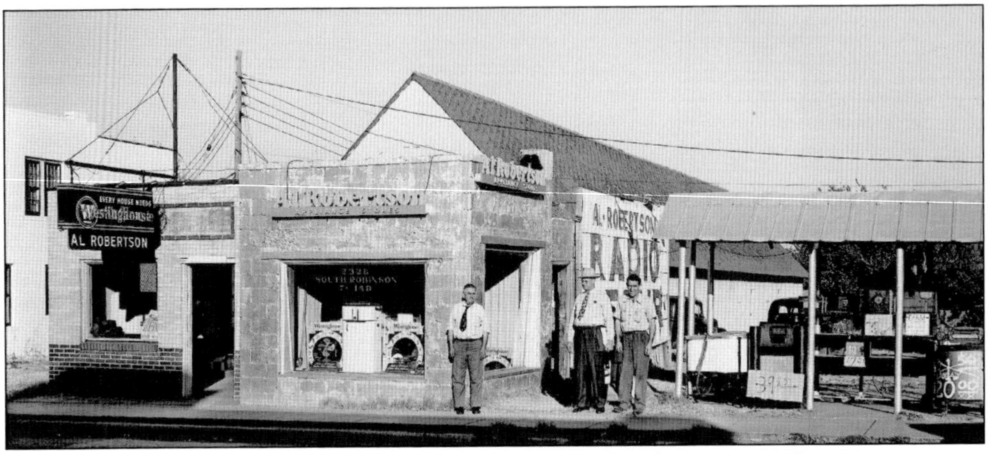

Before television the principal means of entertainment, besides going to the motion picture show, was listening to the radio. From 1920 to the present, Oklahoma City has been connected to the world through radio transmission broadcasting. Early radios used vacuum tubes to transmit sound. As a consequence, radio repair shops sprang up to take care of customers hooked on *Lux Radio Hour* or the *George Burns and Gracie Allen Show*. One such shop was Al Robertson's Appliance Store at 2328 South Robinson Avenue. Photographed in October 1948, by Z. P. Meyer, is the owner and two of his employees. (Courtesy Oklahoma Historical Society.)

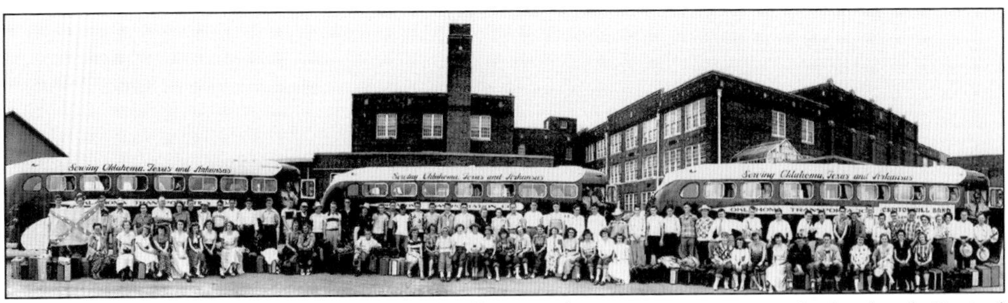

For several years after its founding, Capitol Hill was without a junior or senior high school. Capitol Hill Junior High was started in 1919, then nearly a decade later, the high school was established in 1928. For more than 20 years, Capitol Hill High School was the only school of secondary education. The image here is of the school band, taken in June 1950 by Ginter of Oklahoma City. (Courtesy Oklahoma Historical Society.)

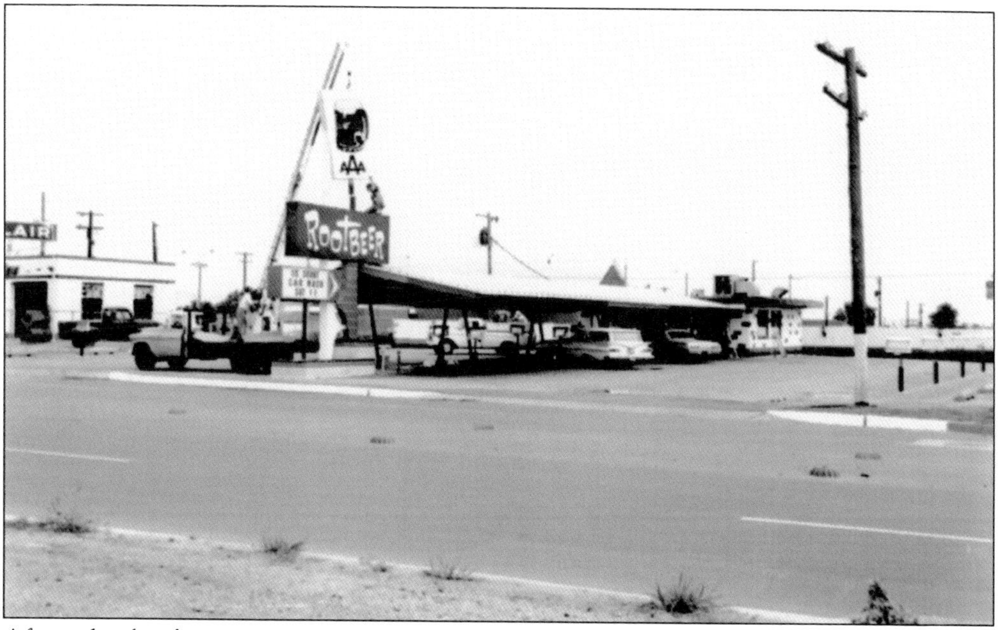

After school a favorite pastime was to go to the local drive-in restaurant for a cold drink, perhaps a burger with fries or maybe a milk shake. The AAA Root Beer Drive Inn at 1020 Southwest Twenty-ninth Street was one such place to "hang out" after school. This late-1950s or early-1960s image was taken by Meyers Photo Shop of Oklahoma City. (Courtesy Oklahoma Historical Society.)

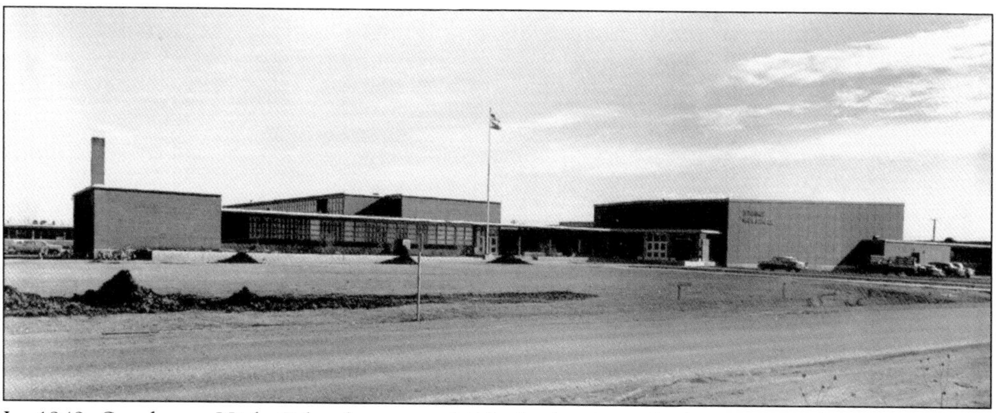

In 1949, Southeast High School was established. As the suburbs continued to move south yet another high school, U.S. Grant, was built in 1953. Located at 5000 South Pennsylvania Avenue, it, along with Capitol Hill and Southeast High Schools, had larger student populations especially in the 1960s through the 1980s with baby boomers coming of high school age. Grant was fairly new in 1958, as seen here, but is slated to have a new facility built (opened in January 2007) under the MAPS for Kids sales tax revenue. The old building is soon to be demolished. (Courtesy Oklahoma Historical Society.)

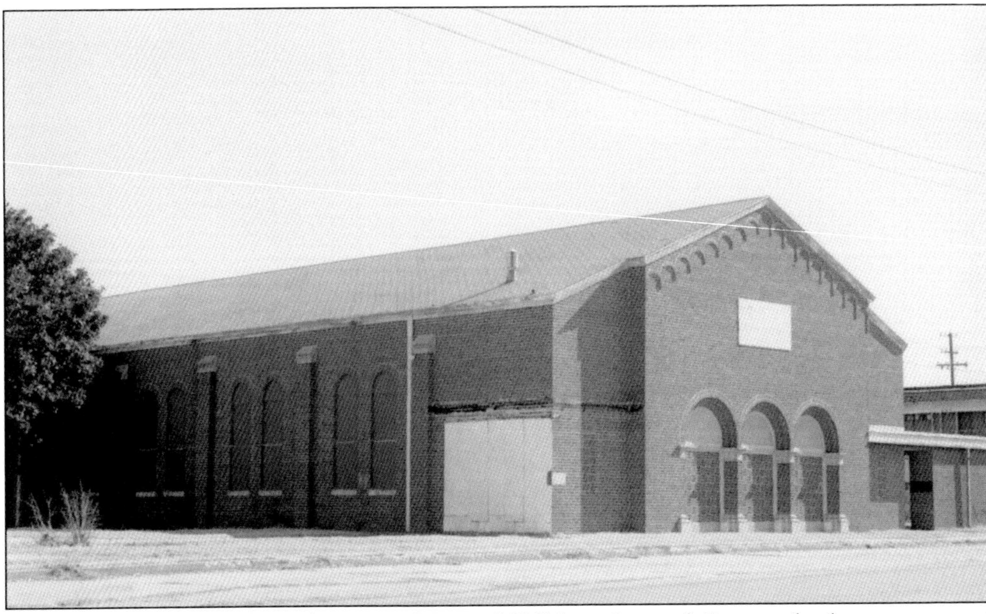

Since the 1970s, the ethnic diversity of Capitol Hill has changed. For nearly three-quarters of a century, the dominant ethnicity has been Caucasian. Since the mid- to late 1980s an influx of Native American, Asian, and Latino people have moved into the older portion of Capitol Hill from the Riverside neighborhood, just south of the North Canadian River to Southwest Fifty-ninth Street. To provide greater access to services and to provide communication to various ethnic communities, facilities such as the Native American Center were established to meet those needs. The center, located in an old Church of Christ at 2900 South Harvey Avenue, is photographed here by Choctaw-Chickasaw tribal member Chester R. Cowen. (Courtesy Oklahoma Historical Society.)

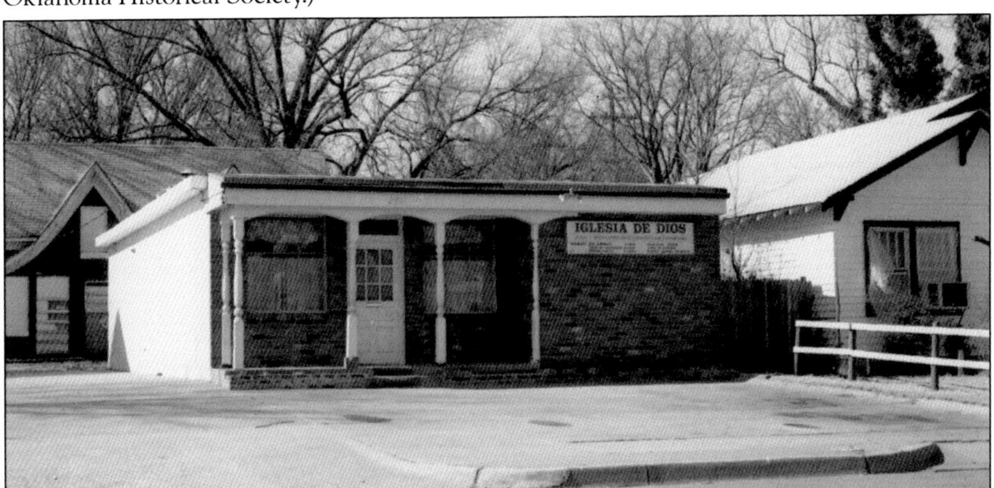

For most of the 20th century, events such as parades were common on the Hill. For many years, the 1889er Society would hold parades every April to commemorate the land run that founded central Oklahoma. With the large influx of Latinos living in the community, street festivals have been the norm, such as Primavera Fest. As the population shifts, new businesses emerge, such as Iglesi de Dios, located at 2817 South Harvey Avenue, photographed here by Chester R. Cowen in February 1996. (Courtesy Oklahoma Historical Society.)

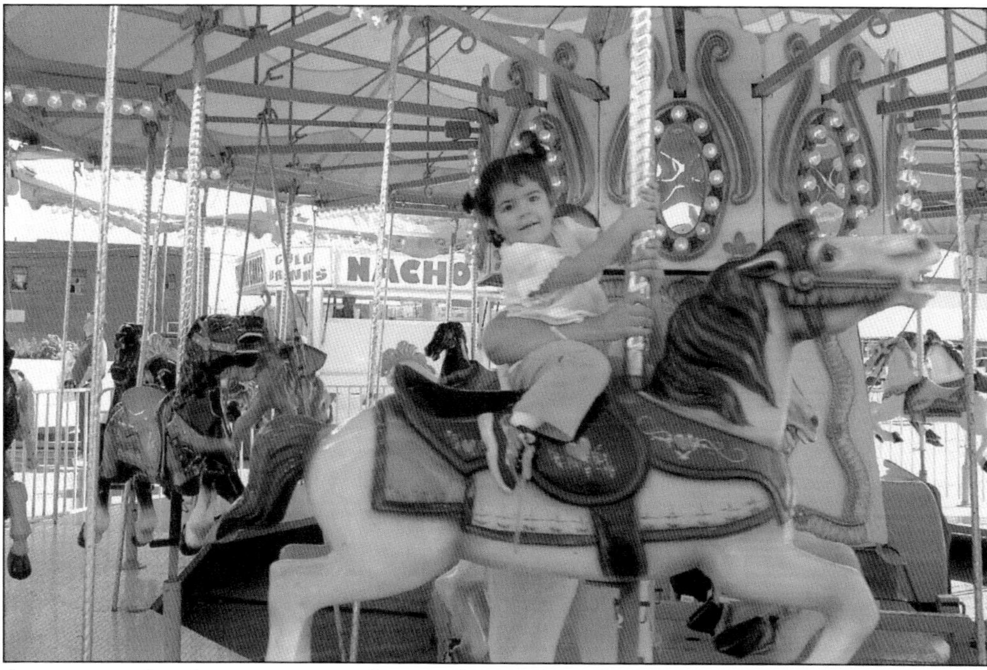

As mentioned earlier, many special events have taken place on Commerce Street. Primavera Fest, started in 2003, is one such activity that encourages the interaction of the community to enjoy the flavor of different societies. This photograph of a small Latino girl enjoying the merry-go-round at the 2004 Primavera Fest was taken by W. D. Welge. (Courtesy Oklahoma Historical Society.)

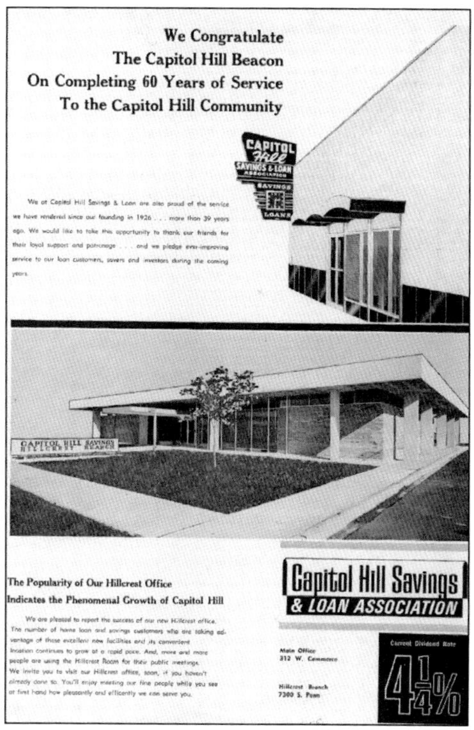

Financial institutions have been a mainstay for most communities. The Capitol Hill Savings and Loan Association was founded in 1926. With two locations, 312 West Commerce Street and 7300 South Pennsylvania Avenue, the association provided home loan and saving accounts. Its South Pennsylvania Avenue branch also provided a meeting room for groups to use. (Courtesy Capitol Hill Beacon.)

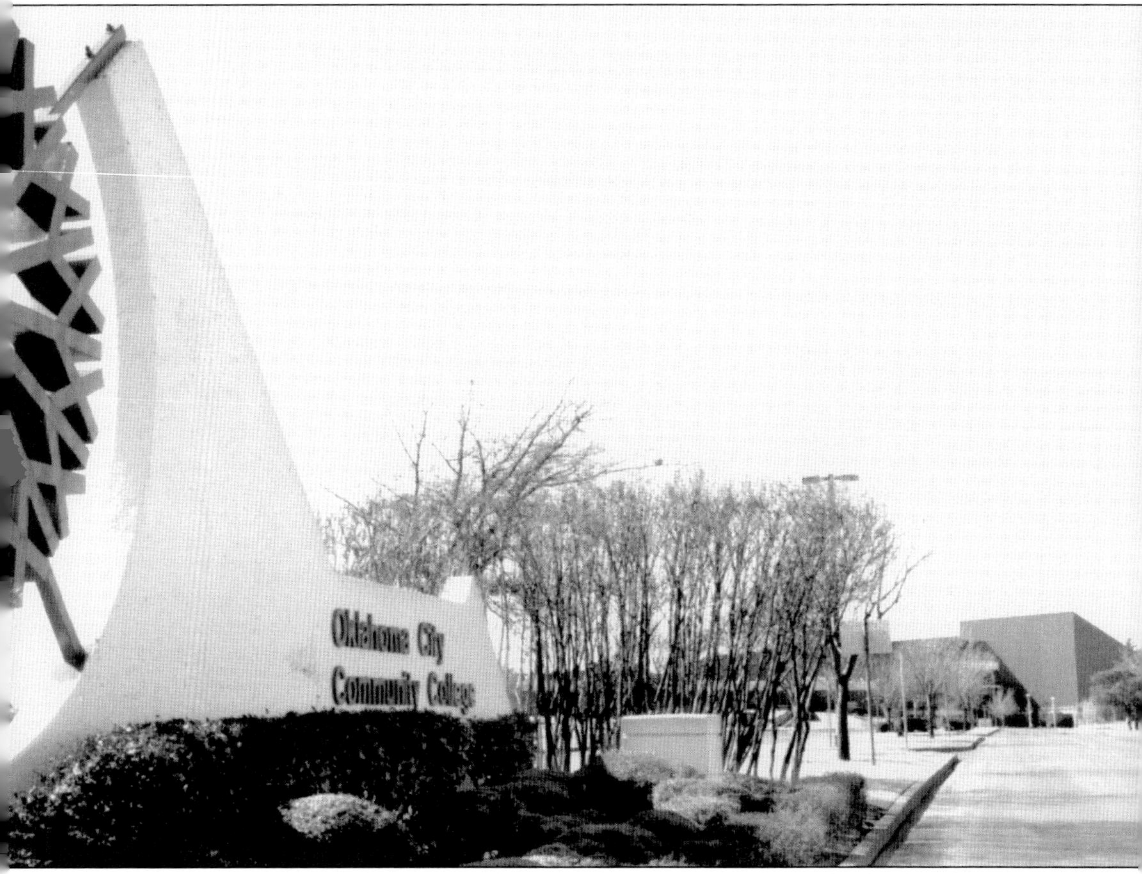

In 1970, the South Oklahoma City Chamber of Commerce and civic leaders banded together to enlighten citizens of South Oklahoma City of the need for a junior college. Midwest City to the east had established Oscar Rose Junior College with great success. The growing educational needs of an ever-expanding population demanded such an institution for the greater Capitol Hill area. In order for the dream to become a reality, it would take a vote of the people to tax themselves so that the school could be established. An election providing for a tax levy was set for June 23, 1970, to vote to raise between $180,000 to $200,000 for operational funds for the college. By less than two percent of the total number of registered voters, the tax passed. Construction for an underground facility soon occurred on land between Southwest Seventy-fourth Street and May Avenue. By the fall of 1972, the college opened to students. From a modular form of teaching in a spacious underground facility to a large campus of several acres nearly 35 years later, Oklahoma City Community College has provided an all-around scholastic environment for the residents of the community. This photograph was taken by W. D. Welge, one of the first students to attend the junior college its first semester of operation. (Courtesy W. D. Welge.)

Four

Second Street, the Lure of Deep Deuce

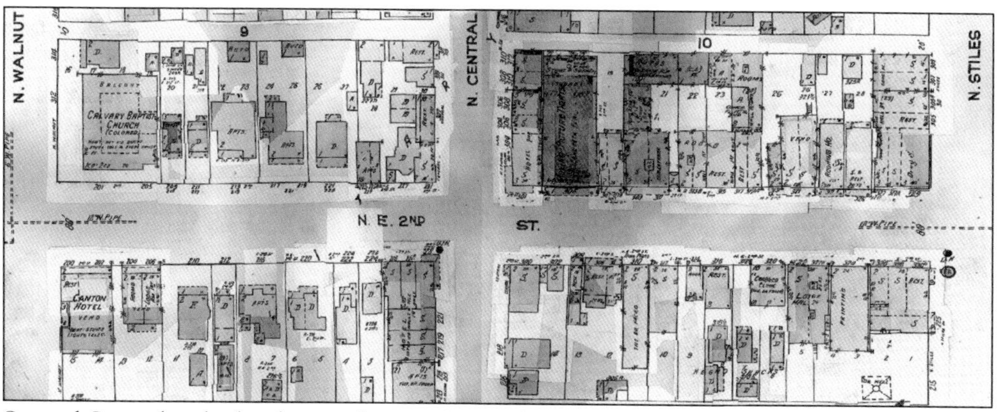

Second Street has had a distinct history. Located just east of downtown Oklahoma City past the Santa Fe railroad tracks and just north of the warehouse district with the Rock Island Railroad serving as a barrier, Second Street, also known as Deep Deuce, was the black business and entertainment sector of town. The map shown here, from 1922, indicates the diversity of residential, business, and entertainment venues. The 300 block contained such important businesses as the Aldridge Theatre, the *Black Dispatch* newspaper, the Lyon's Den, Ruby's Grill, and Randolph Drug Store. (Courtesy Oklahoma Historical Society.)

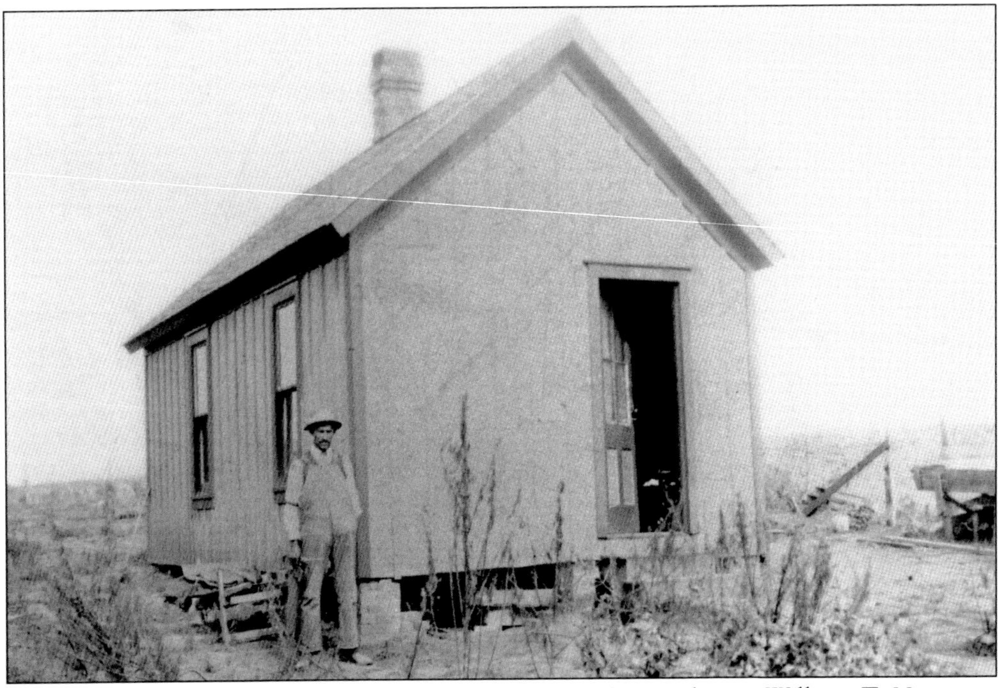

Second Street, as stated earlier, had many visionaries. One such was William T. Vivette, a carpenter by trade and early developer of Second Street. Born in Tennessee in 1876, he migrated to Oklahoma Territory. Among the important buildings he developed were Randolph Drug and Dr. Wyatt A. Slaughter's home, as well as Dr. William L. Haywood's residence. This image dates from around 1902. Vivette passed away in 1962 at the age of 86 and is buried at Trice Hill Cemetery. (Courtesy Black Liberated Arts Center, Inc.)

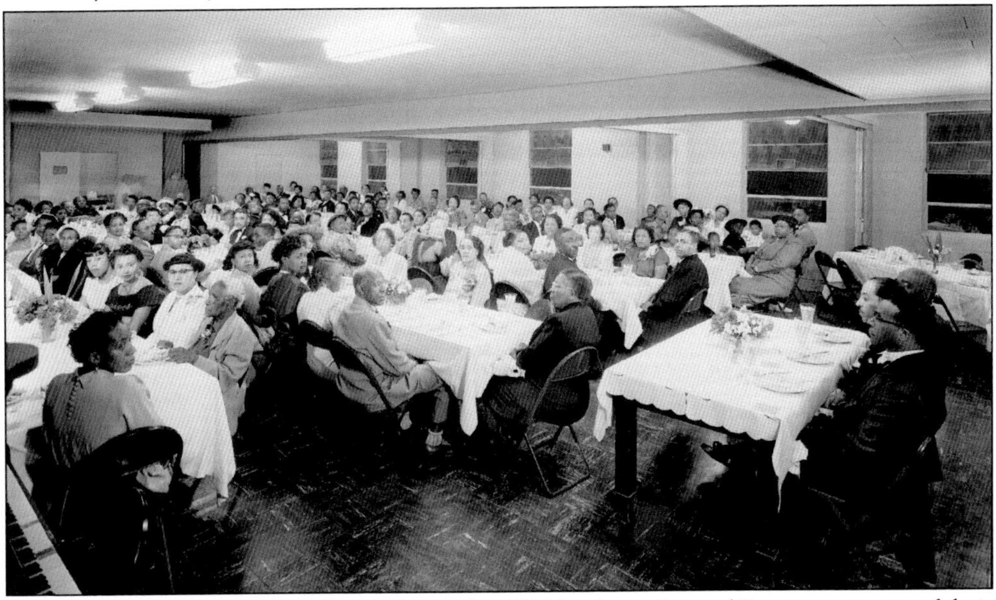

Members of St. John's Baptist Church, located at 801 Northeast Second Street, are at one of their special events sometime in the 1940s. This photograph is by Meyers Photo Shop of Oklahoma City. (Courtesy Oklahoma Historical Society.)

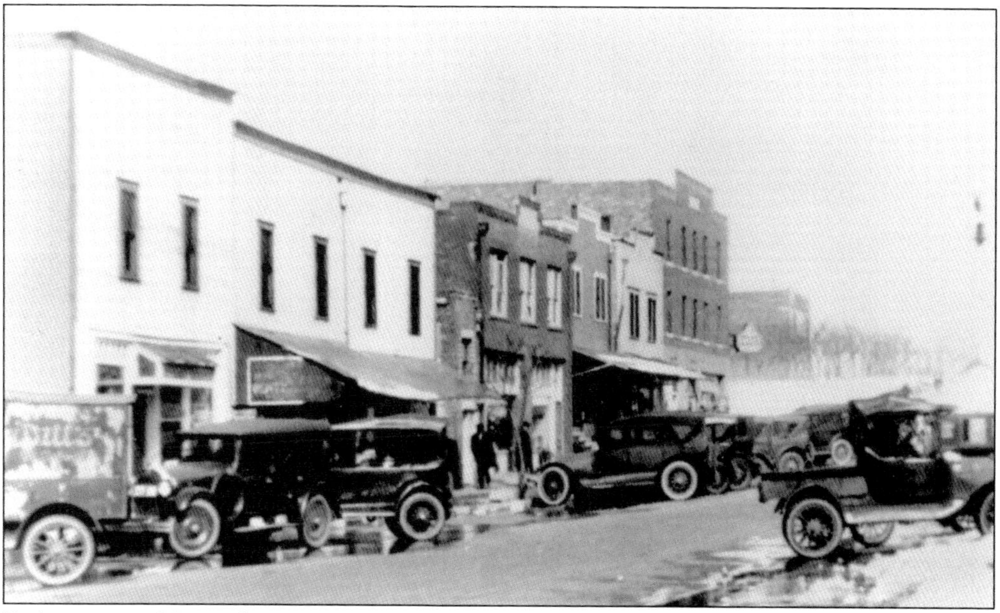

Early images of Second Street are scarce. What does exist are in private collections of families who either lived or worked in the neighborhood. What few have surfaced were taken by commercial photographers or the *Black Dispatch* newspaper. However, the photographic morgue of the newspaper is not available for use. There were two photographers located in the area, Don Simmons at 1009 East Sixth Street and the Hooker Studio, operated by J. H. Hooker, located at 220 Northeast Second Street. None of their collections have been found. This image by an unknown photographer was taken of the main business district on Second Street. Judging by the scene depicted, it was taken during winter sometime in the 1920s. (Courtesy Black Liberated Arts Center, Inc.)

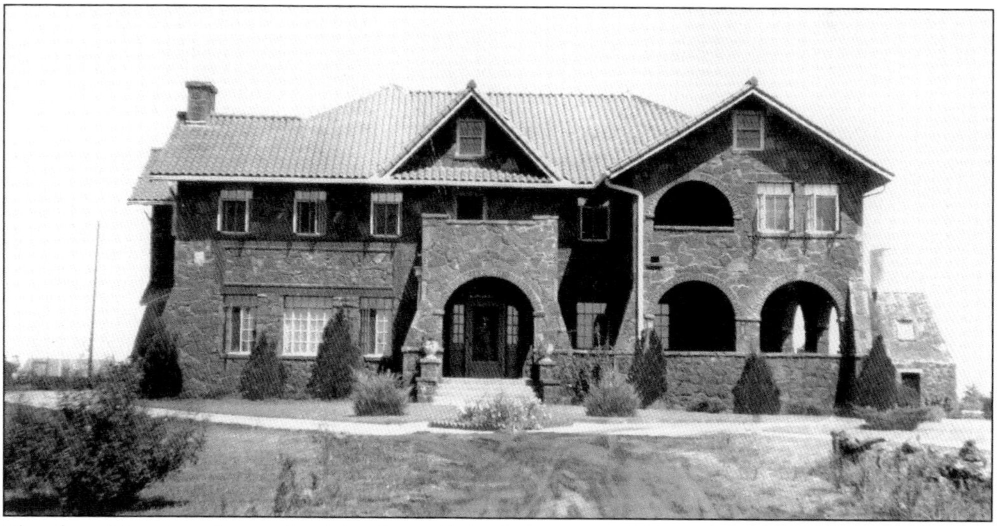

Slaughter Mansion, located at Northeast Fiftieth Street and Bryant Avenue, was the home of Dr. Wyatt A. Slaughter, a longtime physician whose office was located at 331½ Northeast Second Street. The home was built in the 1920s by William T. Vivette mentioned earlier. Constructed of red stone, the home is now the Red Stone Inn Bed and Breakfast operated by owners Mark and Ann Amme. (Courtesy Red Stone Inn Bed and Breakfast.)

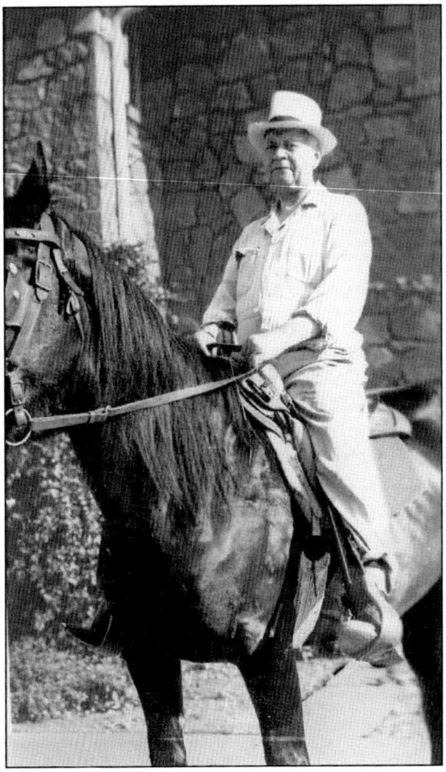

One of the most recognized leaders in the African American community was Dr. Wyatt A. Slaughter. Born in Sheffield, Alabama, in 1872, Slaughter attended Walden University in Nashville and then received his medical degree from Meharry Medical College in 1903. Slaughter moved to Oklahoma and was practicing his profession by 1904. He was instrumental as chair of a committee to enable black physicians to be admitted to the staff of the university hospital in Oklahoma City. He owned and operated a pharmacy and was cofounder of the Great Western Hospital for blacks located at 1824 Northeast Fourth Street in Oklahoma City. Slaughter is seen here at his home near Northeast Fiftieth Street and Bryant Avenue around the 1930s. He died in 1952 and in 1984 was inducted into the African American Hall of Fame located at the Omniplex at Northeast Fiftieth Street and Martin Luther King Boulevard. (Courtesy Red Stone Inn Bed and Breakfast.)

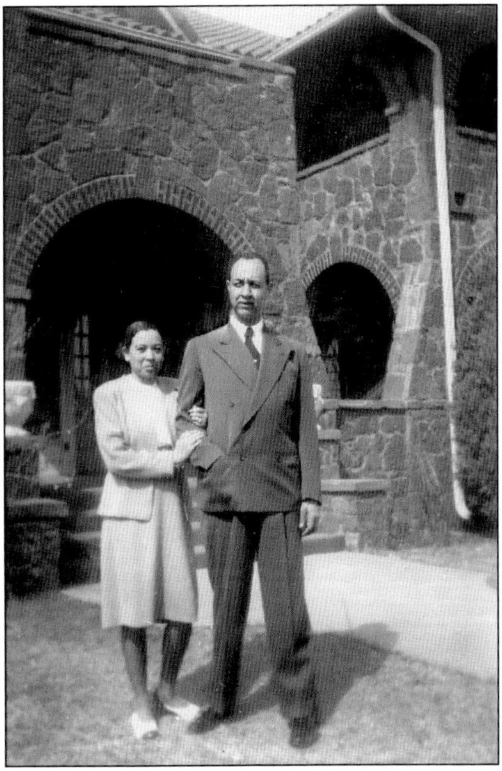

A family dynasty has continued to reign in the African American community lasting more than a century. With the marriage of Slaughter to Edna Randolph in 1907, the children of this marriage included Wyatt Handy and Saretta Slaughter. Son Wyatt also became a doctor, and Saretta married Dr. Gravelly Finley Sr. Seen here at Slaughter Mansion are Saretta and Gravelly around the early 1930s. (Courtesy Red Stone Inn Bed and Breakfast.)

Education is one of the first institutions established in a community, besides religious and government institutions. The first black school founded in Oklahoma City was in March 1891 at the corner of West California Avenue and Harvey Street. The first teacher was J. D. Randolph, a native of Galatin, Tennessee. What became Douglass High School was moved to 112 South Walnut Avenue where the AT&T Ball Park is located today in Bricktown. The first graduating class from Douglass was the class of 1903. It was also that same year that the school burned to the ground. The school relocated to 221 East California Avenue. Seen here is a rare document pertaining to the school. It is an invitation to the 1924 senior class graduation to be held at Tabernacle Baptist Church. (Courtesy Black Liberated Arts Center, Inc.)

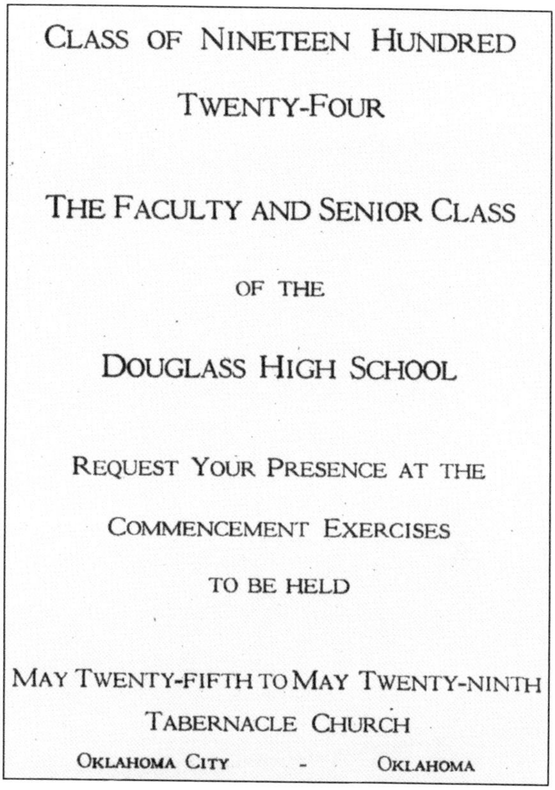

CLASS OF NINETEEN HUNDRED

TWENTY-FOUR

THE FACULTY AND SENIOR CLASS

OF THE

DOUGLASS HIGH SCHOOL

REQUEST YOUR PRESENCE AT THE

COMMENCEMENT EXERCISES

TO BE HELD

MAY TWENTY-FIFTH TO MAY TWENTY-NINTH

TABERNACLE CHURCH

OKLAHOMA CITY - OKLAHOMA

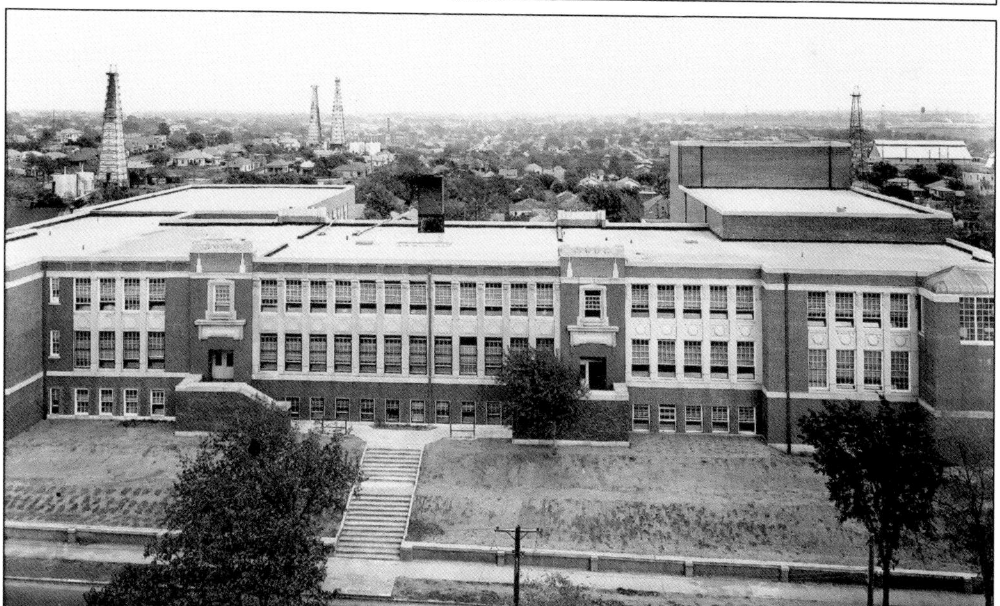

Douglass High School has had several addresses in its long history. In January 1934, the cornerstone was laid for the new Douglass High School at Sixth and High Streets. The school was dedicated on August 31, 1934, as it was ready to receive students. Note the oil derricks in the background. This photograph was taken by Z. P. Meyers of Oklahoma City. (Courtesy Oklahoma Historical Society.)

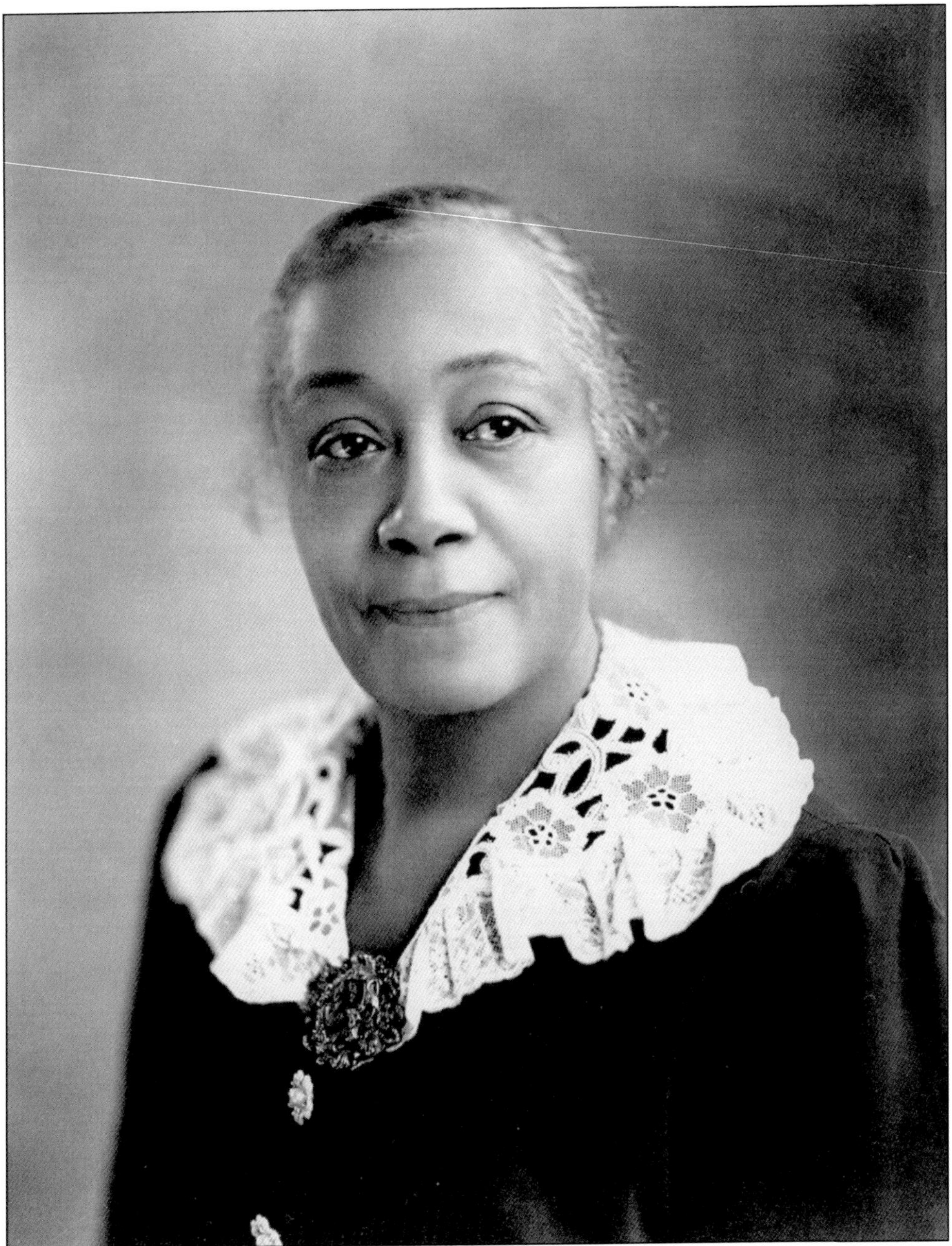

There were many teachers and administrators who were associated with Douglass High School. None was more closely associated and had the greatest impact on her students than Zelia Page Breaux. Breaux, the daughter of Inman Page, first president of Langston University, was the music teacher at Douglass. She began her teaching assignment at the school in 1918. In February 1944, Breaux was elected president of the Oklahoma Association of Negro Teachers, becoming only the second woman to be president of the organization. Breaux retired from Douglass in August 1948 after 30 years of service. She, along with F. E. Whitlow, built the Aldridge Theatre in 1919. This image was taken by Harry Watton, early Oklahoma City portrait photographer. (Courtesy Oklahoma Historical Society.)

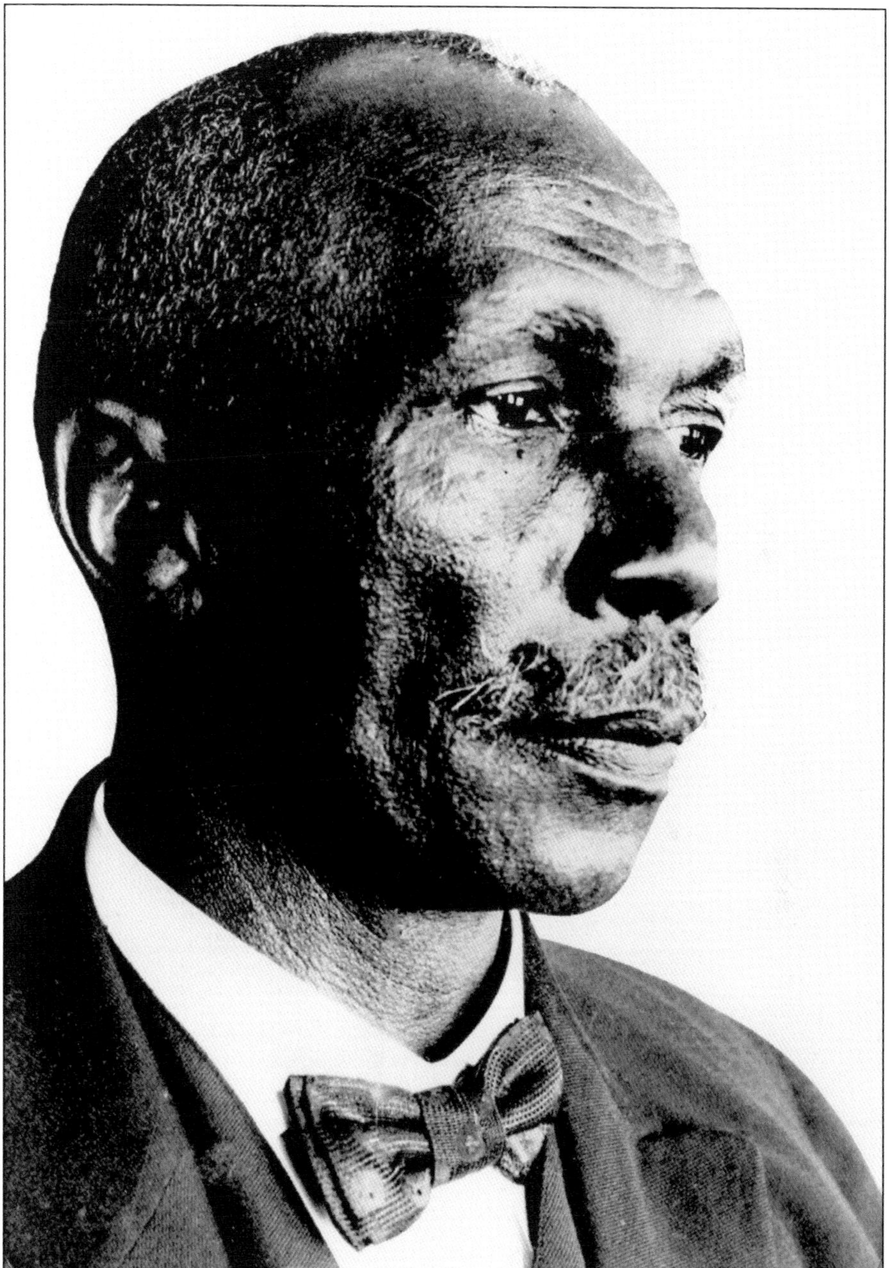

Inman Page, like his daughter Zelia, is synonymous with African American education. Born into slavery in 1852 on a Virginia plantation, Page was not destined for common labor. During the Civil War he made his way to Washington, D.C., where he had the advantage of educational opportunities. He eventually graduated from Brown University in 1877. He secured a professorship at Roger Williams University in Nashville, Tennessee. In 1898, he became the first president of the Colored Agricultural and Normal University at Langston, Oklahoma Territory. The last dozen years of his life he was a supervising principal in various African American schools in Oklahoma City. He died within six months of retiring from the school system in 1935. (Courtesy Oklahoma Historical Society.)

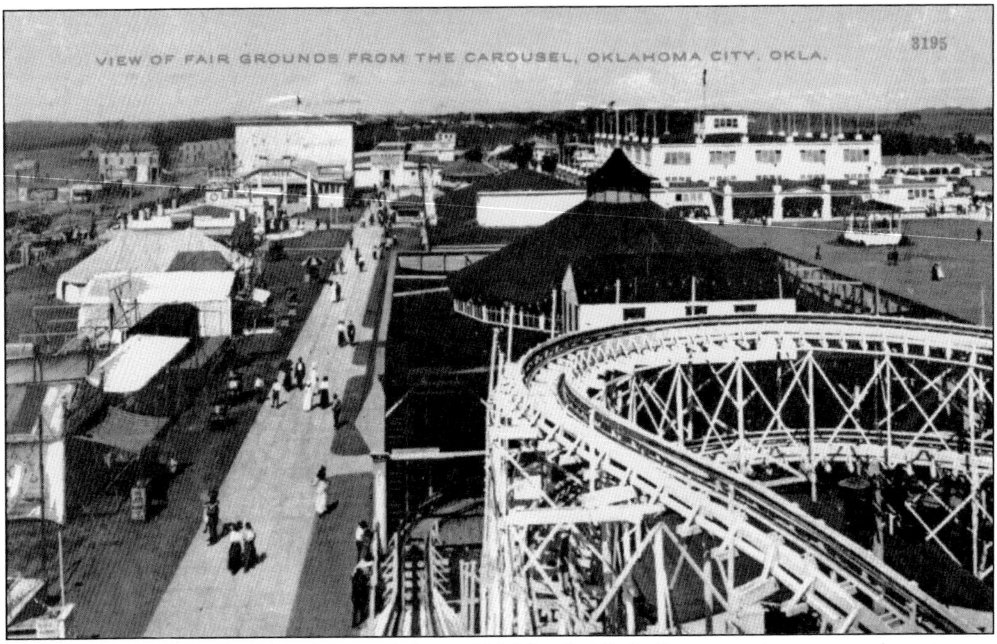

Before Douglass High School moved from 600 North High Street to its present location at 900 North Eastern Avenue (now Martin Luther King Boulevard), the old Oklahoma State Fair grounds was located there. This view of the grounds, taken from the carousel, is dated from around the mid-1920s. This picture postcard is from the James E. Stewart collection. (Courtesy Oklahoma Historical Society.)

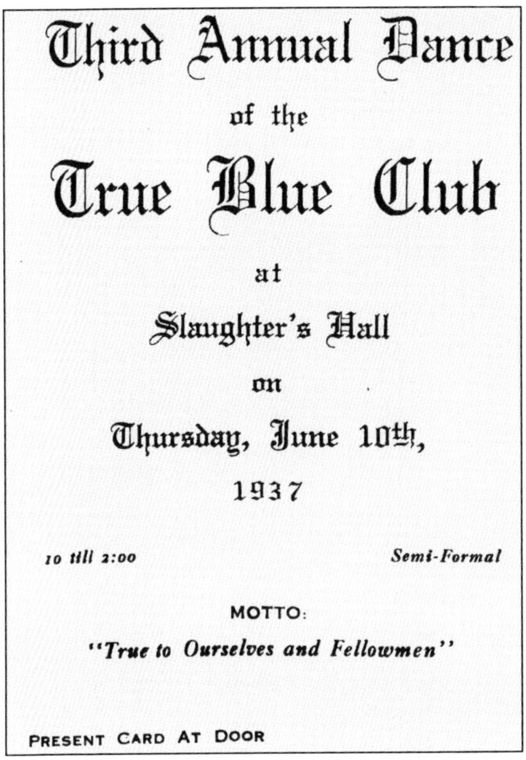

Third Annual Dance

of the

True Blue Club

at

Slaughter's Hall

on

Thursday, June 10th,

1937

10 till 2:00 *Semi-Formal*

MOTTO:

"True to Ourselves and Fellowmen"

PRESENT CARD AT DOOR

Mention the name Slaughter's Hall to individuals who lived near Second Street and the surrounding area and one will receive many treasured memories. Located on the second floor over the True Blue Club at 331½ Northeast Second Street, it was in the heart of Deep Deuce. Every blues or jazz musician of any consequence jammed or performed at Slaughter's Hall. Every Friday night a dance was held at Slaughter's Hall. It was the "in place to be" on Second Street. (Courtesy Black Liberated Arts Center, Inc.)

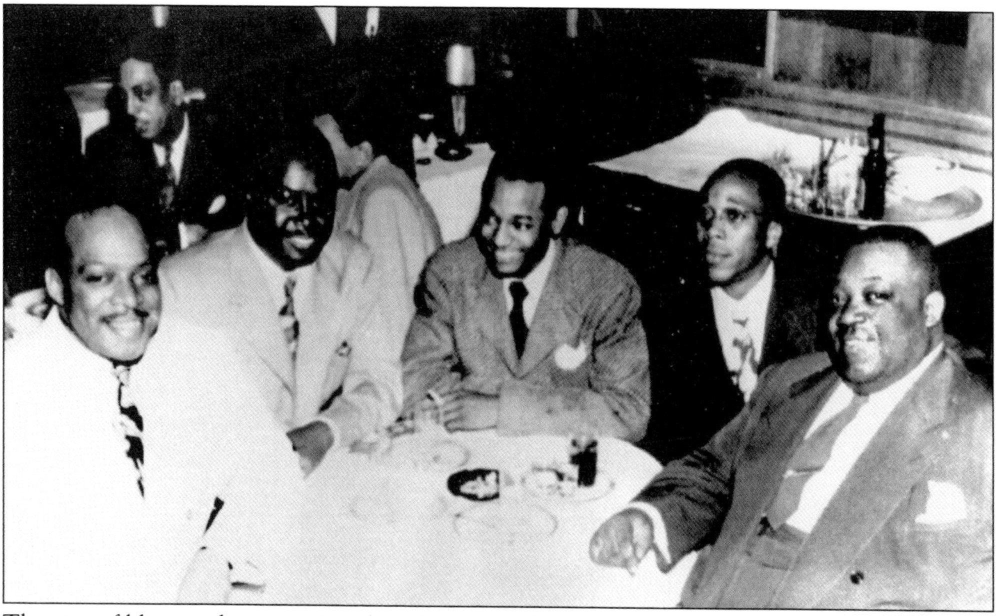

The rise of blues and jazz was incubated in Deep Deuce or Second Street. No other place had more to do with the development of these musical genres than Second Street. Notables such as Charlie and Eddie Christian, Leslie Sheffield, the Blue Devils, Leroy Parks, or Jimmy Rushing (Mr. Five by Five) all honed their musical talents at places such as Slaughter's Hall, the Hole, Ruby's Grill, and the list goes on. Here in this rare image are on the far left Count Basie, second from right Charlie Christian, and on the far right Rushing. It is not known where they were when this photograph was taken, but it came from the files of the *Black Dispatch* newspaper in the early 1940s. (Courtesy Black Liberated Arts Center, Inc.)

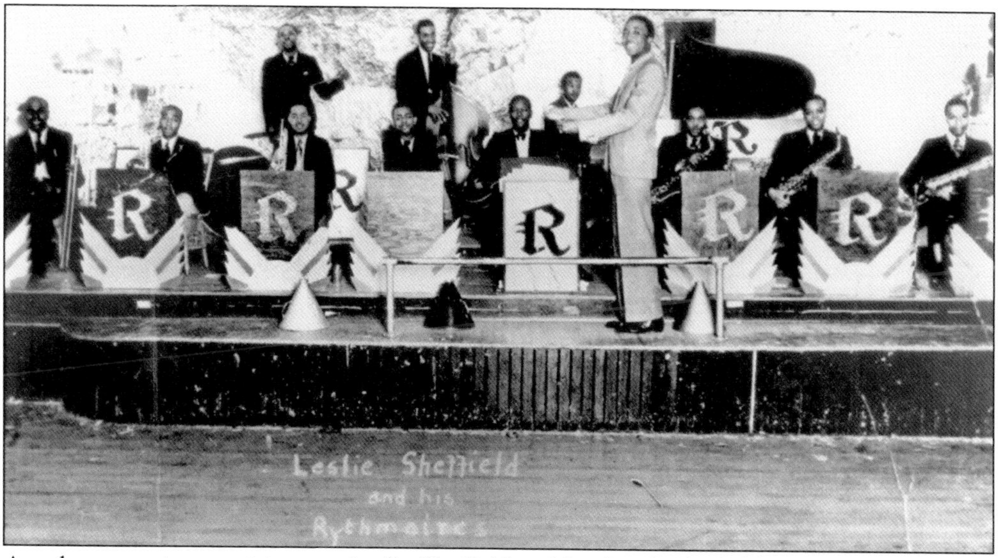

Another great jazz musician was Leslie Sheffield and his band. Sheffield is seen here directing the band, saxophonist Leroy Parks stated that this performance was at the 330 Club on West California Avenue in Oklahoma City. It was white club, and Sheffield's band played there often. Sheffield was not only an accomplished pianist, but also arranged and composed musical pieces as well. (Courtesy Black Liberated Arts Center, Inc.)

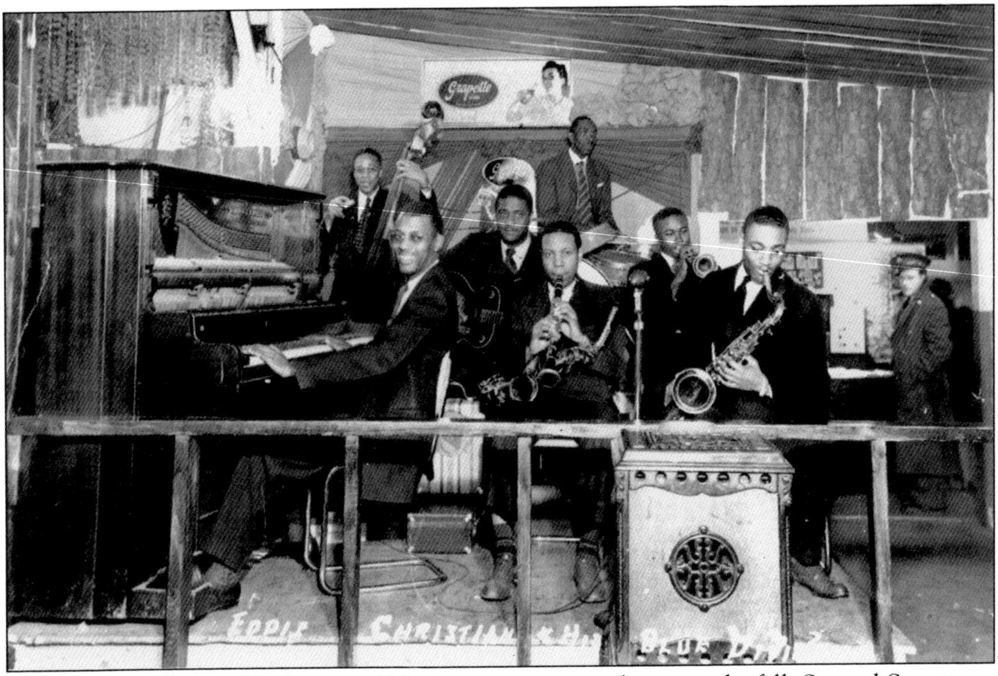

Second Street during the day was all business enterprises, but as night fell, Second Street was transformed, the atmosphere was decidedly different, and one could feel the excitement. The depth of the blues and jazz tradition ran very deep in northeast Oklahoma City. Eddie Christian, older brother to jazz guitarist Charlie Christian, played many times at the local venues on Second Street. In the photograph shown here, Eddie can be seen playing the piano while Leroy Parks, at the far right, is playing the saxophone. (Courtesy Black Liberated Arts Center, Inc.)

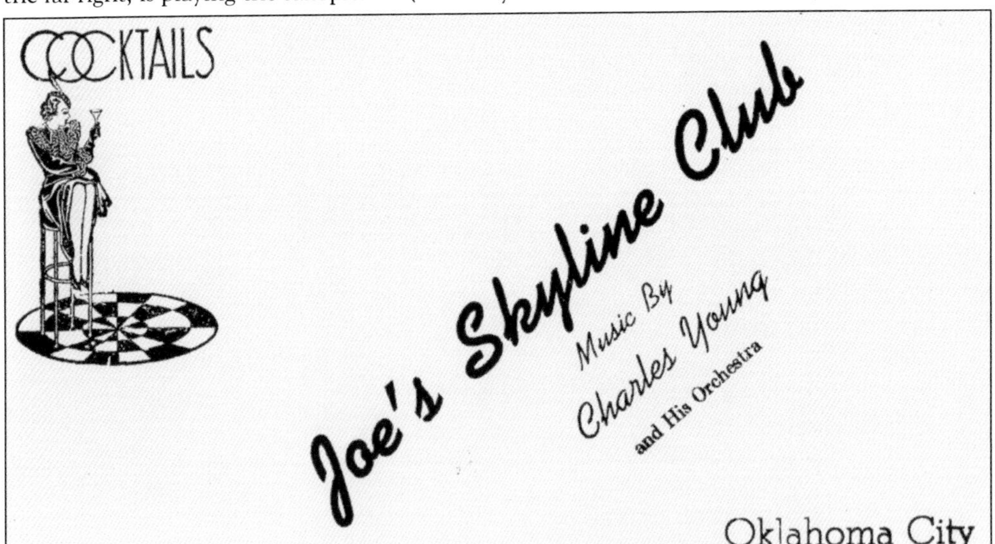

Nightclubs provided the patron with a means to escape ordinary life even for just a little while. It was an opportunity to share with friends a good time with drinks, dancing, or listening to the band play until close. One such venue was Joe's Skyline Club at the southeast corner of Northeast Fourth Street and Eastern Avenue now Martin Luther King Boulevard. At one time Leroy Parks managed the club. (Courtesy Black Liberated Arts Center, Inc.)

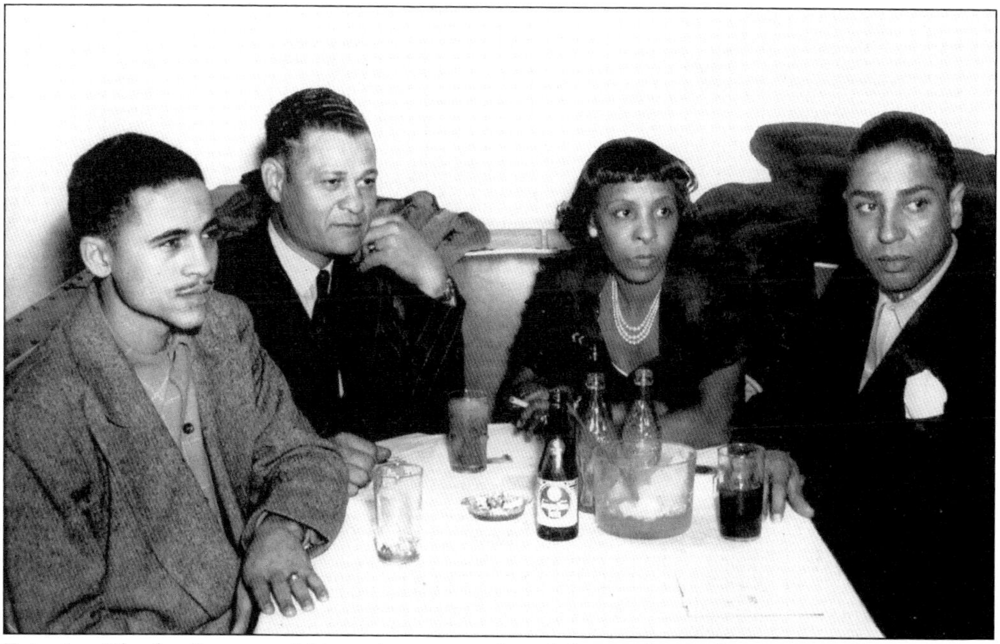

Enjoying Charles Young and his orchestra are, from left to right, Willie Ray Jr., Ellsworth, I. V., and Jack Kirk at Joe's Skyline Club. The photographer is unknown. (Courtesy Black Liberated Arts Center, Inc.)

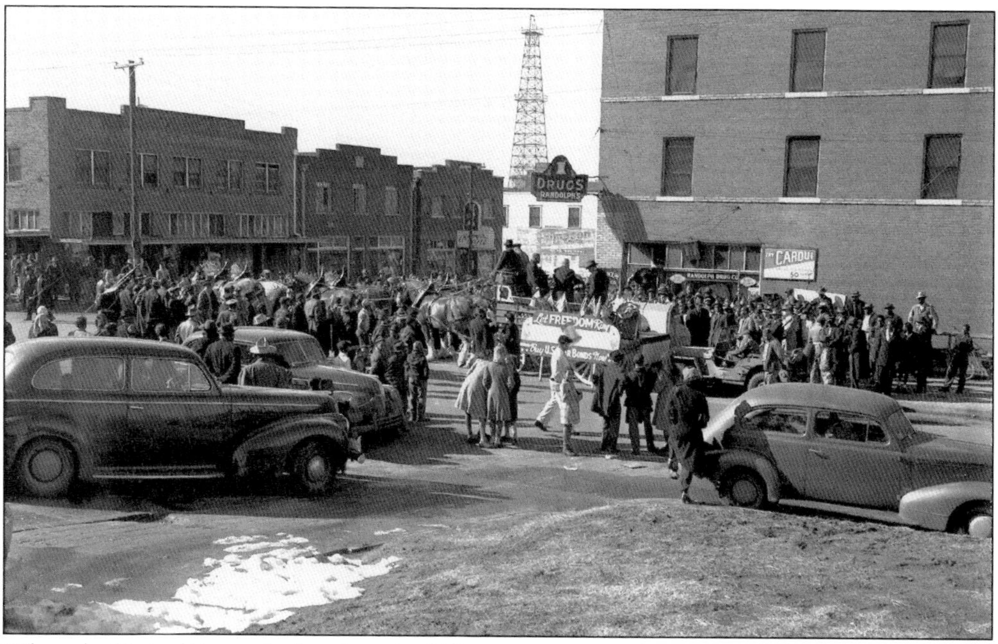

When the United States declared war in 1941, many patriotic events were held across the country in support of the war effort. On Second Street, parades were held as well as rallies to gain the spirit of sacrifice to win the war. In 1942, photographer Z. P. Meyers captured several scenes of a rally to galvanize the public. This image, taken across the street from Randolph Drug Company at 331 Northeast Second Street, shows a good crowd gathering to hear dignitaries give rousing speeches. (Courtesy Oklahoma Historical Society.)

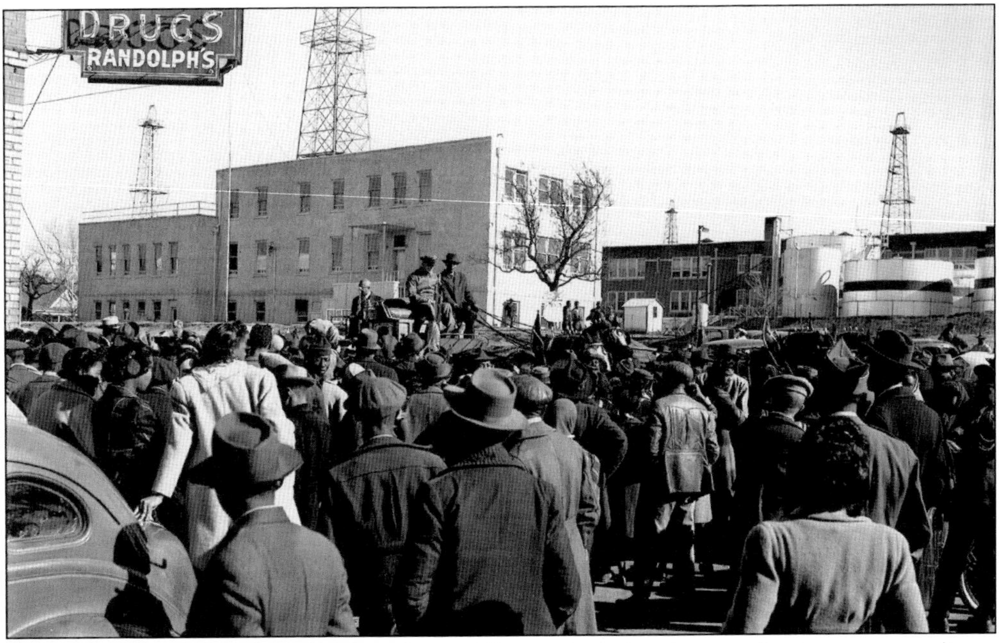

This is another view of the rally along Second Street capturing the crowd as it prepares to listen to the speakers about the war effort. Here Z. P. Meyers photographs from in front of Randolph Drug Company. (Courtesy Oklahoma Historical Society.)

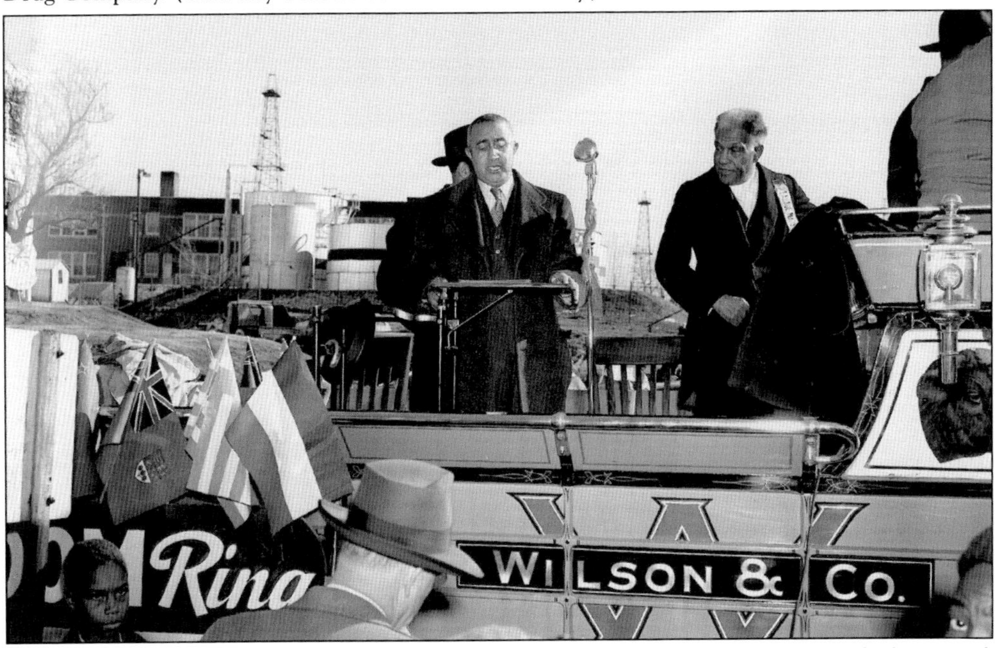

A close-up view of the speaker reveals that at the podium is the publisher of the *Black Dispatch* Roscoe Dunjee. The *Black Dispatch* was established in 1917 and had not only a local following, but a national one as well. The newspaper continued operating at 324 Northeast Second Street until 1982 when it ceased publication. Dunjee arrived in Oklahoma City in 1892 and was a powerful voice for the African American community for many years. This photograph is by Meyers Photo Shop of Oklahoma City. (Courtesy Oklahoma Historical Society.)

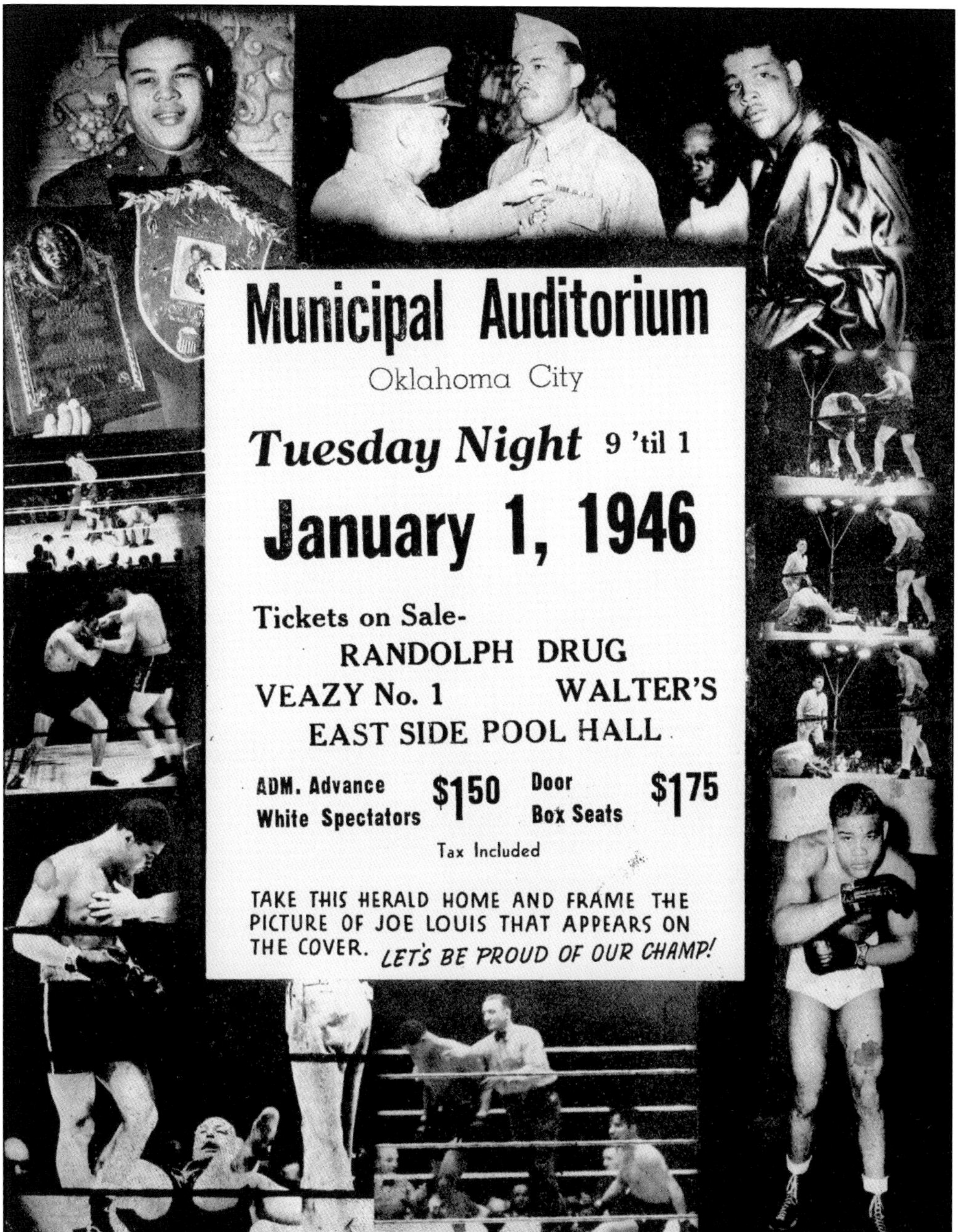

Special events of all kinds added to the quality of life in northeast Oklahoma City. On New Years day 1946, boxing champion Joe Louis would appear in Oklahoma City at the Municipal Auditorium. Tickets were available at Randolph Drug Company and East Side Pool Hall. (Courtesy Black Liberated Arts Center, Inc.)

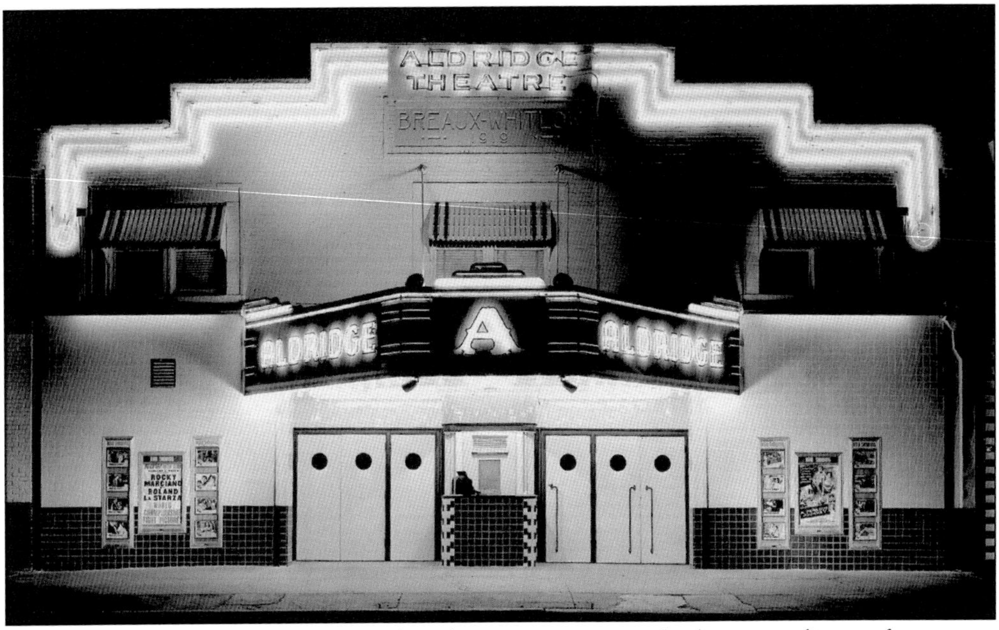

Probably the most central gathering place for entertainment, whether it was live performances, music, drama, or comedy, including motion pictures, was at the Aldridge Theatre. Built by Zelia Page Breaux and F. E. Whitlow in 1919, the Aldridge was the first theater built in the black community. It was not uncommon for individuals to have their own photographs taken in front of the Aldridge. This night view of the theater was taken by Ray Jacoby, a local Oklahoma City photographer. (Courtesy Oklahoma Historical Society.)

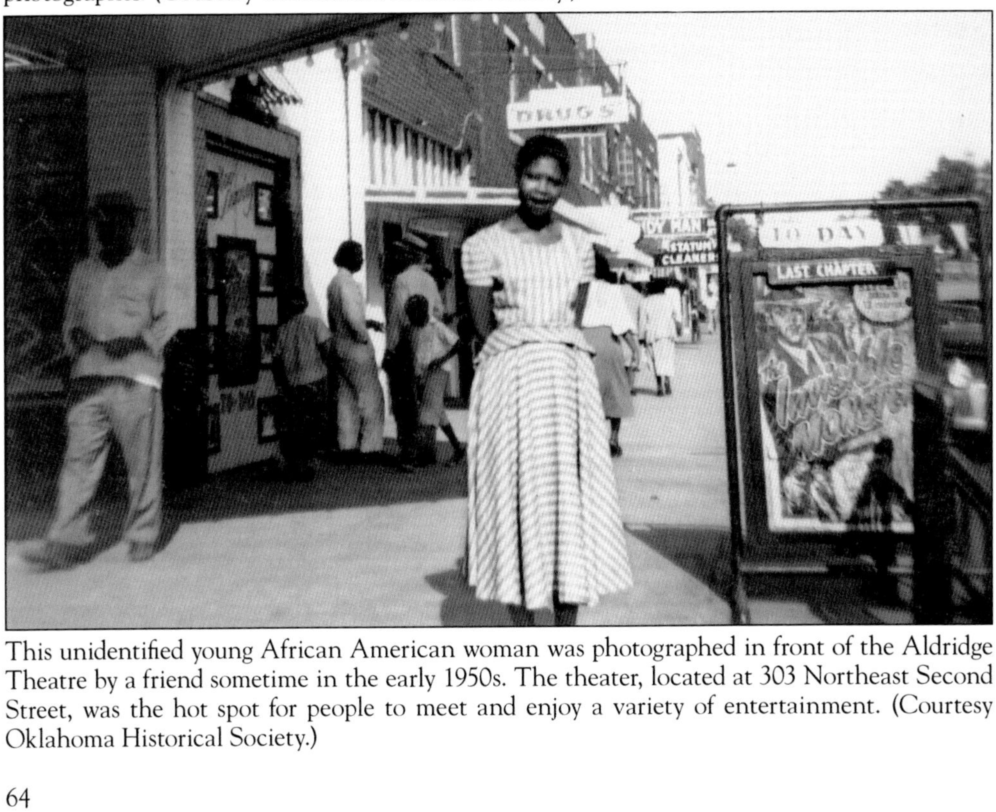

This unidentified young African American woman was photographed in front of the Aldridge Theatre by a friend sometime in the early 1950s. The theater, located at 303 Northeast Second Street, was the hot spot for people to meet and enjoy a variety of entertainment. (Courtesy Oklahoma Historical Society.)

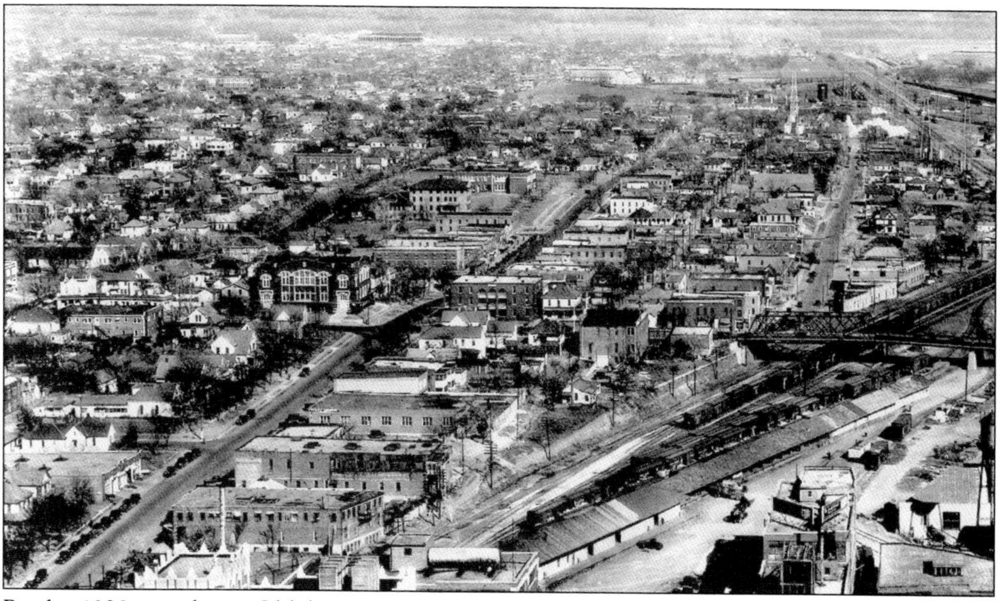

By the 1930s northeast Oklahoma City was expanding beyond the set boundaries that blacks could live or establish business concerns in. This aerial view demonstrates that growth. Near the center of the image is Calvary Baptist Church, a mainstay in the African American community. To the right is the Canton Hotel where many notable blacks would stay when visiting the city. With segregation still evident, prominent persons such as Joe Louis, Count Basie, Marian Anderson, and many other African Americans were barred from staying at the Skirvin or Biltmore Hotels until after the late 1960s when segregation was abolished. (Courtesy Oklahoma Historical Society.)

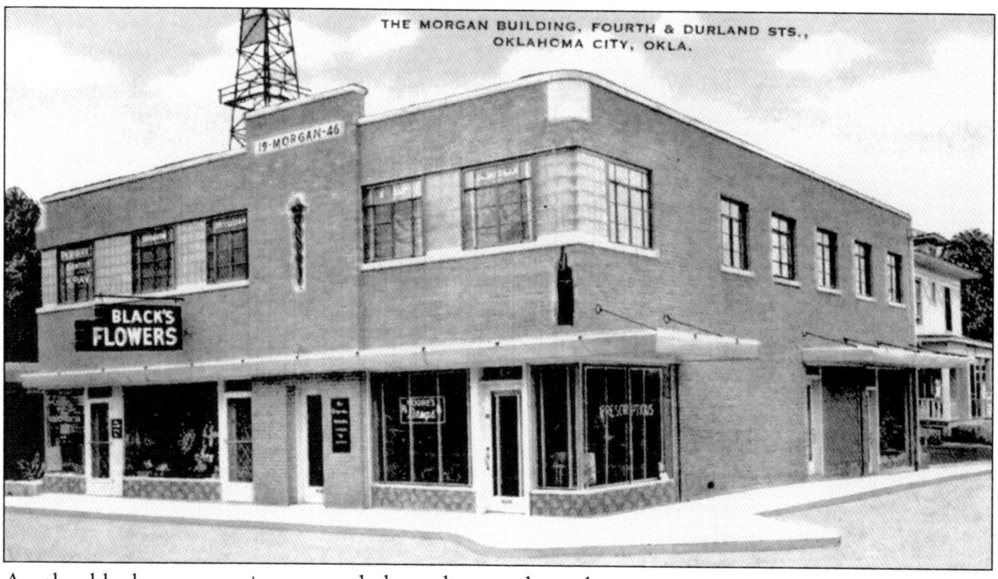

As the black community expanded to the north and east, new construction was evident, especially after World War II. In 1946, the Morgan building was built by Dr. C. Wesley Morgan. Located at Northeast Fourth Street and Durland Street, the building housed a dental office, Black's Flowers, a beauty salon, and several other small businesses. The Morgan building still stands, however, it is not in use. (Courtesy Oklahoma Historical Society.)

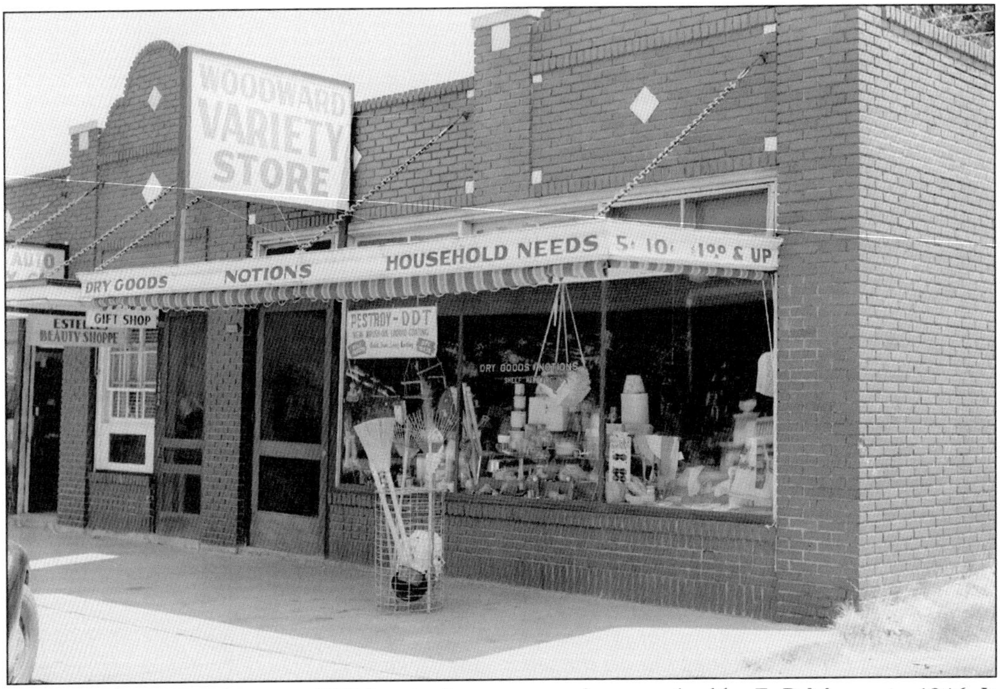

Woodward's Variety Store at 1308 Lottie Avenue was photographed by Z. P. Meyers in 1946. It was typical of the small neighborhood businesses that sold household items. (Courtesy Oklahoma Historical Society.)

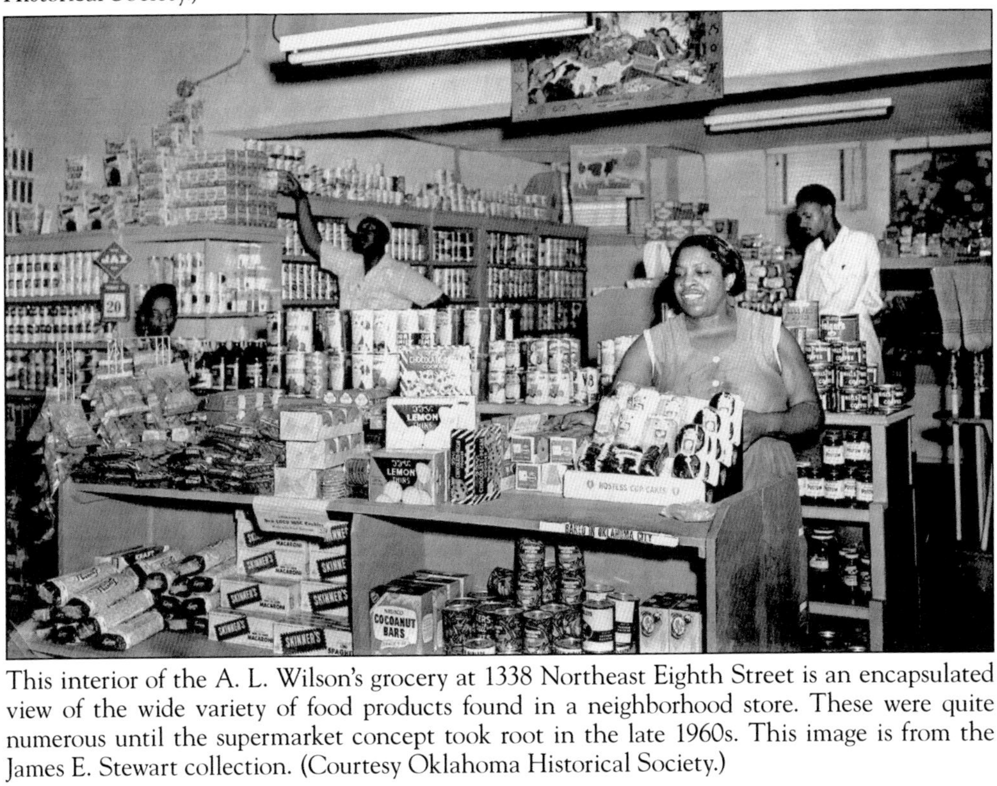

This interior of the A. L. Wilson's grocery at 1338 Northeast Eighth Street is an encapsulated view of the wide variety of food products found in a neighborhood store. These were quite numerous until the supermarket concept took root in the late 1960s. This image is from the James E. Stewart collection. (Courtesy Oklahoma Historical Society.)

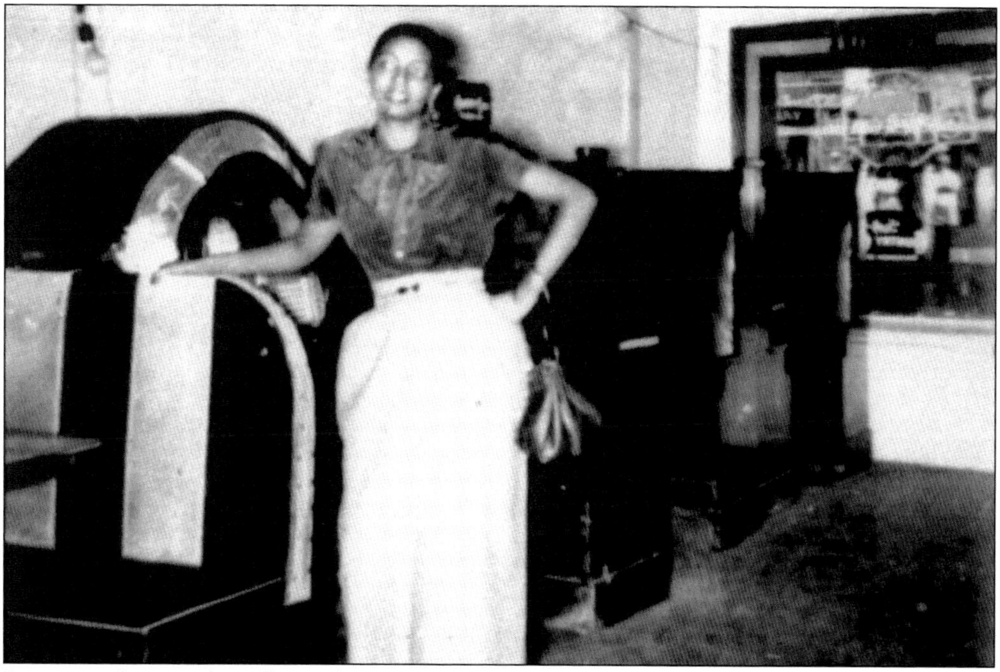

Businesses large and small were located along Northeast First through Fourth Streets for several blocks in any direction. However, Second Street was considered by all to be the hub of the business district in northeast Oklahoma City. One such enterprise was the Busy Bee Beer Garden at 325 Northeast Second Street. This interior view has Hazalle Smith posing in front of the jukebox. The photographer is unknown, but the image is from 1952. (Courtesy Oklahoma Historical Society.)

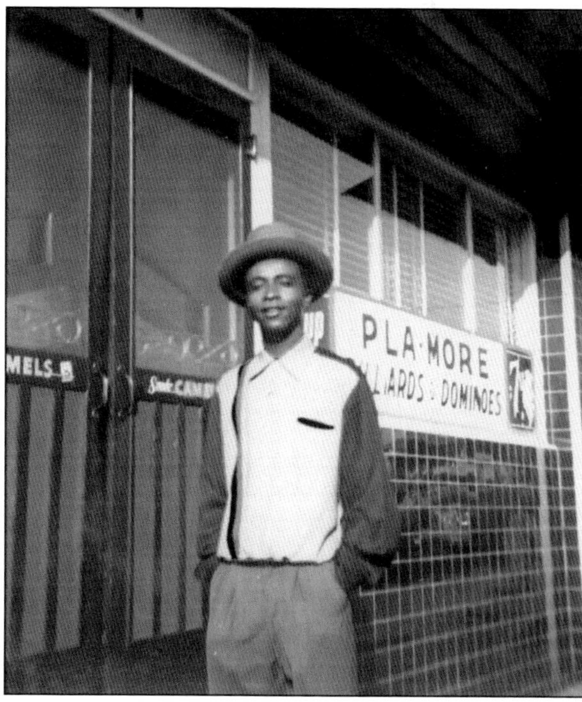

Another business that provided entertainment to its customers was the Pla-More Billiards and Domino Parlor at 321 Northeast Second Street. Ross Minor was the owner of the business. The person standing in front of the business is identified only as Jimmy in this 1952 photograph. (Courtesy Oklahoma Historical Society.)

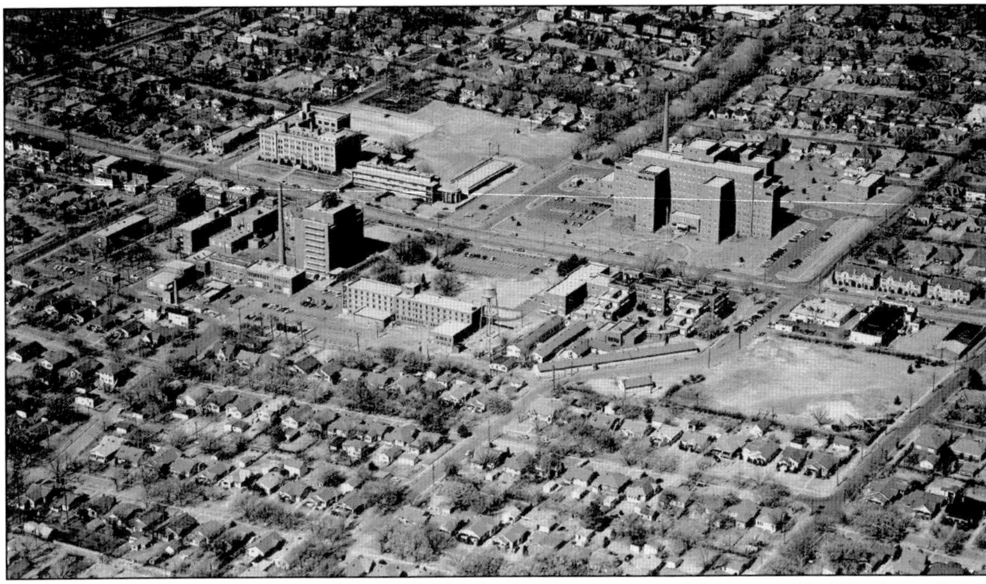

After the World War II, the population of Oklahoma City increased dramatically. The boundaries that inhibited the natural expansion of the black community, due to segregation, were being challenged in the courts. At one time no African American could live past California Avenue, then Northeast Fourth Street, then Eighth Street. Although open housing laws would not take effect in Oklahoma City until 1968, the migration of the black population beyond the "set boundaries" stipulated by the white-dominated society took place. This aerial view of a vibrant neighborhood near Northeast Thirteenth Street includes University Hospital. This image was taken by Meyers Photo Shop in the early 1950s. (Courtesy Oklahoma Historical Society.)

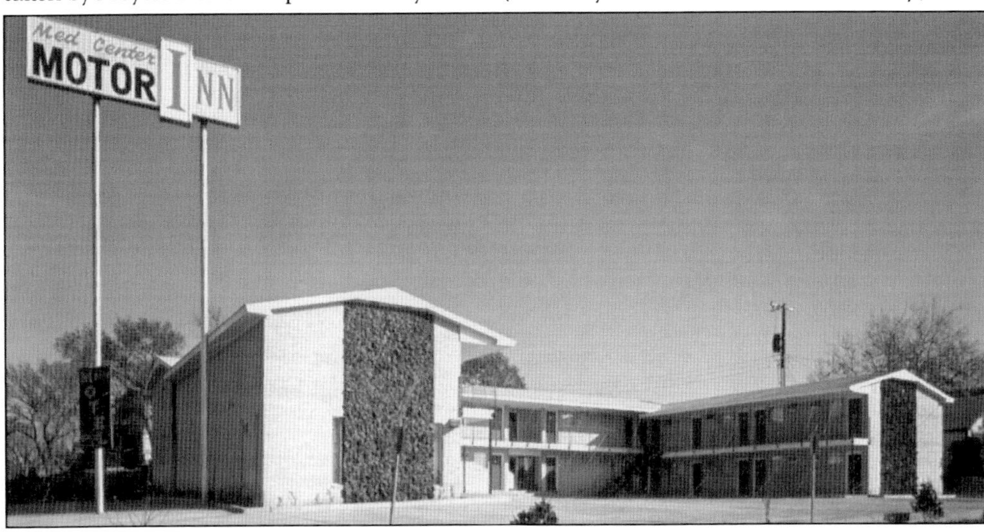

A growing medical facility along the Northeast Thirteenth Street corridor, east of Lincoln Boulevard, over time supplanted the residential neighborhood. Along with University Hospital, the Veterans Hospital was added, Presbyterian now O. U. Medical Center and Children's Hospital has transformed the area into a huge medical complex. To cater to patrons visiting patients, motels began to emerge nearby. This 1950s vintage postcard of the Med Center Motor Inn at Northeast Thirteenth Street and Stonewall Avenue filled that need. (Courtesy Oklahoma Historical Society.)

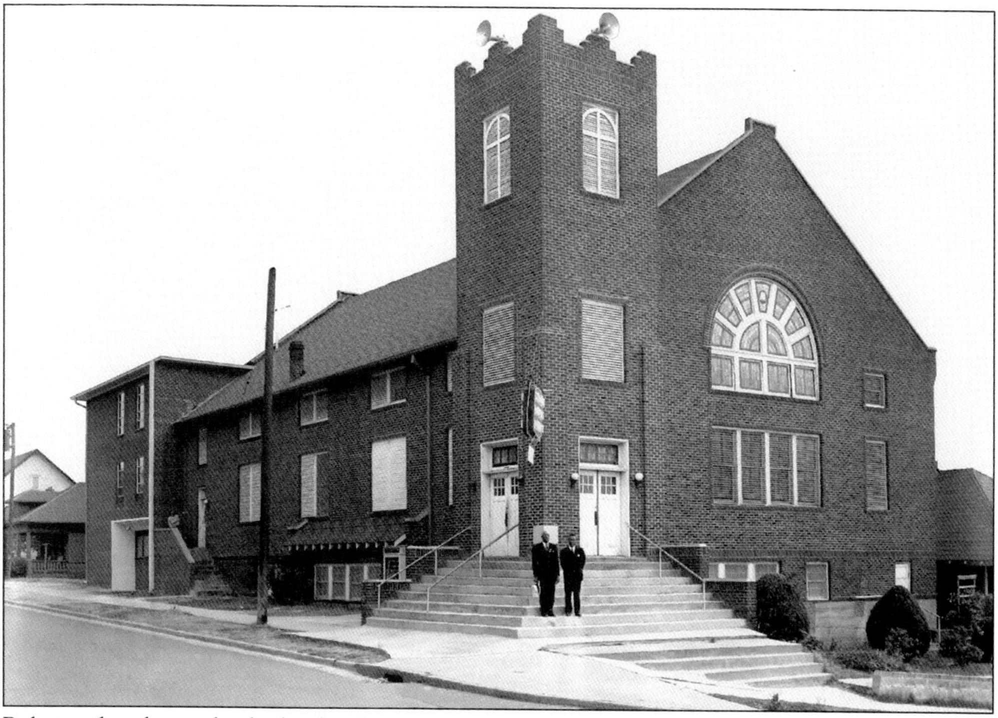

Religion has been the bedrock of society. Regardless of the many businesses that seemed to dominate the Deep Deuce area that provided entertainment that was considered by many religious denominations to be sinful such as dance halls, beer taverns, or billiard rooms, churches of every type were, and continue to be, a major presence in the life of residents in northeast Oklahoma City. One can see houses of worship practically on every corner. St. John Baptist Church at 801 Northeast Second Street is seen here in May 1952. (Courtesy Oklahoma Historical Society.)

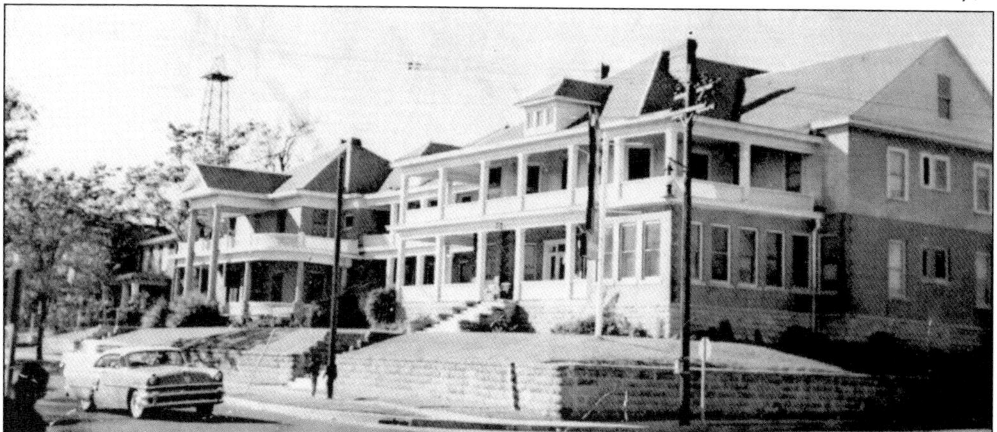

HOTEL YOUNGBLOOD - 325 N.E. 4th & Stiles - OKLA. CITY, OKLA.

Another famous landmark near Deep Deuce was the Hotel Youngblood at 325 Northeast Fourth Street and Stiles Avenue. The hotel opened to the public in 1954 and was owned by Dr. Stafford R. and Verona Youngblood of Oklahoma City. The imposing building contained 75 rooms and was a fixture in the community until it closed in 1982. In the late 1980s, the building was demolished to make room for the Centennial Expressway or what is now Interstate 235. This image is from the James E. Stewart collection. (Courtesy Oklahoma Historical Society.)

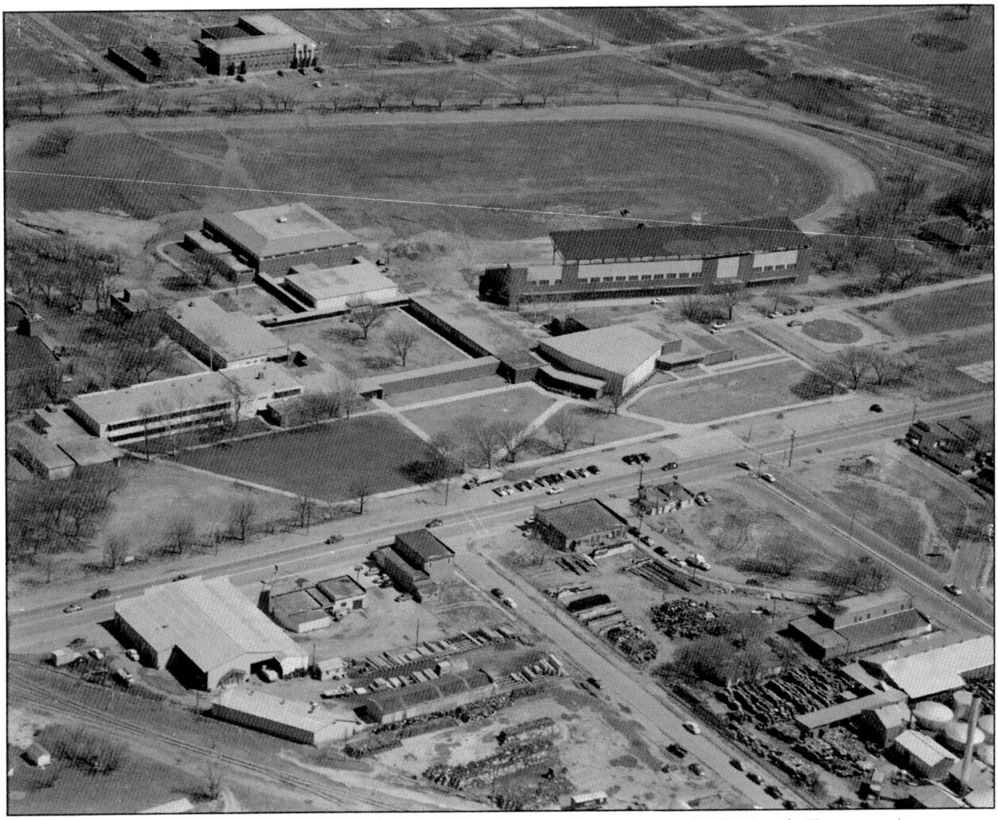

This aerial view of Douglass High School shows its new location at 900 North Eastern Avenue or what is now Martin Luther King Boulevard. The student population grew dramatically during the 1940s and 1950s, outgrowing its former building at 600 North High Street. In 2006, the school seen here was replaced with a modern facility to accommodate an ever-growing student body. The photograph was taken in April 1955 by Z. P. Meyers. (Courtesy Oklahoma Historical Society.)

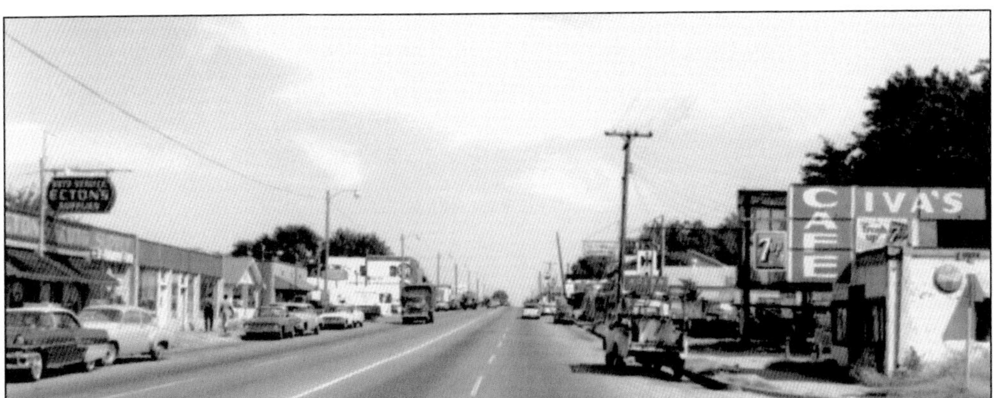

Not far from the high school is this scene, looking south from North Eastern Avenue and East Park, of the various businesses along the street. The photograph was taken by Barney Hillerman in September 1960. (Courtesy Oklahoma Historical Society.)

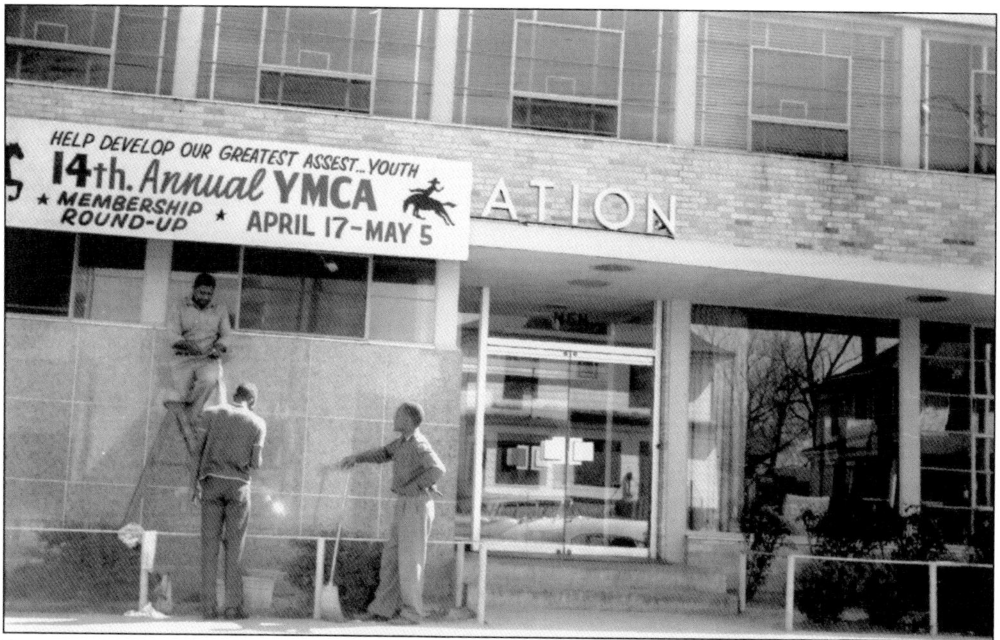

Preparation for the annual membership campaign for the northeast YMCA located at 614 Northeast Fourth Street is underway. This photograph was taken by James C. Gatewood, director of the East Side YMCA, in April 1961. (Courtesy Oklahoma Historical Society.)

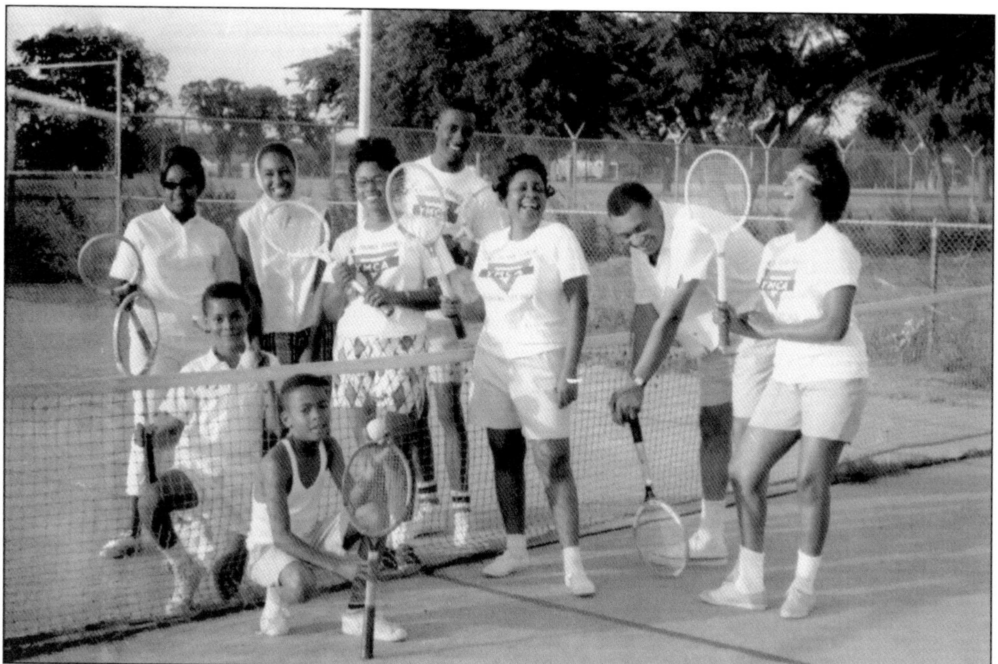

Because of limited opportunities for recreational activities for both men and women, the East Side YMCA provided a venue for women to enjoy the benefits of team sports. This women's tennis team is seen here hamming it up for the photographer James C. Gatewood. Gatewood took this image on August 8, 1961. (Courtesy Oklahoma Historical Society.)

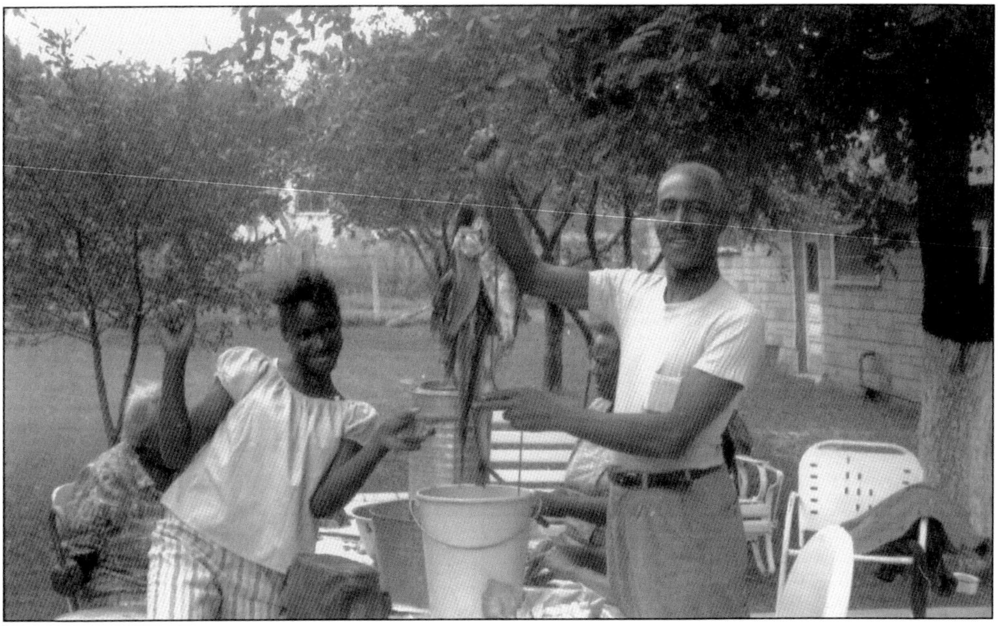

The number one recreational activity in the United States is hunting and fishing. On any given weekend, hundreds of thousands of people will be enjoying the benefits of the great outdoors. Here a family has arrived home from a fishing trip and is exhibiting its catch of the day. It must have been one of those warm winter days Oklahoma is noted for as this photograph was taken by James C. Gatewood on December 20, 1961. (Courtesy Oklahoma Historical Society.)

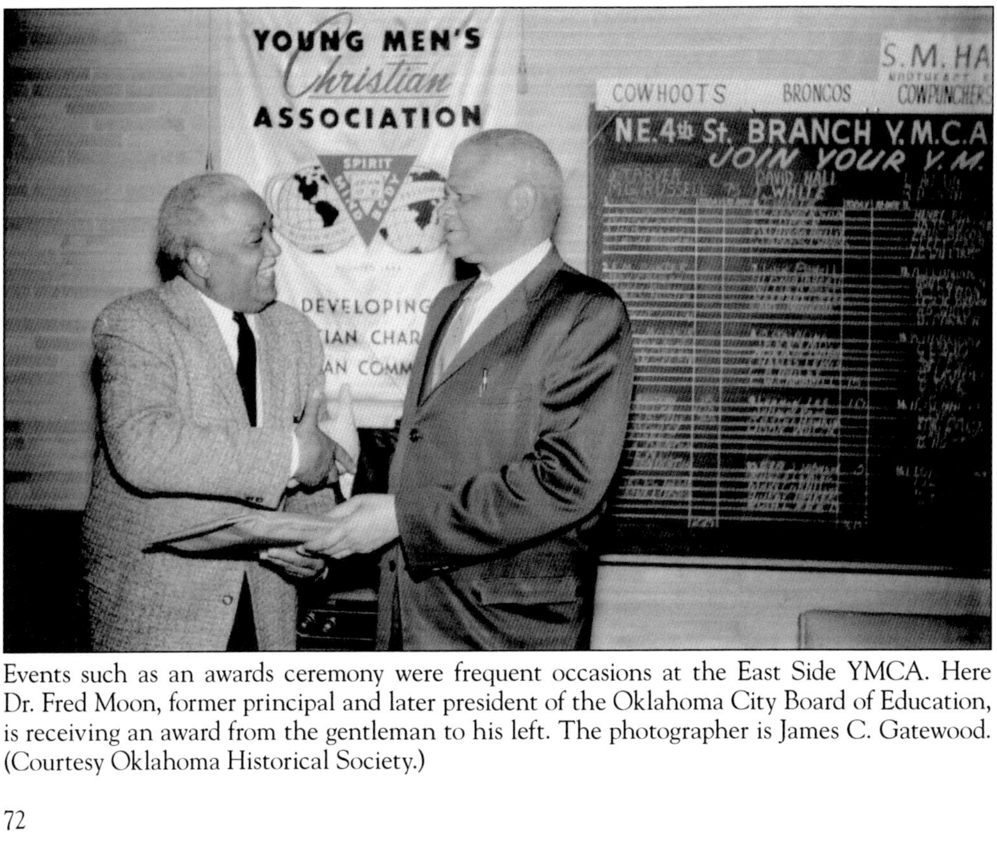

Events such as an awards ceremony were frequent occasions at the East Side YMCA. Here Dr. Fred Moon, former principal and later president of the Oklahoma City Board of Education, is receiving an award from the gentleman to his left. The photographer is James C. Gatewood. (Courtesy Oklahoma Historical Society.)

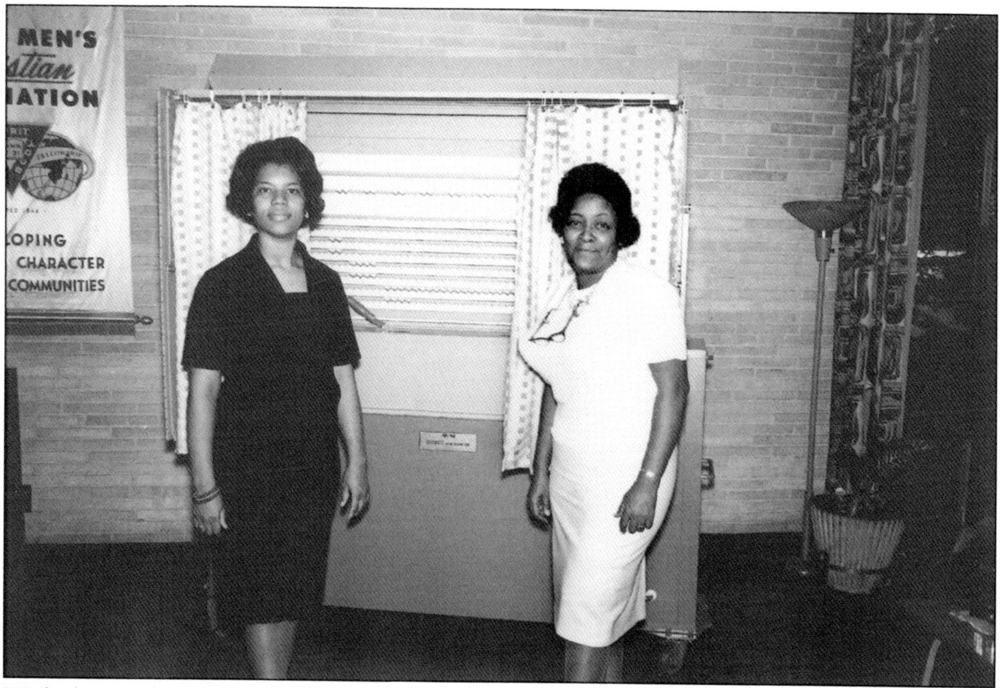

With the Civil Rights Act of 1964 and the subsequent voter rights that was passed by Congress, literacy tests and the hated poll tax became things of the past. Threats and intimidation at the ballot box came to an end. The significance of this image cannot be overstated. For the first time black Americans could vote in their own neighborhoods without fear. The voting booth seen here is in the lobby of the East Side YMCA with two unidentified poll workers. This photograph was taken by James C. Gatewood around 1964. (Courtesy Oklahoma Historical Society.)

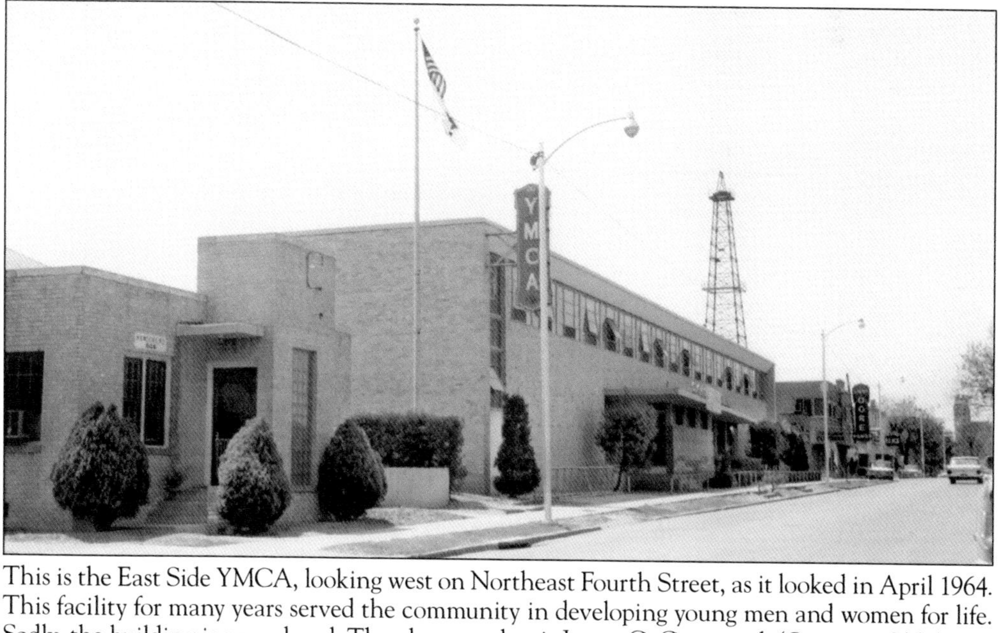

This is the East Side YMCA, looking west on Northeast Fourth Street, as it looked in April 1964. This facility for many years served the community in developing young men and women for life. Sadly, the building is now closed. The photographer is James C. Gatewood. (Courtesy Oklahoma Historical Society.)

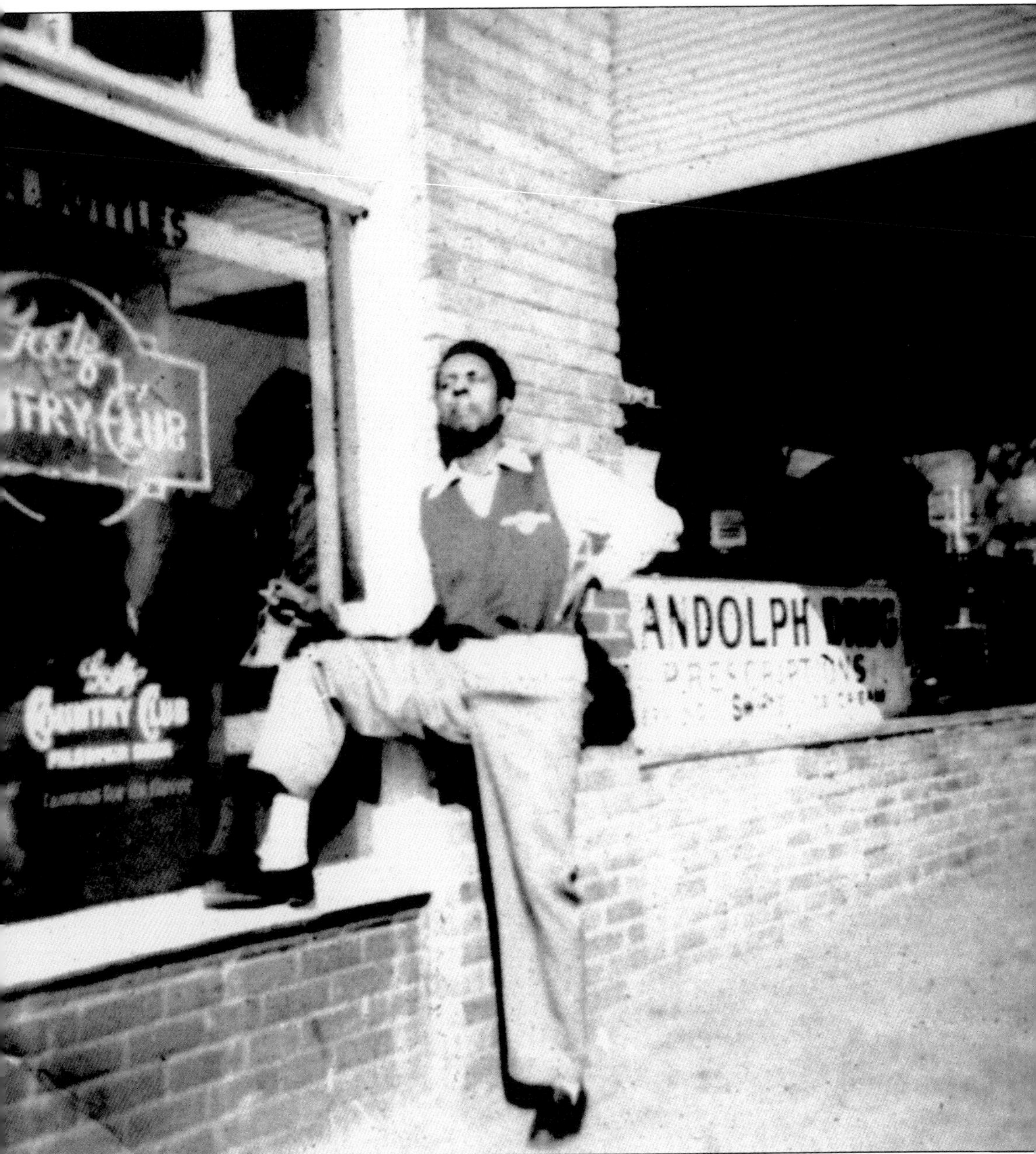

This personal photograph is of Billy Jack Fisher in front of Randolph Drug Company along Second Street in its heyday in 1952. In a few short years, many changes would occur and Deep Deuce, the heart and soul of Second Street and the African American community, would be gone. (Courtesy Oklahoma Historical Society.)

Five

THE WAREHOUSE DISTRICT

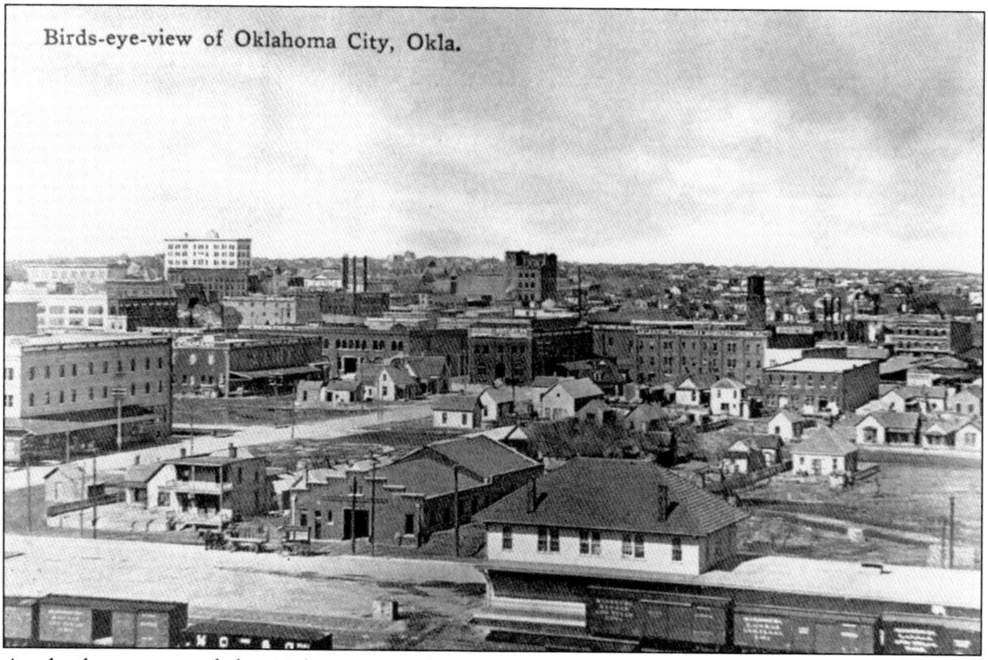

At the beginning of the 20th century, the *Daily Times-Journal* issued a detailed chronicle of the progress of Oklahoma City in terms of population, banking, manufacturing, business, and residential construction. The special edition of the newspaper provides an interesting glimpse into the tremendous growth of the city. This image dates from around 1910 and shows multistoried brick structures dotting what once was open prairie. In the foreground is the Wells Fargo and Company Livery Stable located at 115 East Reno Avenue. Built in 1906, this building is listed on the National Register of Historic Places. As late as 2006, it was used as a curio shop. (Courtesy Oklahoma Historical Society.)

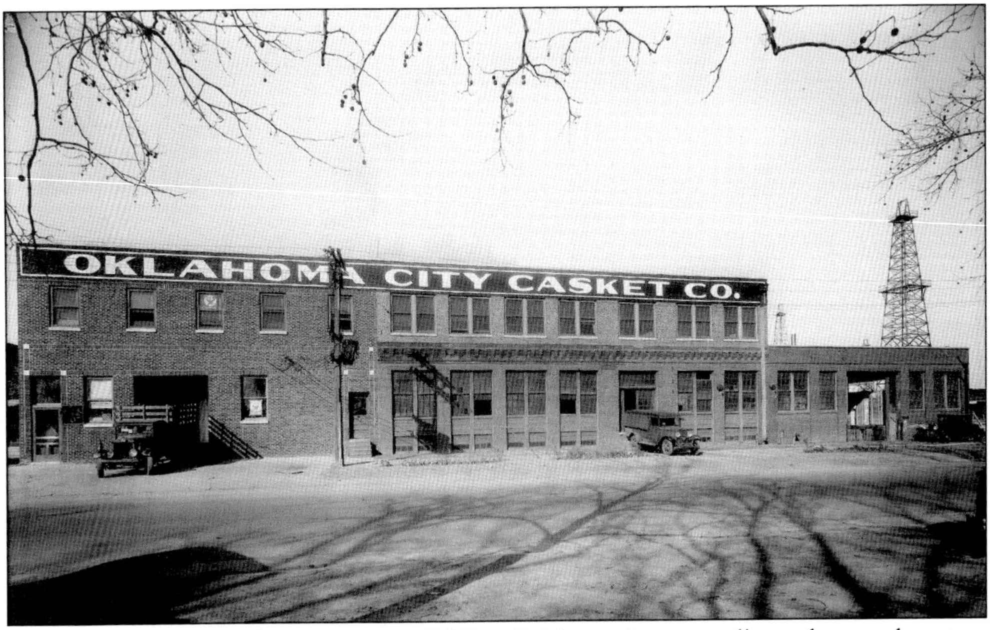

The Oklahoma City Casket Company at 413 East California Avenue really needs no explanation. This image was taken in the late 1920s by Z. P. Meyers. In later years, the building adjacent was torn down and a building similar in size to the its neighbor became the Oklahoma Restaurant Supply Company. Seeing the two buildings side-by-side was a bit of comic irony. (Courtesy Oklahoma Historical Society.)

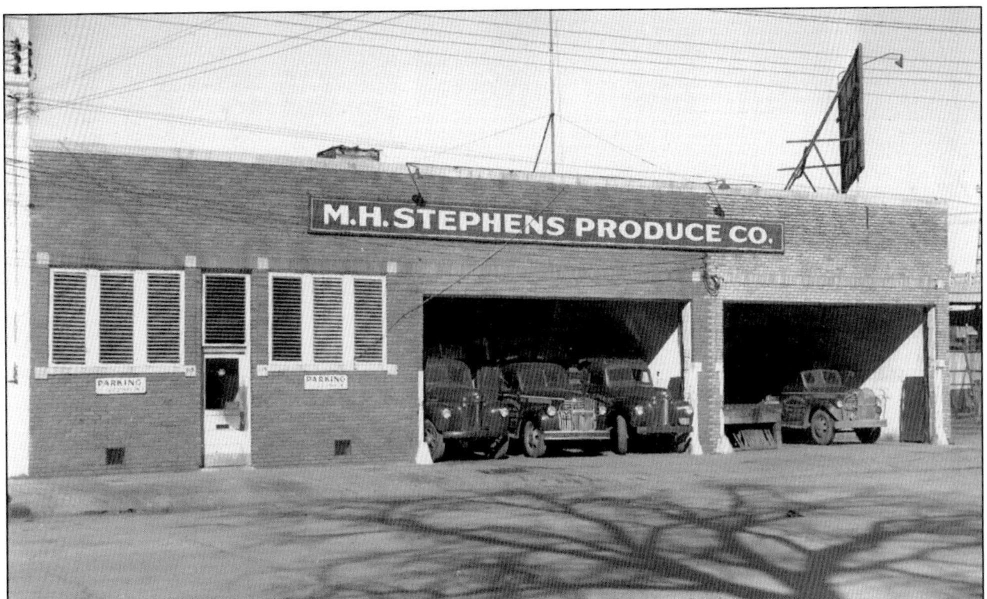

Next door to the Mideke Supply Company building was the M. H. Stephens Produce Company at 113 East Main Street. This single-story building delivered agricultural products to various customers around the city. This image was taken in the mid-1930s; however, the photographer is unknown. (Courtesy Oklahoma Historical Society.)

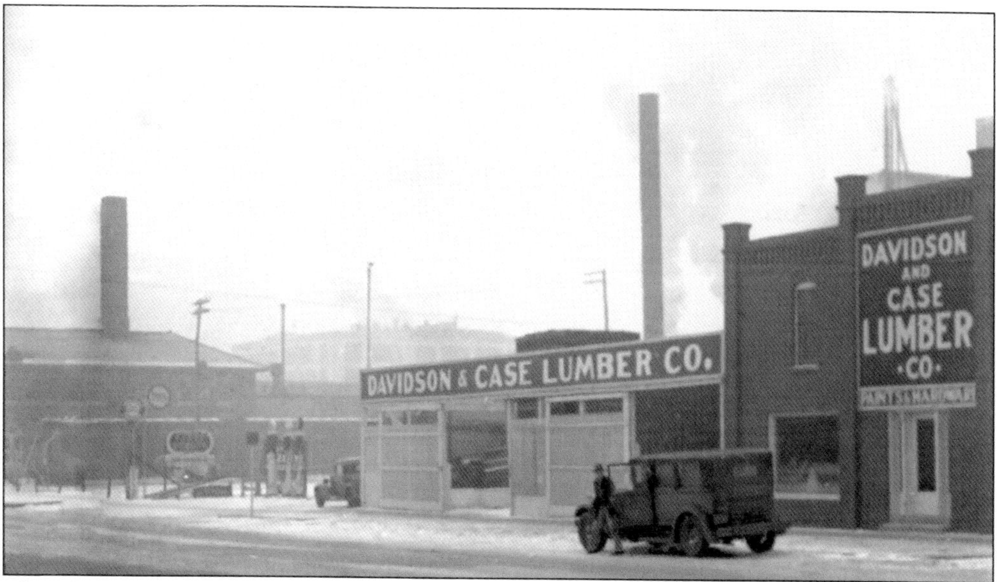

This photograph of a frosty morning in Oklahoma City was taken in the mid-1930s by Meyers Photo Shop. The Davidson and Case Lumber Company at 24 West Reno Avenue was just west of the main warehouse district of Oklahoma City. The company specialized in building materials, repairs, and remodeling. (Courtesy Oklahoma Historical Society.)

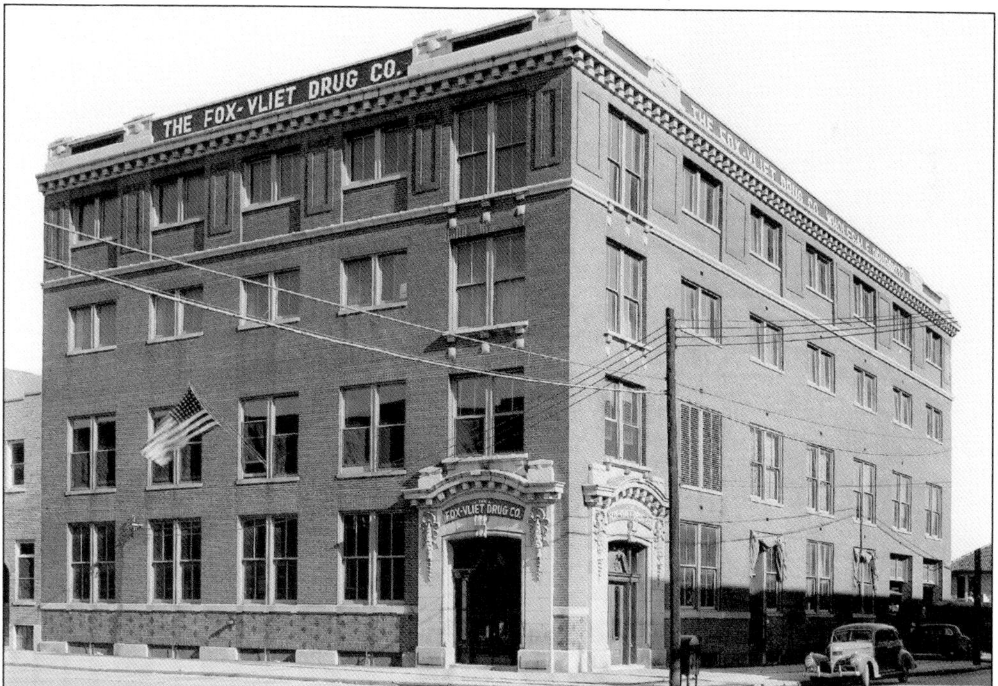

This ornate structure is one of the oldest buildings in Bricktown. It was built in 1910 as a four-story facility to the Kingman-Moore Implement Company located at 100 East California Avenue. In 1915, the company was sold to the Emerson-Brautingham Implement Company. In 1924, it was sold again and was renamed the Fox-Vliet Drug Company. This photograph dates from the 1940s and was taken by Meyers Photo Shop. (Courtesy Oklahoma Historical Society.)

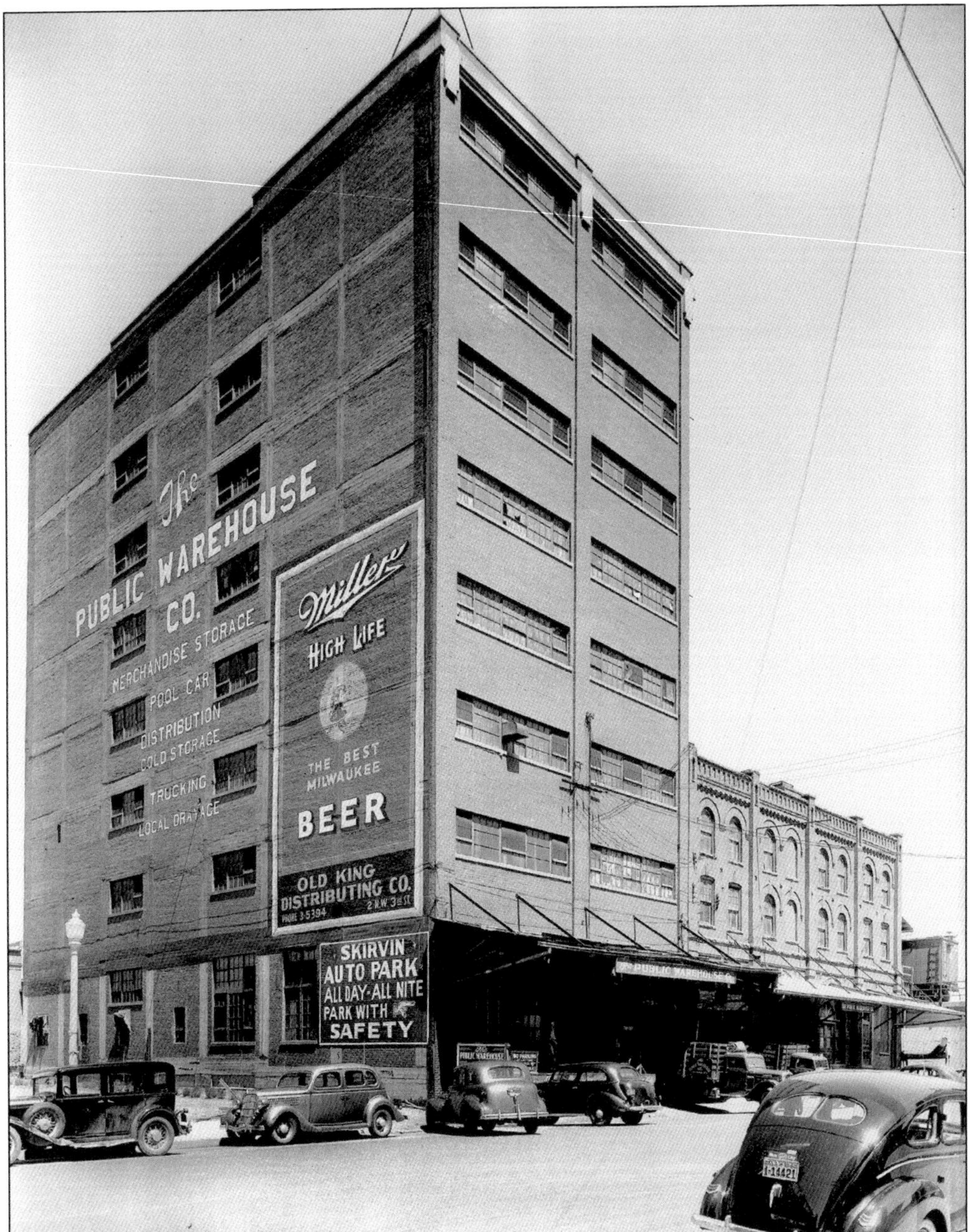

This eight-story building was the Public Warehouse Company located at 1–7 Northwest First Street. Curtice B. Robertson was president at the time this image was taken. The building no longer exists as it succumbed to urban renewal in the 1970s. This photograph was taken in the 1940 by Meyers Photo Shop. (Courtesy Oklahoma Historical Society.)

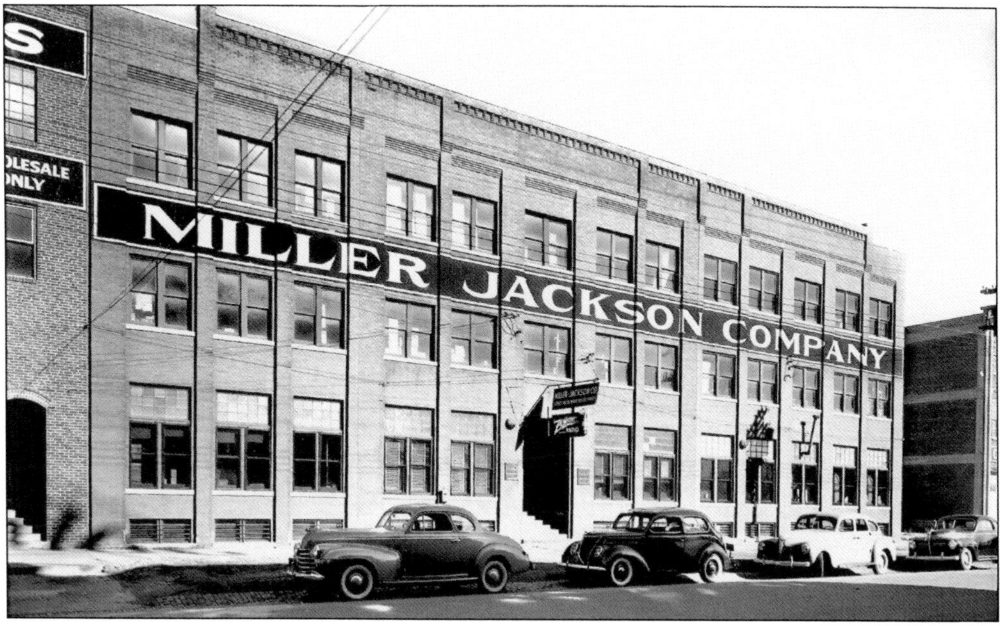

One of the mainstays of Bricktown is the Miller Jackson Building at 121 East California Avenue. The building was constructed in 1909 and was the state's largest wholesaler of tin and wooden products. By the 1980s the company was a distributor for modern appliances. This image was taken by Meyers Photo Shop in the 1940s. (Courtesy Oklahoma Historical Society.)

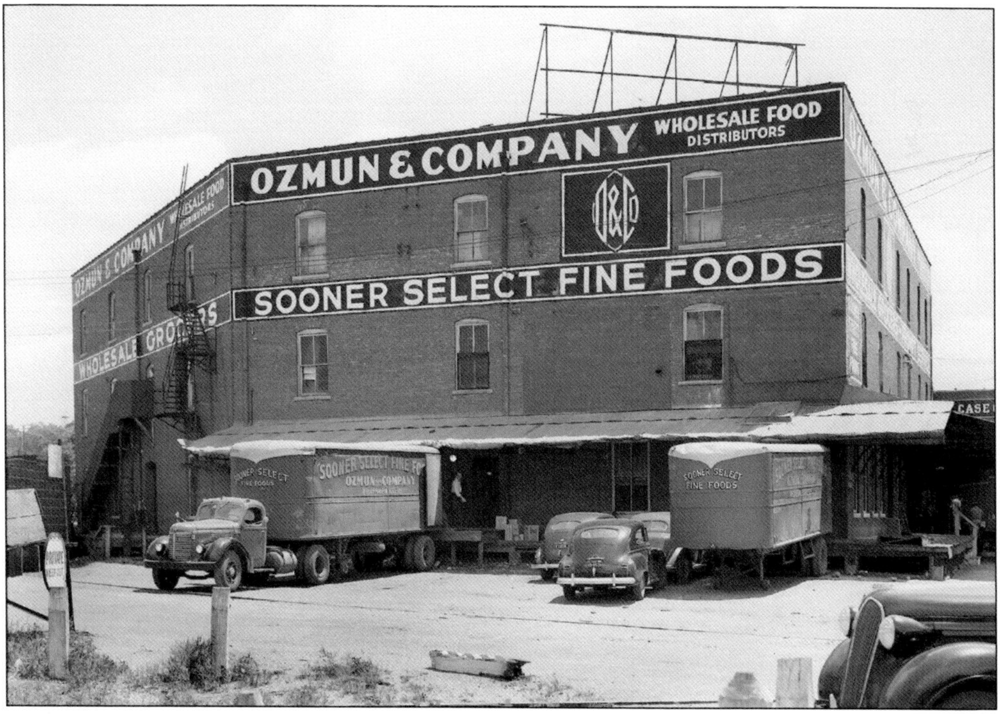

Ozmun and Company was a wholesale distributor of fine foods. Grover C. Ozmun was president and manager of the company. Located at 3–9 East Main Street, this photograph was taken by Meyers Photo Shop in May 1947. (Courtesy Oklahoma Historical Society.)

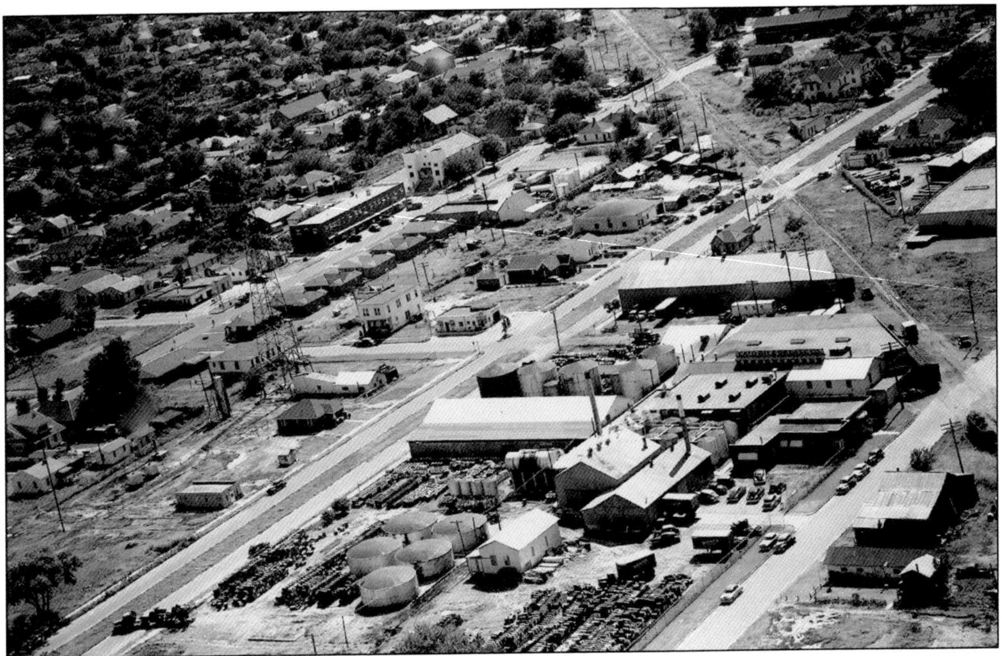

At the extreme eastern edge of the warehouse district is Cato Oil and Grease, located at 915 North Eastern Avenue. The company is a distributor and exporter of petroleum products and engineered lubrication. This aerial view was taken by Meyers Photo Shop in the late 1940s. (Courtesy Oklahoma Historical Society.)

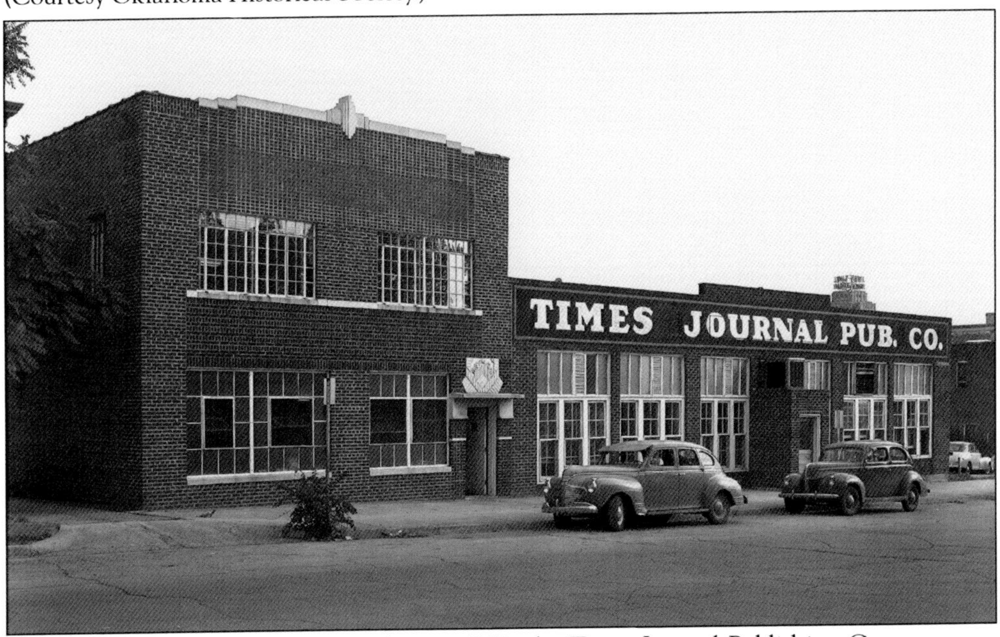

At the time this photograph was taken in 1950, the Times Journal Publishing Company was the oldest operating business in the warehouse district, having been founded in 1889. At one time the company published afternoon additions except for Sunday. They also were jobbers for bookbinding and printing. This photograph was taken by Meyers Photo Shop. (Courtesy Oklahoma Historical Society.)

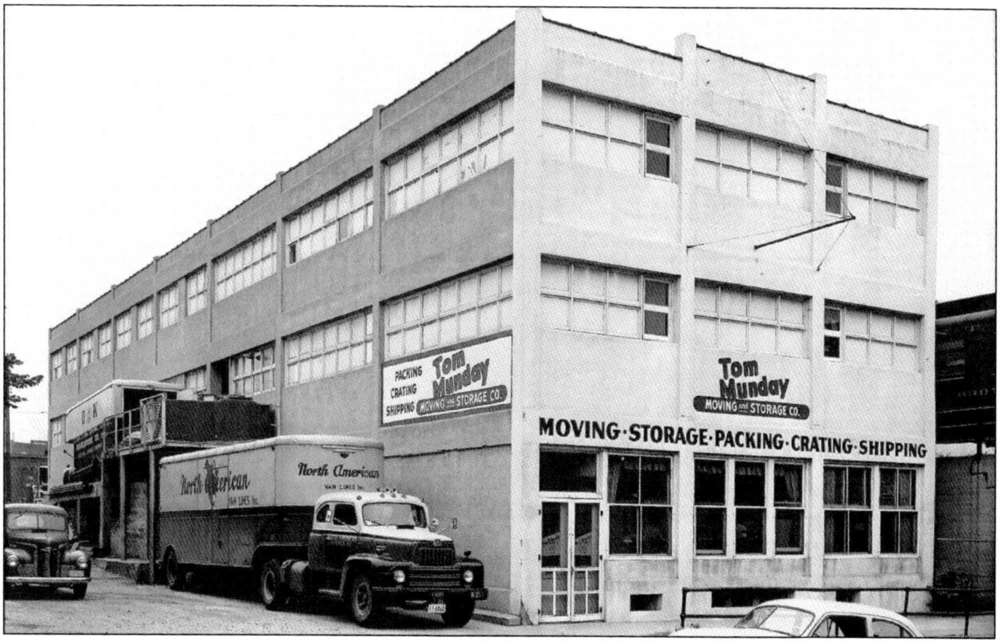

Americans are seemingly always on the move. After World War II, population shifts, an increase in the birth rate, and more military funding for Tinker Air Force Base meant more families were moving to Oklahoma City and surrounding communities. This movement of people and their possessions provided a boom for moving companies. Tom Munday Moving and Storage Company assisted in that process. Located at 6 Northeast Sixth Street, it were an all-purpose moving company. This photograph, taken in October 1950, is by Meyers Photo Shop. (Courtesy Oklahoma Historical Society.)

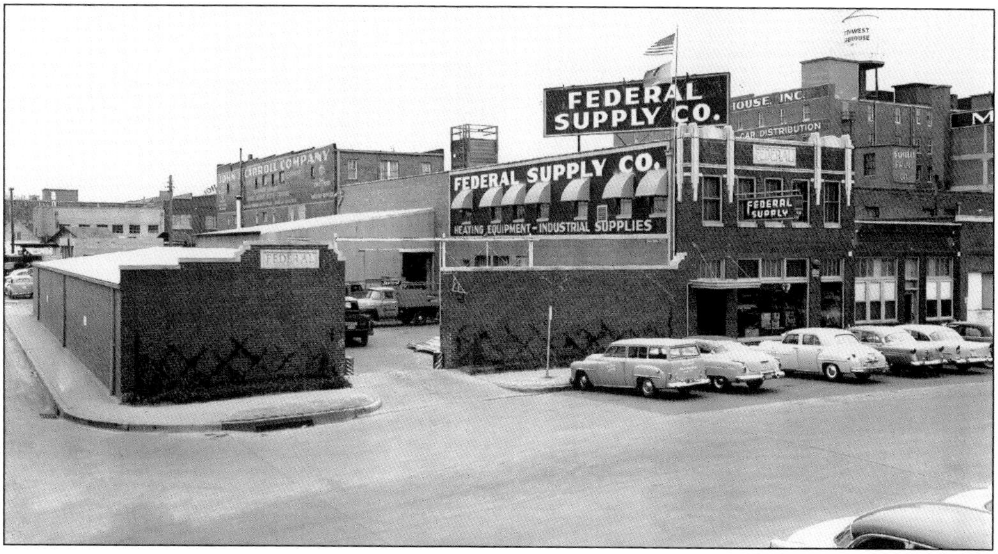

The warehouse district contained many wholesale distributors of various products. One such company was Federal Supply Company at 120 East Main Street. Located immediately west of the historic Walnut Avenue Bridge, the company handled heating equipment and industrial supplies for major manufacturers. Noted commercial photographer Ray Jacoby took this shot in January 1956. (Courtesy Oklahoma Historical Society.)

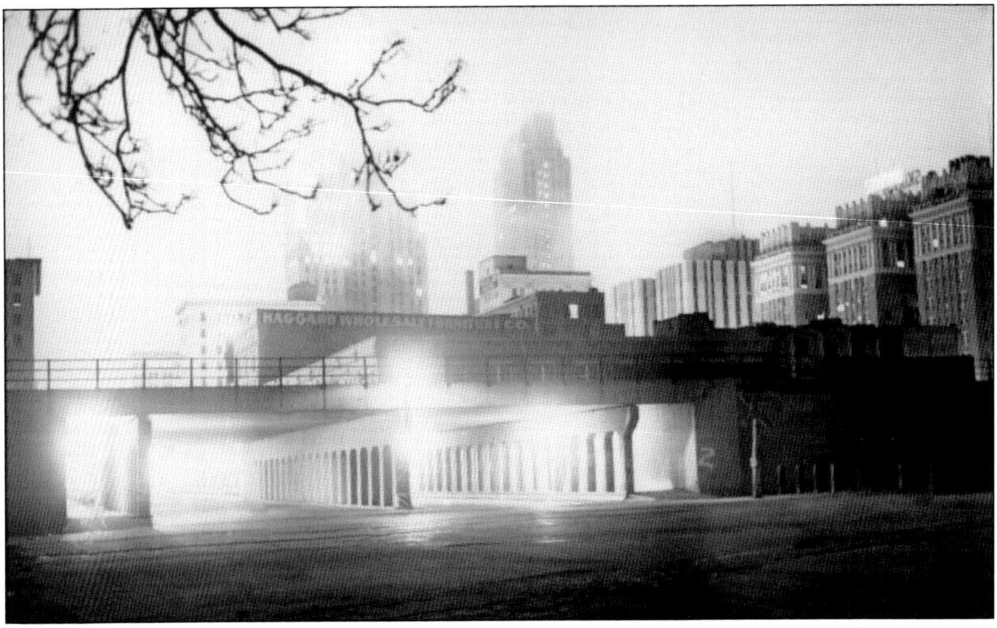

This tranquil night scene was taken at the western edge of Bricktown in the mid-1950s along East Main Street. Here the Santa Fe railroad crossing overpass, the Haggard Wholesale Furniture Company on West Main Street, and, at the far right, the decorative Skirvin Hotel can be seen. This image was taken by Clayton E. Soule. (Courtesy Oklahoma Historical Society.)

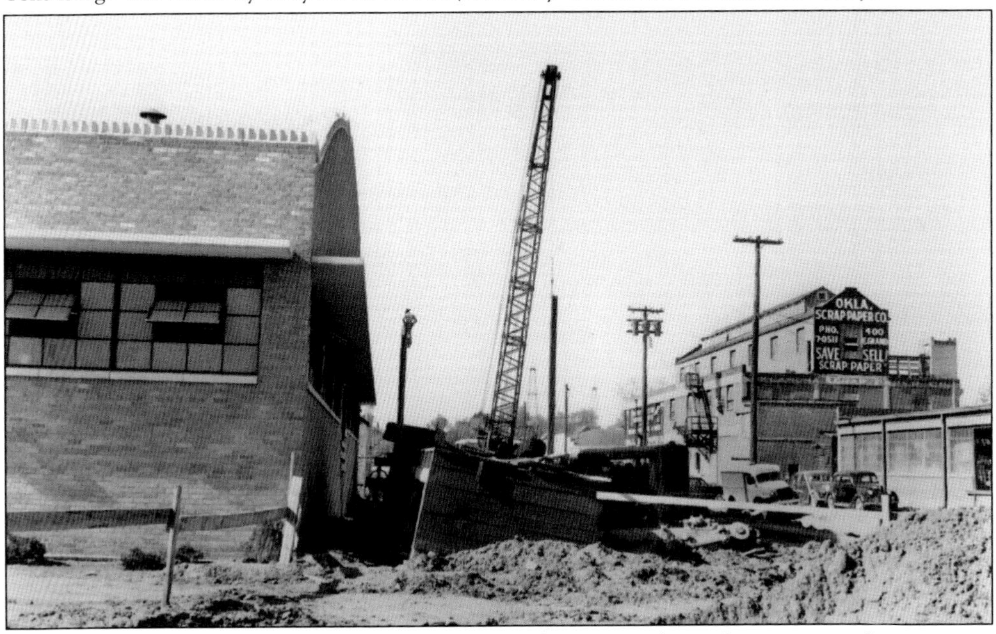

After World War II, the warehouse district entered into a prolonged transition of stagnation. With the rise of suburbia, construction of the interstate highway system and new developments of retail leaving the downtown sector of the city, several of the wholesale and distribution firms left downtown. Evidence of that transition can be seen here with deteriorating buildings. This image was taken along the 400 block of East Grand Boulevard by Meyers Photo Shop. (Courtesy Oklahoma Historical Society.)

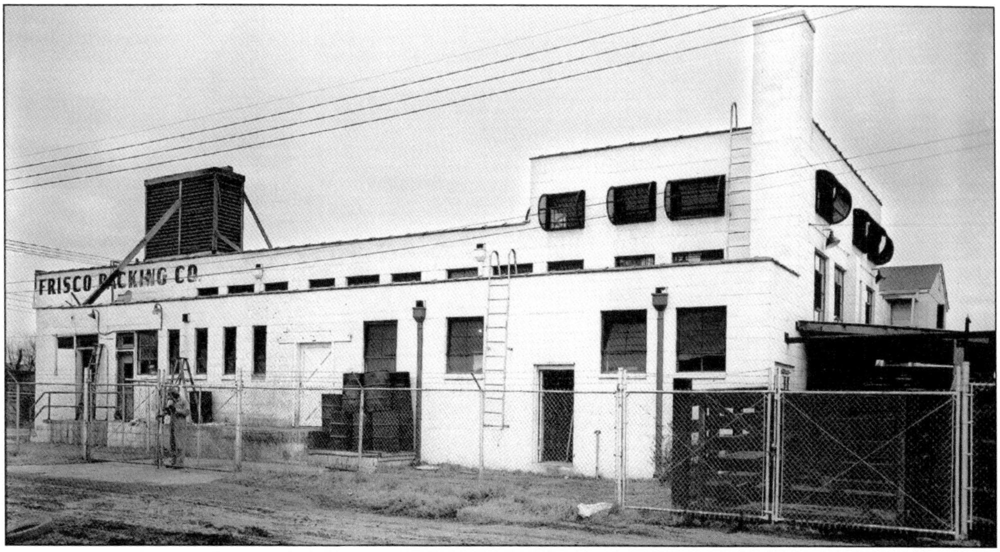

As the warehouse district began to decline from the 1940s on, a number of brick structures were replaced with glass and concrete monoliths. By 1980, the central core of the downtown commercial district was all but replaced due to urban renewal. Here is an example of the slow decline of the once vibrant warehouse district. The Frisco Packing Company at 544 South Walnut Avenue was photographed by Barney Hillerman sometime in the early 1960s. (Courtesy Oklahoma Historical Society.)

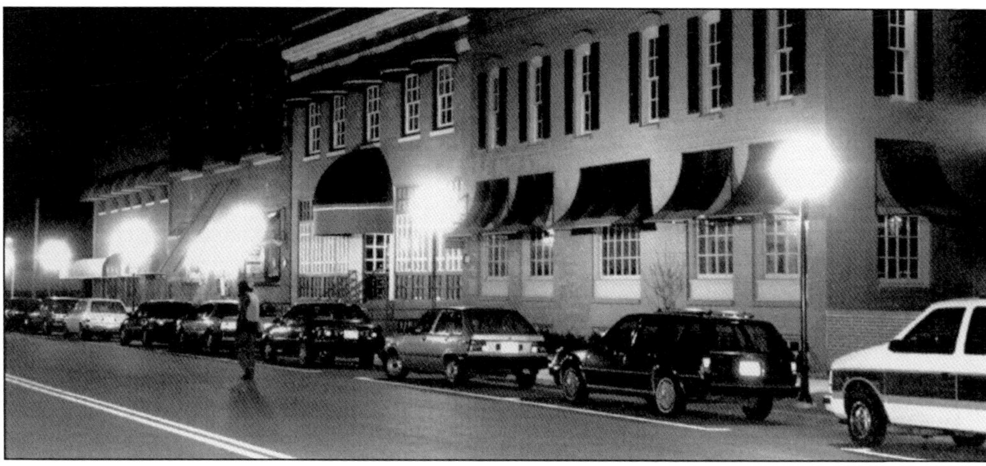

With the decline of the central business district in downtown Oklahoma City from the 1950s forward, city leaders looked for solutions to reverse the trend. In 1964, a design plan created by architect I. M. Pei was proposed to the leadership. The plan was adopted and implemented by the Urban Renewal Authority, a federally funded program. Many of the majestic buildings from the early 1900s were razed to make room for glass and concrete structures in the vain hope that people would come back downtown during the evening. It was a partial success. In 1979, real estate developer Neal Horton had a vision. He began buying property in the old warehouse district east of downtown. By the fall of 1981, Horton began to promote his plan: Brick Town USA. Horton unfortunately was about 10 years ahead of his time. The first of the renovated brick structures that Horton renovated can be seen here at 114 to 124 East Sheridan Avenue with a series of offices occupying the buildings. This image was captured by W. D. Welge in December 1988. (Courtesy Oklahoma Historical Society.)

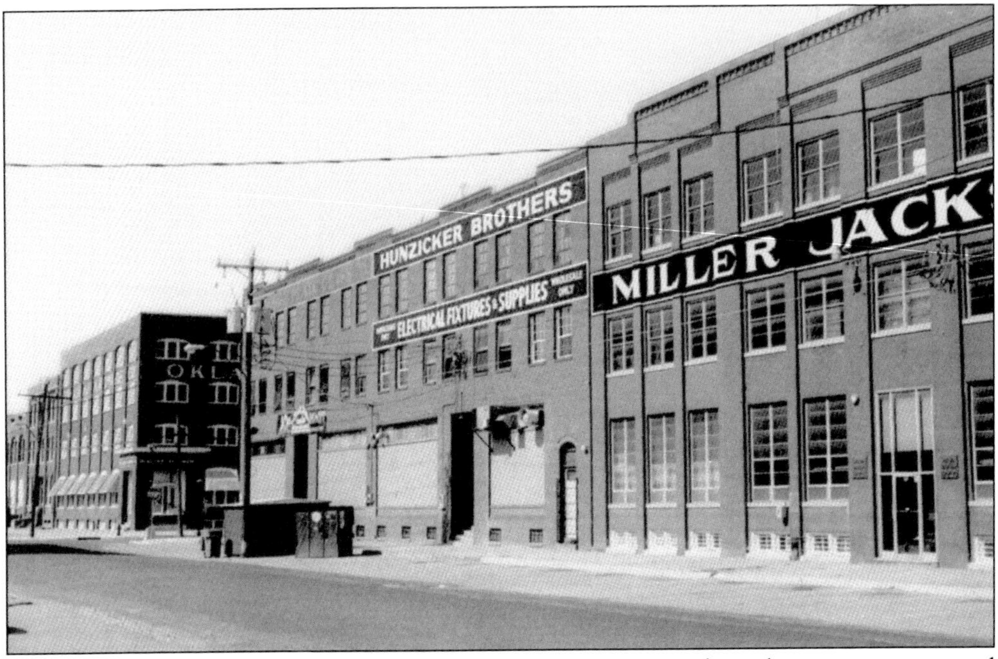

Neal Horton's vision for the revitalization of Bricktown, as it was now being known, was continued after his company filed for bankruptcy. In the fall of 1985, three individuals, Jim Tolbert, Don Karchmer, and Jim Brewer, become major property owners in the district. With a vote of the people in 1993, voters approved the Metropolitan Area Projects (MAPS) that includes a canal much like that of San Antonio, Texas. Construction of the canal would begin in the mid-1990s. California Avenue, east of the Santa Fe railroad, was chosen as the site for the canal. Buildings that would front along it were rapidly being acquired for redevelopment purposes. Seen here is Hunzicker Brothers Electrical Supply Company on East California Avenue and Miller Jackson Company before construction began in 1996. These photographs were taken by W. D. Welge in January 1995. (Courtesy Oklahoma Historical Society.)

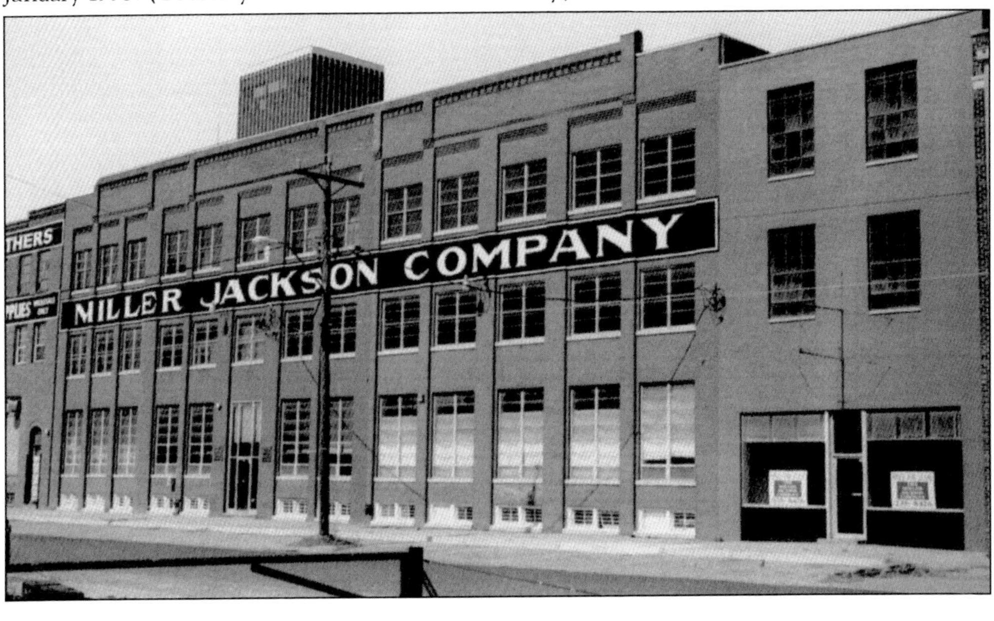

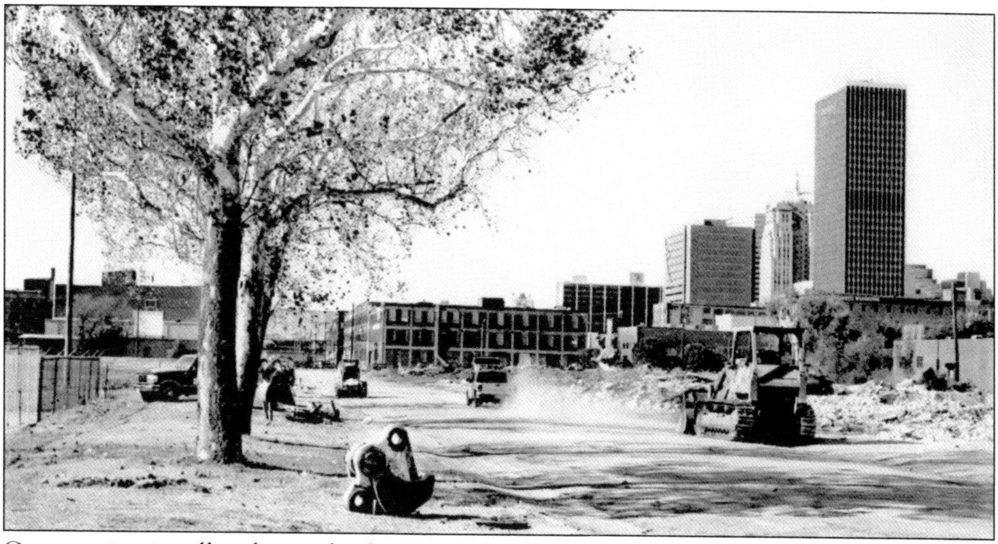

Construction is well underway for the proposed canal that will wind its way through Bricktown. This photograph was taken by W. D. Welge in 1996. (Courtesy Oklahoma Historical Society.)

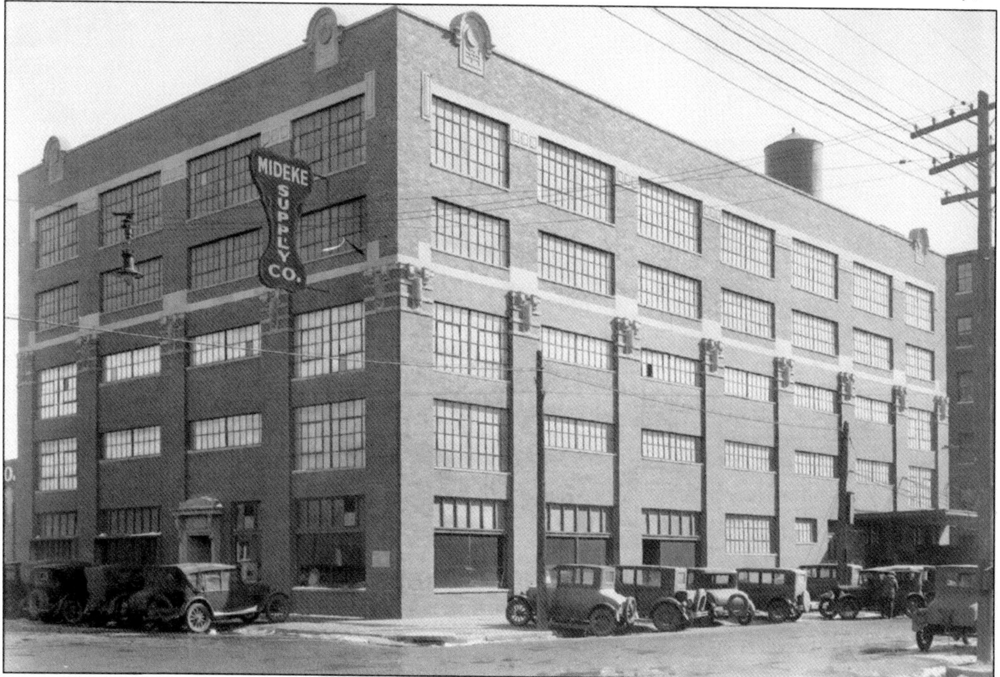

The warehouse district, located east of the Santa Fe railroad in downtown Oklahoma City, expanded during two periods of economic growth (1898–1912 and 1920–1930). Both periods of economic prosperity resulted in the construction of all the buildings that comprise Bricktown. The Mideke Supply Building at 100 East Main Street is one of the largest structures in the warehouse district. The building consists of red brick, like most of the buildings in the district. It was originally a one-story building constructed in 1919. In 1928, the company expanded to the five-story facility. Mideke was a supply house specializing in various construction materials for cotton gins, grain elevators, power plants, and oil field and road building equipment. (Courtesy Oklahoma Historical Society.)

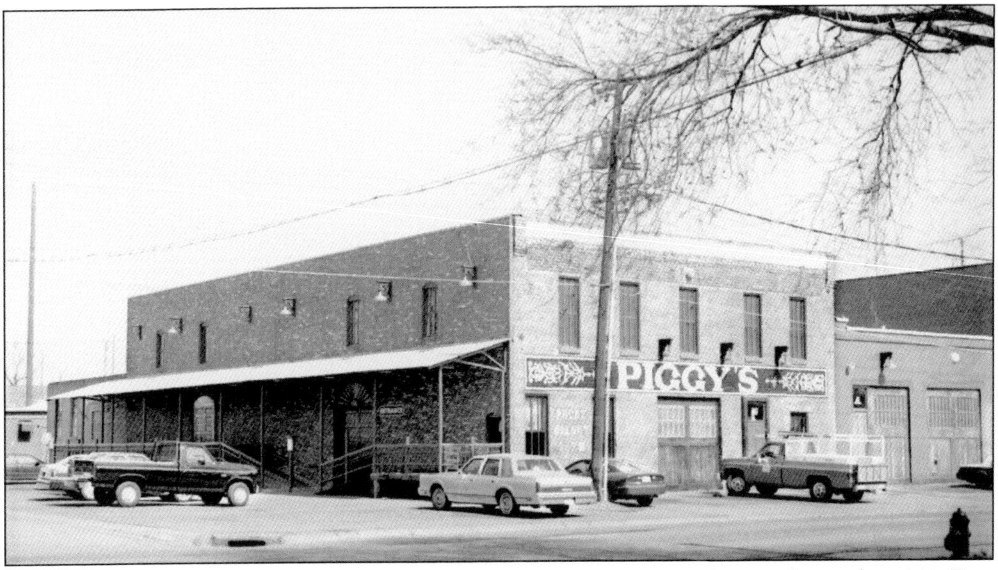

One of the first restaurants to open in Bricktown was Piggy's Barbeque, located at 303 East Sheridan Avenue. For several years it was the best place to eat hickory-smoked barbecue. It had three barbecue sauces for the customer's palate: mild, hot, and nuclear. On the containers for the nuclear sauce there was a disclaimer, "where even piggy's fear to tread." This photograph was taken in the early 1990s by W. D. Welge. The restaurant is now Crabtown, serving seafood dishes. (Courtesy Oklahoma Historical Society.)

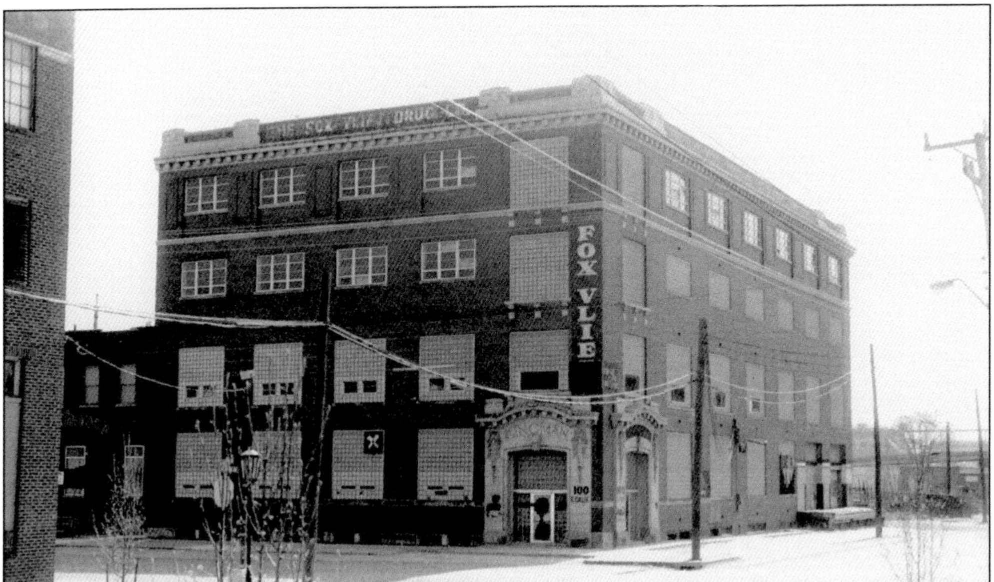

The old Fox-Vliet Building (Kingman Building), located at 100 East California Avenue, is 97 years old since its construction. It is less than three years from reaching the century mark as a structure. The building was photographed by W. D. Welge in January 1995. (Courtesy Oklahoma Historical Society.)

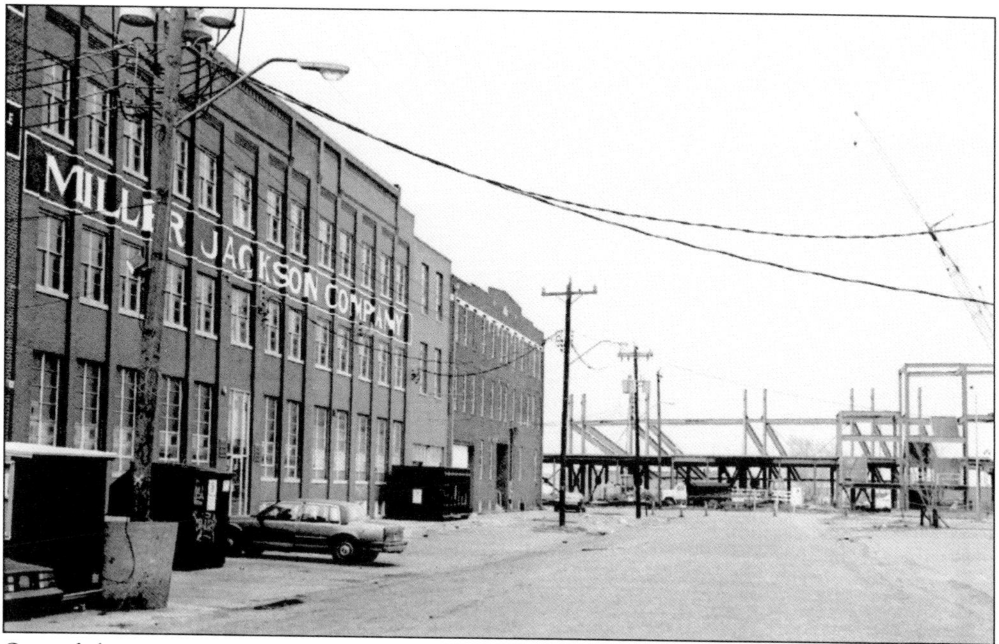

One of the tangible signs of progress of MAPS is seen here with the steel framework of the Bricktown Ball Park under construction. This is looking east on California Avenue in 1996. This image was taken by W. D. Welge. (Courtesy Oklahoma Historical Society.)

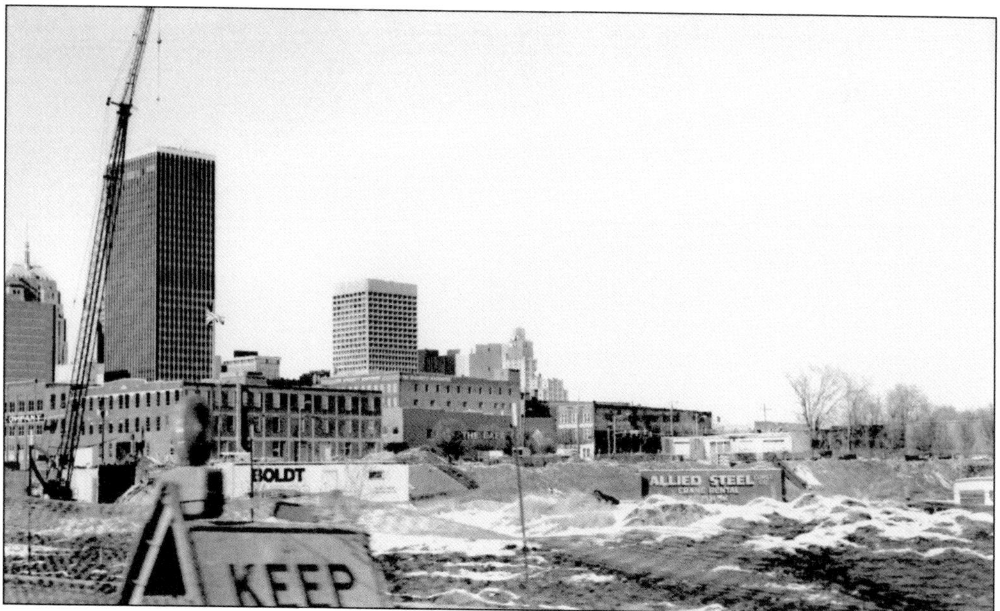

Construction was well underway in 1996 for the different projects planned for Bricktown. Various historic structures were renovated and given a new lease on life as the area attracted attention by local residents and out-of-town visitors. This image was taken by W. D. Welge along East Reno Avenue. (Courtesy Oklahoma Historical Society.)

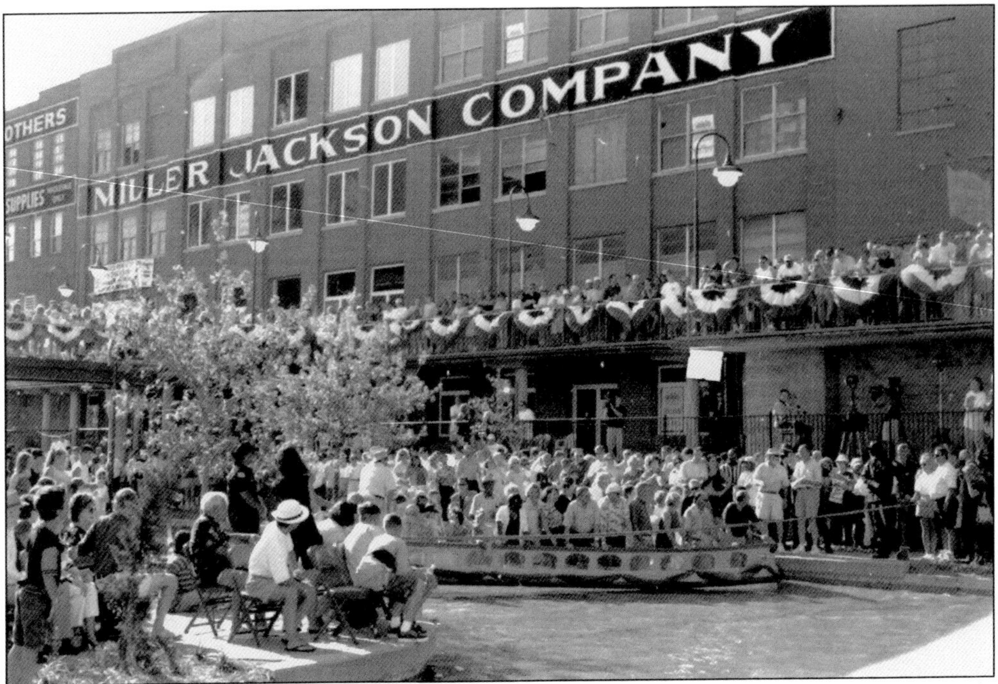

Seen here, with much fanfare, the Bricktown canal opens on July 2, 1999, with throngs of people in observance. Since its opening, the water taxis that operate on the canal have been extremely popular with visitors. Note the Miller Jackson Building in the background. This photograph was taken by W. D. Welge. (Courtesy Oklahoma Historical Society.)

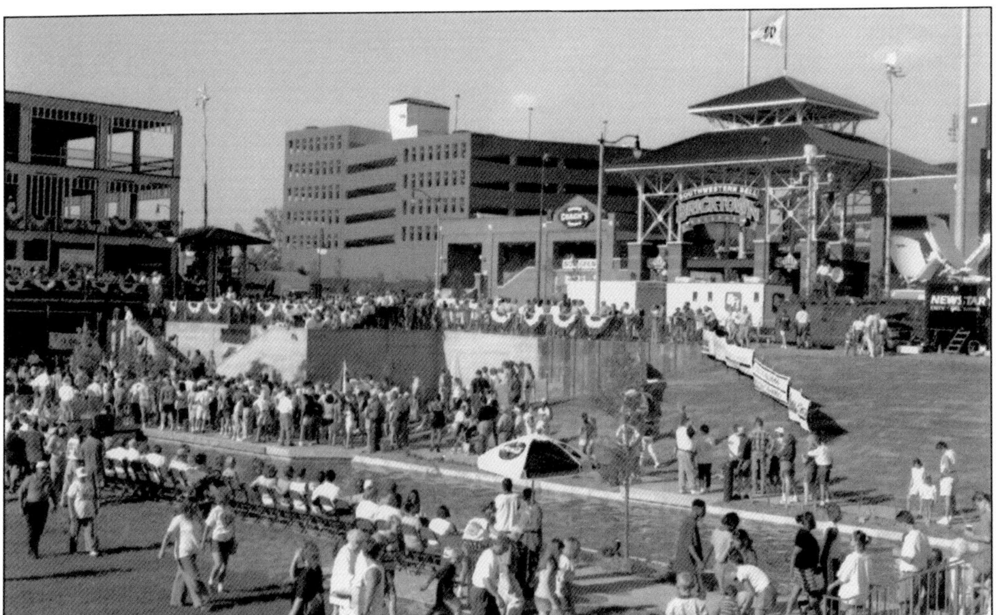

This is the dedication of the Bricktown canal on July 2, 1999, with the SBC Bricktown Ball Park seen in the background. The ballpark opened a year earlier and has been very popular with baseball fans. This photograph was taken by W. D. Welge. (Courtesy Oklahoma Historical Society.)

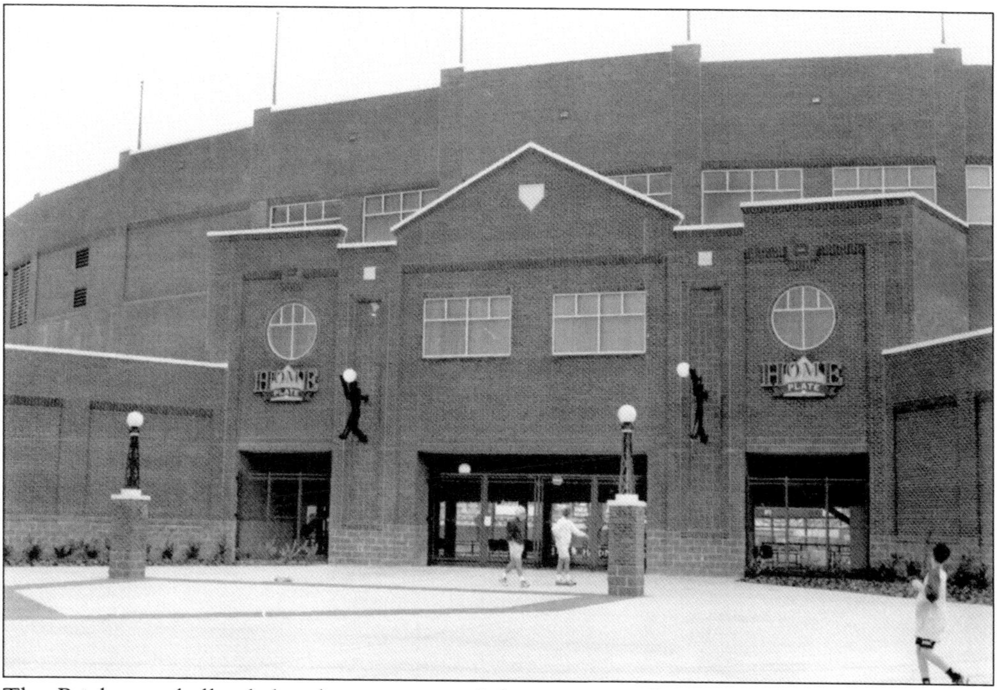

The Bricktown ballpark has become one of the more popular venues for entertainment in Oklahoma City. This image was taken of the home plate entrance in 2004 by W. D. Welge. (Courtesy Oklahoma Historical Society.)

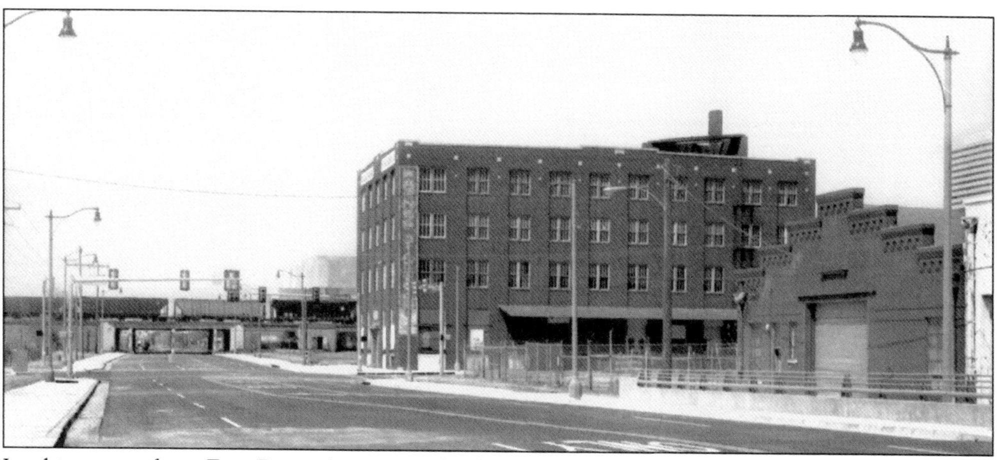

Looking west from East Reno Avenue is the four-storied Rock Island Plow Building, located at 29 East Reno Avenue. Built in 1909, it was a subsidiary of the Rock Island Corporation of Chicago. The building was sold in 1932 during the Depression to Reinhart and Donovan, a regional construction firm. In 2007, the building has been for sale for some years. At right is the Wells Fargo building, before it was opened as Boone's Store, a curio shop, in 2005. The photograph was taken in 2004 by W. D. Welge. (Courtesy Oklahoma Historical Society.)

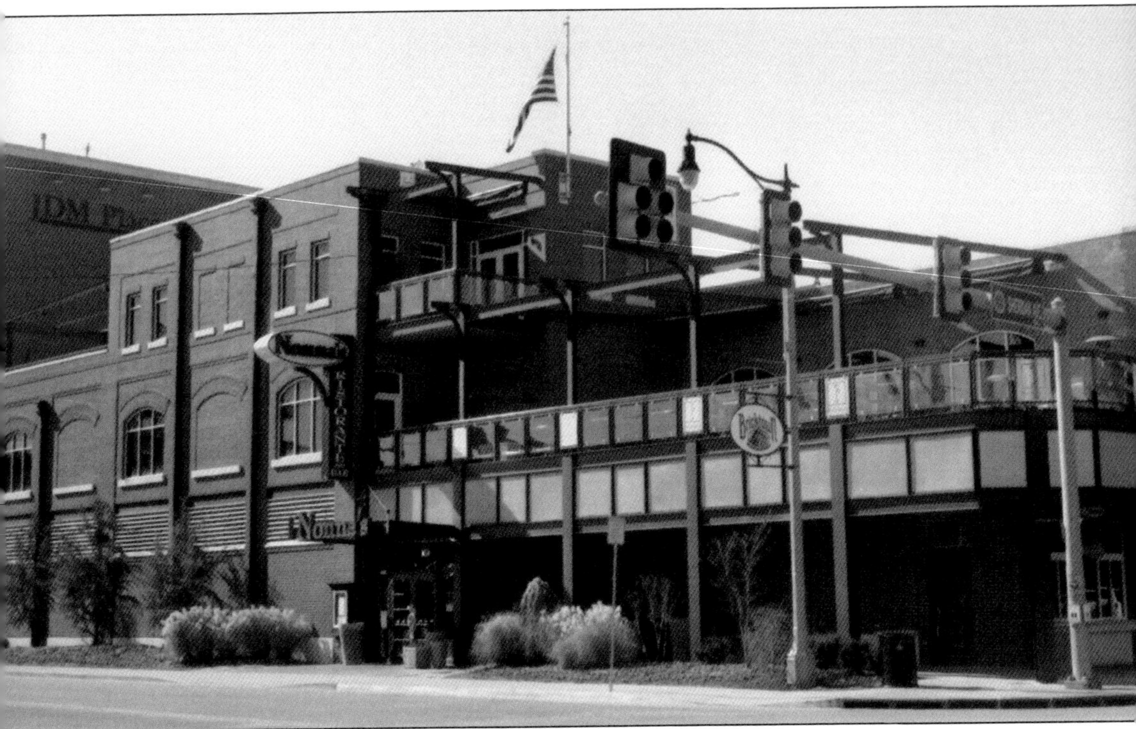

The most recent addition to the flourishing businesses of Bricktown is Nonna's Euro-American Ristorante and Bar at 1 Mickey Mantle Drive (formerly Walnut Avenue). Converted from a warehouse to a trendy restaurant, Nonna's opened in February 2005. Nonna's was built in 1906 and was originally Henry Brown's Drug Store. In 1921, it was California Auto Livery, and after 1926, it was Doc and Bill's Furniture Company. Since 1984, it has had a myriad of businesses operate in the facility. It is altogether fitting that Bricktown has been a success. The vision of Neal Horton, the father of Bricktown, was on the verge of success when his untimely death occurred. If he were alive today he would be extremely proud of his long-range vision of an entertainment district for Oklahoma City. (Courtesy W. D. Welge.)

Six

DEEP DEUCE TODAY

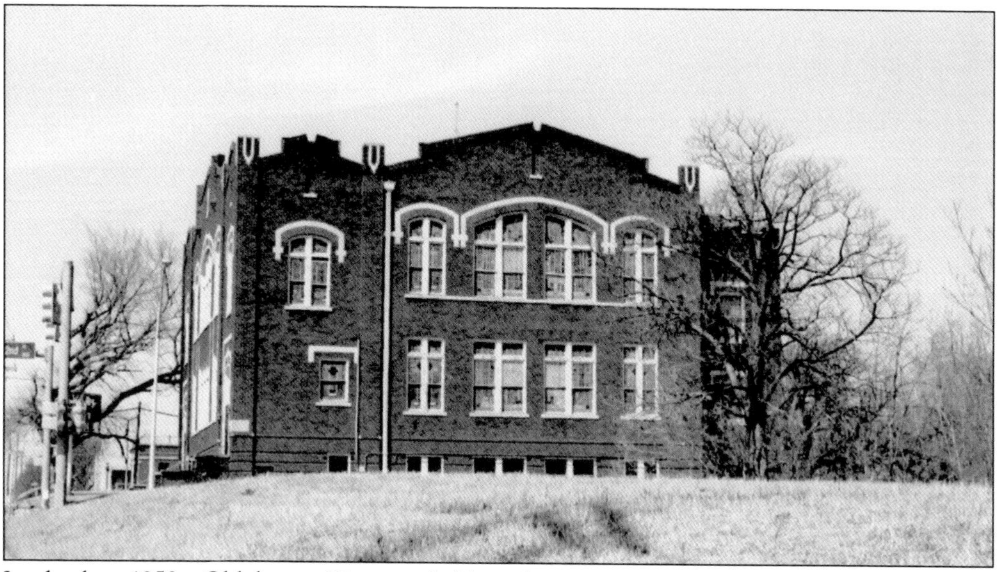

In the late 1950s, Oklahoma City, much like other cities across America, came face-to-face with racism and a segregated society that had existed since its founding in 1889. Courageous men and women, young and old, banded together to fight this battle not with clubs or fists, but with economic clout that would eventually overcome the stigma of separation of the races. A cornerstone to that battle was the Calvary Baptist Church at 400 North Walnut Avenue. In 1958, leaders of the African American community met to plan peaceful marches and sit-ins to get the attention of city, civic, and corporate leaders of Oklahoma City. Such notables who led the way at great risk to themselves included Clara Luper, Rev. W. K. Jackson, Jimmy E. Stewart Sr., Jimmy E. Stewart Jr., Roscoe Dunjee, E. Melvin Porter, and many, many other unsung heroes who sought change peacefully for the greater good for all. It is a testament to the people of Oklahoma City that peaceful change was achieved. This photograph was taken by Chester R. Cowen in April 1996. It is probably not coincidental that the image was taken on the anniversary of Dr. Martin Luther King Jr.'s death by an assassin's bullet. (Courtesy Oklahoma Historical Society.)

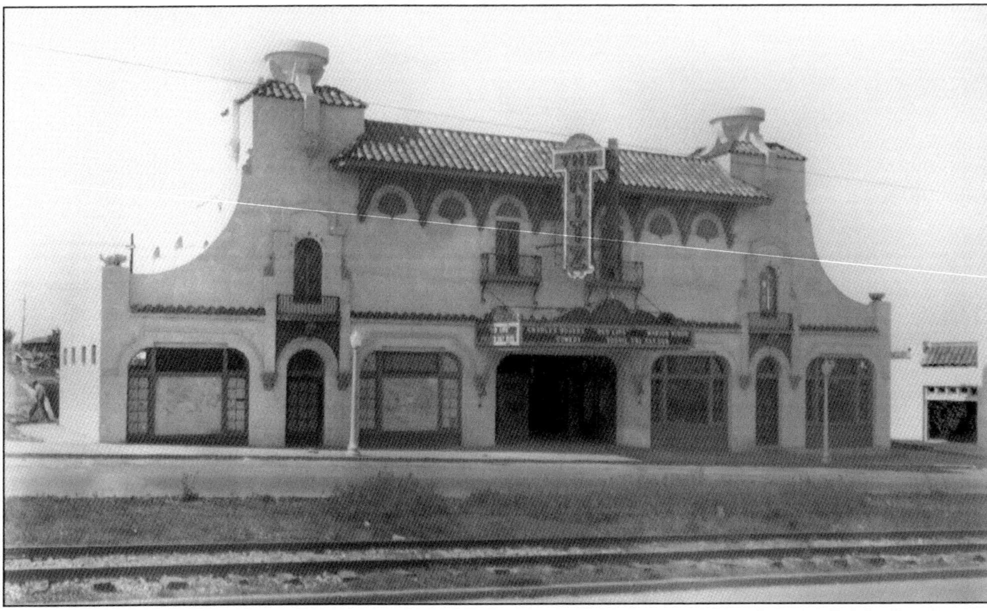

The Ritz Theatre, as it looked in the mid-1930s, was beyond the reach of all blacks due to segregation in Oklahoma. At the time the northern boundary for blacks to live and own businesses did not extend beyond Northeast Thirteenth Street. In fact, the limit was at Northeast Eighth Street. Editor and publisher of the *Black Dispatch* Roscoe Dunjee was also the founder of the local NAACP. His activism in pushing the boundary limits was fought through the courts in Oklahoma. It was not until 1936 that government-supported residential segregation was ended by a decision of the Oklahoma State Supreme Court. This photograph was taken by Meyers Photo Shop. (Courtesy Oklahoma Historical Society.)

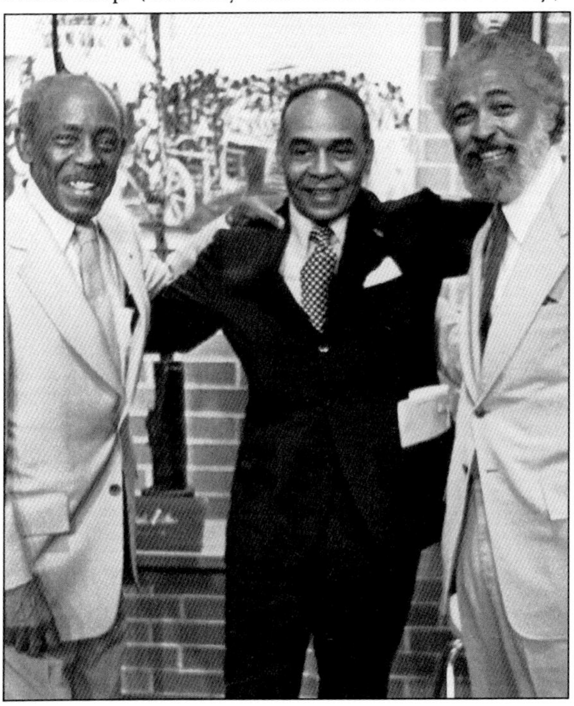

The names of James E. (Jimmy) Stewart Sr. and Ralph Ellison may not register any kind of recognition for non–African American residents. Sad and true as that fact is, both these men were stalwarts in the community. Stewart worked his way up through the ranks at Oklahoma Natural Gas Company where, when he retired from the company, he was a corporate vice president. Ellison was born in Oklahoma City and, like others, attended Douglass High School. He went on to achieve greater fame outside the state, becoming an accomplished author. One of his works, *Invisible Man*, received national acclaim. This image from the James Stewart collection includes, from left to right, Stewart, Ellison, and Ellison's brother. (Courtesy Oklahoma Historical Society.)

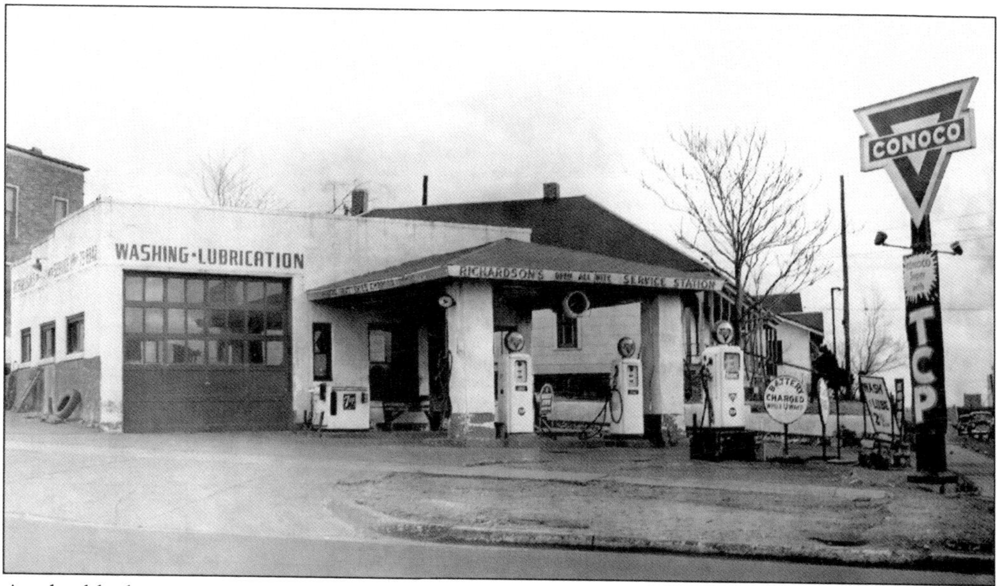

As the black community expanded into newer neighborhoods, businesses followed soon after. As a consequence, the older sector of the community began to decline. By the late 1960s, the immediate area around Second Street was moving toward oblivion. One of the last vestiges left in the neighborhood was Richardson's Conoco Service Station at 400 Northeast Second Street. Operated by L. E. Richardson, it provided the usual service to its customers until it too moved to a newer location. This image by an unknown photographer is from the James Stewart collection. (Courtesy Oklahoma Historical Society.)

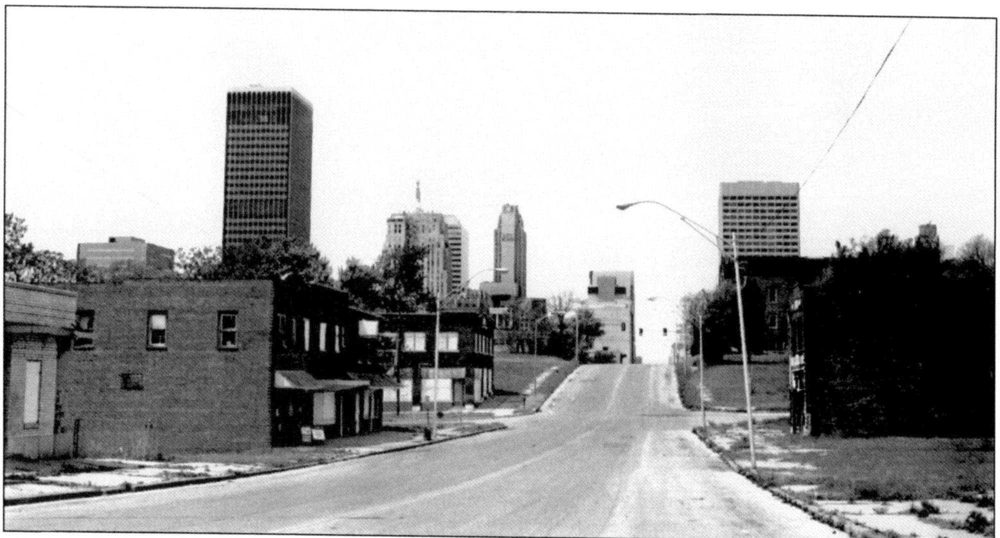

The gradual decline of Second Street and the surrounding area became acute with the platting and construction of the Centennial Expressway that cut through the heart of the neighborhood. With the demolition of residential and business property underway from Stiles Avenue east to Lincoln Boulevard, several of the east–west streets, such as Second Street, were cut off because of the highway. This further hastened the death of Deep Deuce. This image taken in 1995 by W. D. Welge shows very few buildings left on what was Second Street from Stiles Avenue looking west to downtown Oklahoma City. (Courtesy Oklahoma Historical Society.)

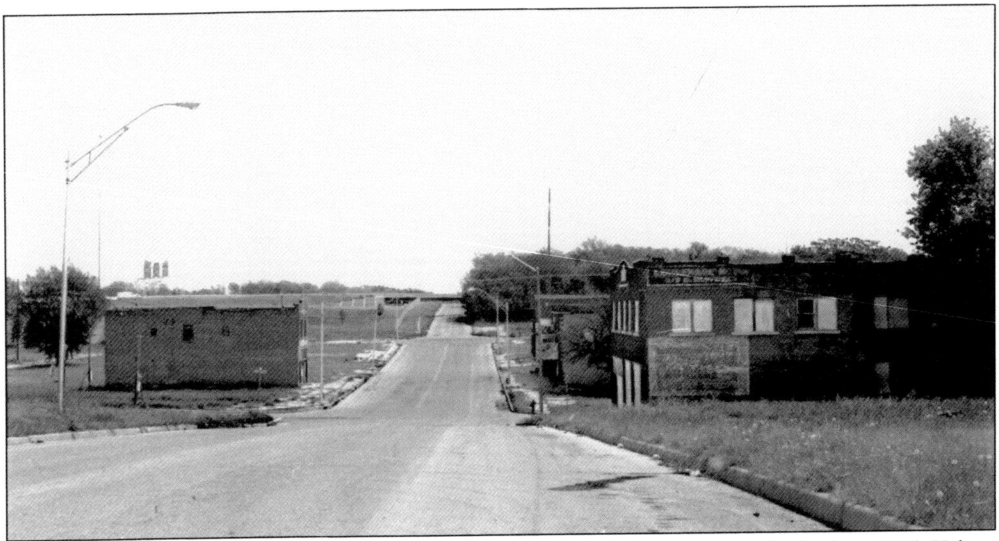

This is another view of Second Street, looking back toward the east, as it looked in 1995. Taken from around Walnut Avenue, only a small number of structures remain of the once jamming Deep Deuce. In the far background is Interstate 235, the concrete barrier that dissected the neighborhood in 1989. (Courtesy Oklahoma Historical Society.)

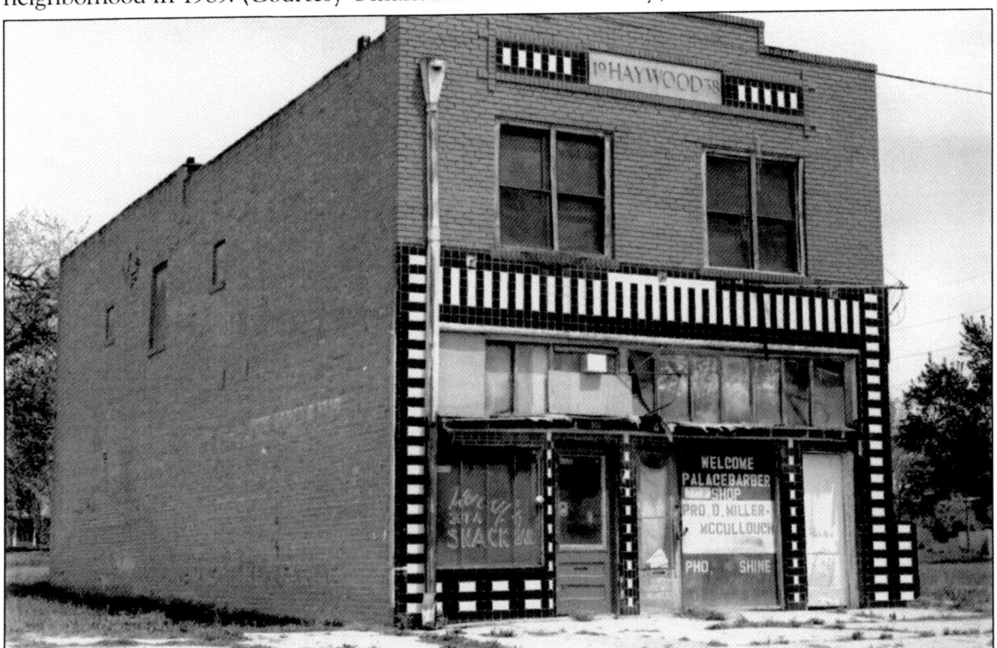

The building pictured here is the Haywood Building, built in 1926 and remodeled by Dr. W. L. Haywood. Located at 307 Northeast Second Street, the structure is a two-story brick commercial-style building. Its peak years of operation were from the 1920s to 1970s. At various times, the building served as a specialty store, clinic, and restaurant. Haywood was not the first owner on record. That distinction belonged to Andrew Rushing, who was the father of legendary blues singer Jimmy "Five by Five" Rushing. The building has been listed on the National Register of Historic Places. The photograph was taken by W. D. Welge in 1995. (Courtesy Oklahoma Historical Society.)

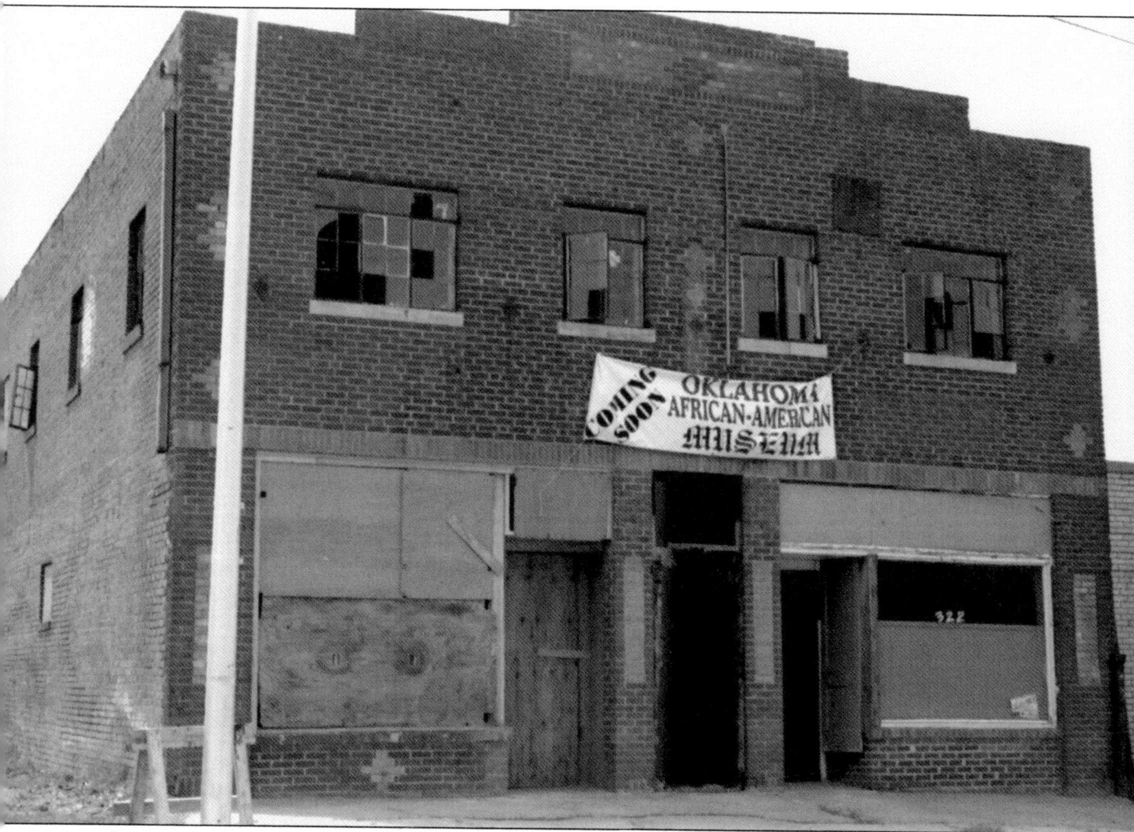

Central among the buildings that dominated Second Street was the Elks Victory Lodge, built by Dr. Wyatt H. Slaughter in 1929. The building served as the Rest for the Elks until 1936. After 1936, the building at 322 Northeast Second Street became the site for several successive restaurants and social clubs. Probably the most notable was Ruby's Grill, established in 1940 by Ruby Lyons, brother to Sidney Lyons. Ruby's Grill became a local nightspot that gained fame across the state. Ruby's Grill offered fine food, musical entertainment, and dancing that continued until 1946. In the mid-1990s, the abandoned building was being proposed as an African American museum. The museum never materialized. This particular photograph was taken in 1995 by W. D. Welge. (Courtesy Oklahoma Historical Society.)

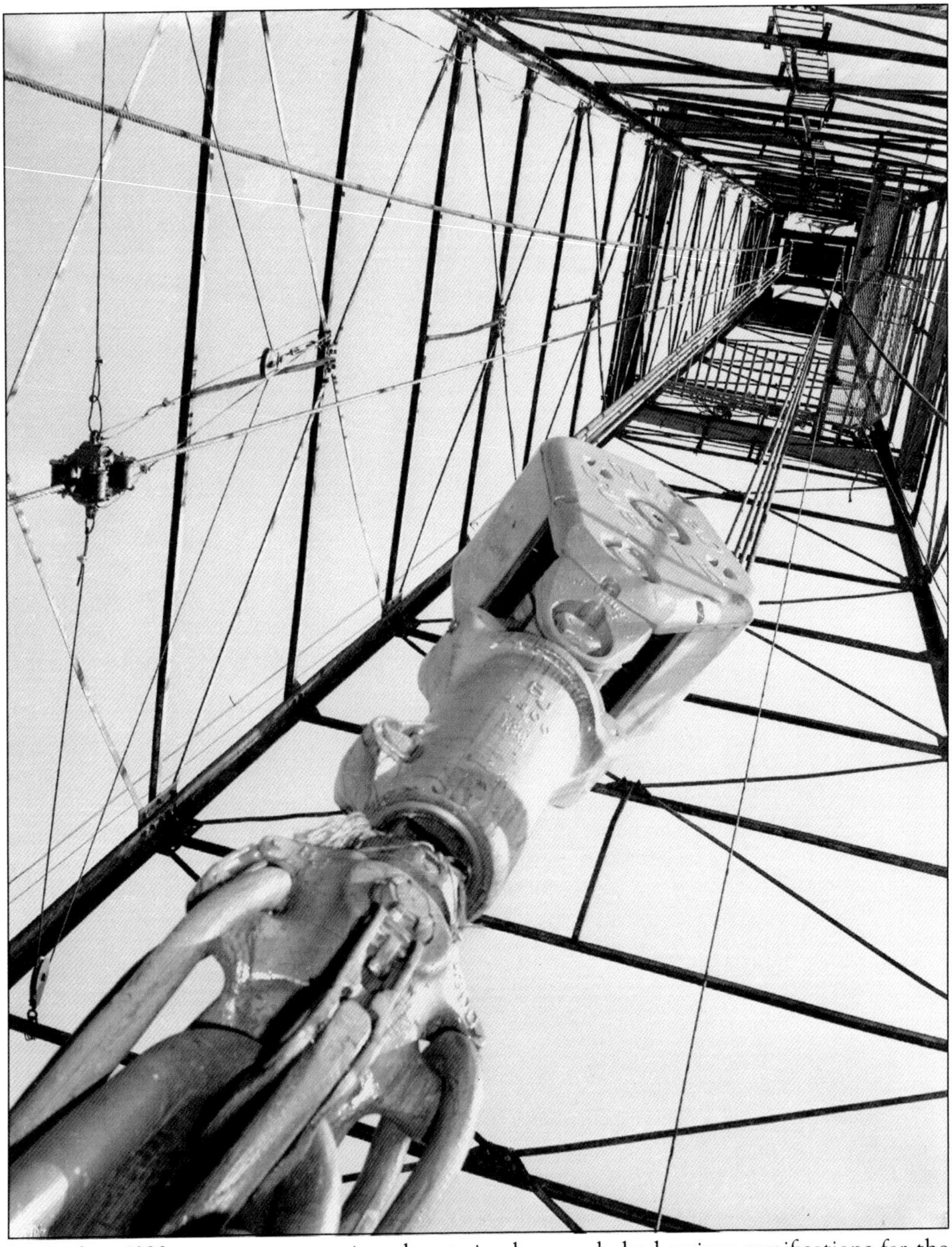

In the late 1920s, two events coming almost simultaneously had serious ramifications for the development that impacted life on Second Street. The first was the discovery of the Oklahoma City field that ran directly underneath the community. This potential gold mine left the community with lower property values; wells could blow out causing dangerous fires and very unpleasant odors came from the drilling and storage of crude. The other was the crash of the stock market in 1929. This artistic image of an oil derrick taken from a distinctive view was photographed by Z. P. Meyers. (Courtesy Oklahoma Historical Society.)

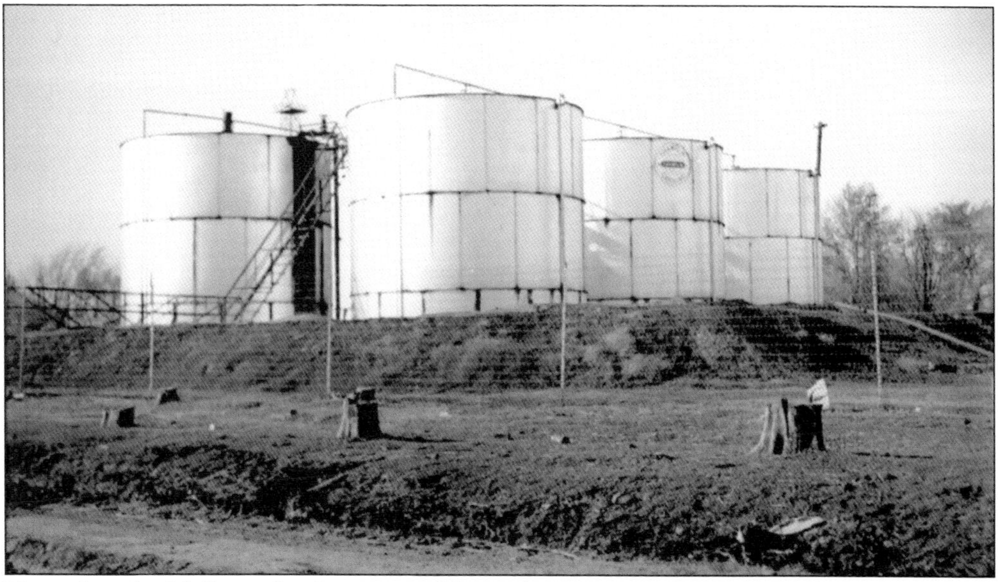

The end result of drilling oil is the storage of the crude as it waits to be transported to a refinery. This oil storage battery located at Southeast Seventeenth Street and Byers Avenue was and is a common site around neighborhoods in northeast and southeast Oklahoma City. This image was taken around 1938 by Clayton E. Soule of Oklahoma City. (Courtesy Oklahoma Historical Society.)

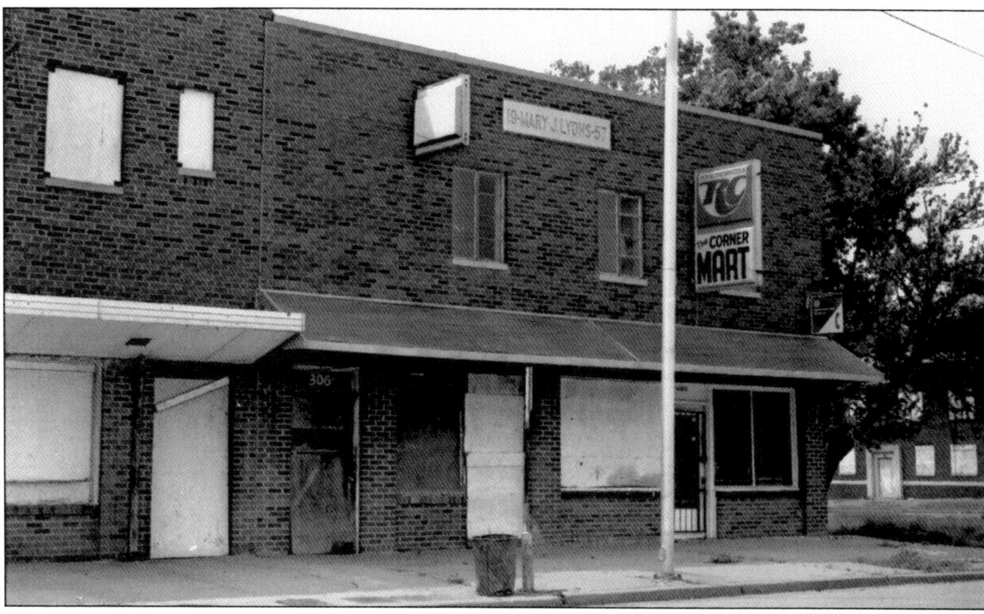

The Mary J. Lyons Building was built in 1957 and was located on the 300 block of Northeast Second Street. Mary Lyons was the wife of successful businessman Sydney D. Lyons, who founded the East India Toilet-Goods and Manufacturing Company. Mary was one of the wealthiest women in Oklahoma City. She and her husband helped build several buildings in the Deep Deuce area. Mary, who owned numerous parcels of land and oil interests, was also the owner of Lyons Park, an amusement park in Edmond. As one of the last remaining structures in Deep Deuce, it was in use until the mid-1990s. This photograph is taken by W. D. Welge in 1995. (Courtesy Oklahoma Historical Society.)

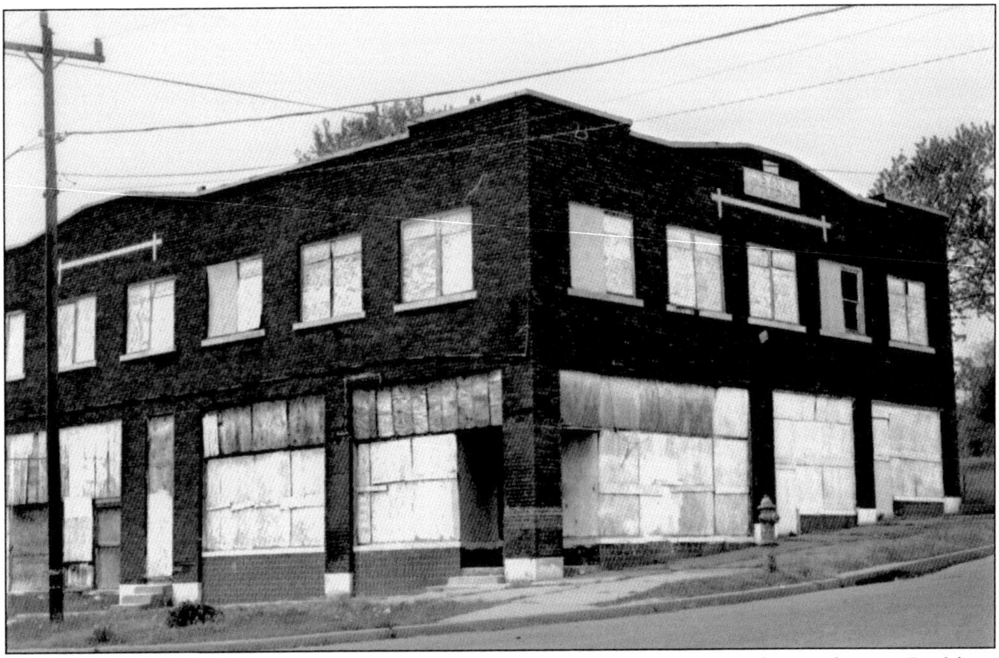

One of the last businesses built during the heyday of Deep Deuce was the Littlepage Building in 1924. Located at 219 North Central Avenue, it served as the M&M Hotel to meet the needs of a thriving commercial interest of African Americans visiting the city. Such notables as Duke Ellington, Count Basie, Joe Louis, Sarah Vaughan, and Nat King Cole registered at the M&M Hotel. The first floor of the two-story redbrick building contained several business enterprises, including a restaurant, a barbershop, and a grocer, it also served as the headquarters for the Blue Devil's Orchestra. The building was in use until late 1990 and since has been boarded up. This image was taken in 1995 by W. D. Welge. (Courtesy Oklahoma Historical Society.)

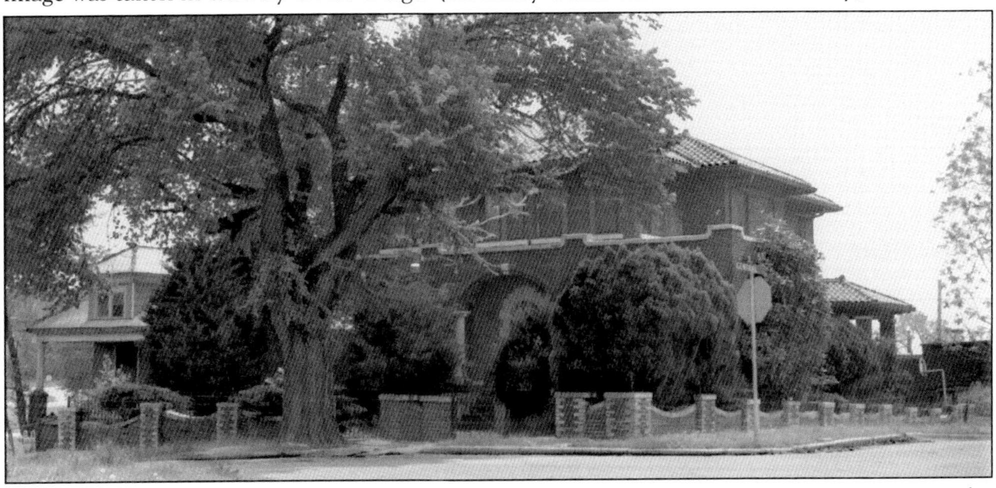

One of the most significant structures still standing and in use in the Deep Deuce area is the Melvin Luster Home at 300 Northeast Third Street. Built in 1926 by Luster's stepfather Sydney Lyons, the home is a two-story wood and brick structure. The interior of the home has a number of ornate features including canvas walls (painted in oils by a commissioned artist), sculptured ceramic tile, stone fireplaces, and beveled glass French doors. This photograph was taken in 1995 by W. D. Welge. (Courtesy Oklahoma Historical Society.)

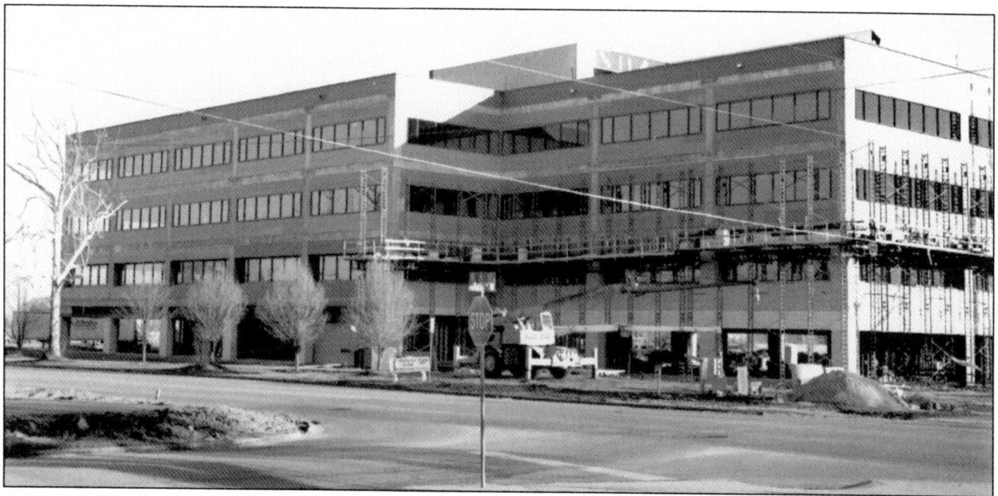

After steady decline from the 1970s through the 1990s, eventually the Oklahoma Department of Transportation saw an opportunity to develop an inner-city highway linking Interstates 40 and 44. In the late 1980s, the Department of Transportation built the Centennial Expressway (now Interstate 235) linking Interstates 35 and 40 to Interstate 44 in far northeastern Oklahoma City. The roadway cut through the neighborhood, thus creating a physical as well as social barrier to Deep Deuce. The land east of the expressway, from Northeast First Street along Lincoln Boulevard, became in a sense an extension of the hospital complex at Northeast Thirteenth Street with the development of a medical research and development complex. From Northeast Fourth to Eighth Streets the Presbyterian Research Foundation has continued to expand through the mid-1990s to the present. Seen here is one of the medical research facilities in the final stages of construction at Northeast Eighth Street and Lincoln Boulevard in 2007. (Courtesy W. D. Welge.)

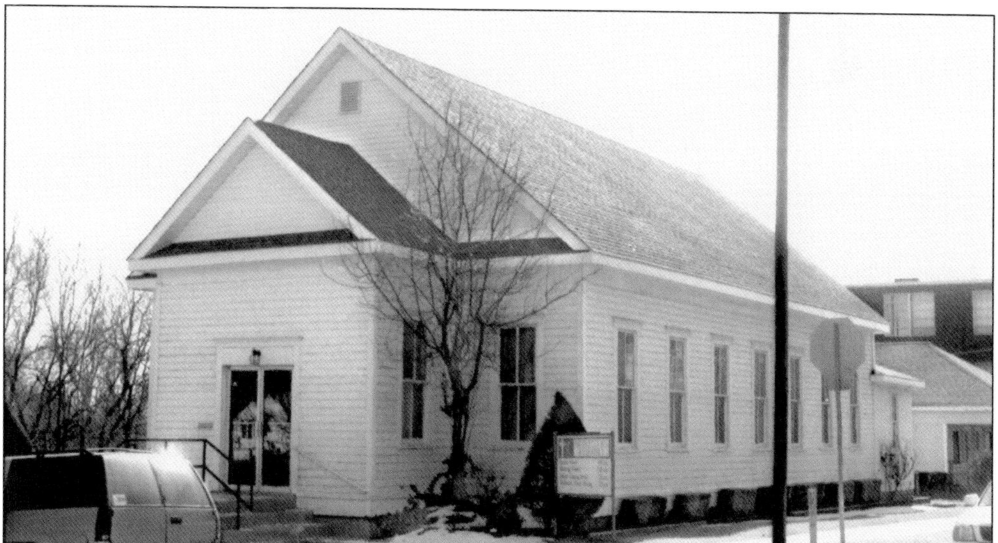

East of Lincoln Boulevard and separated by Interstate 235 is a section of the neighborhood that continues to survive, although the main business district along Second Street has disappeared. Here is one of many churches that hold weekly services for its small, but loyal, congregation. The Harvesters Assembly at Northeast Third and Phillips Streets was photographed in early 2007. (Courtesy W. D. Welge.)

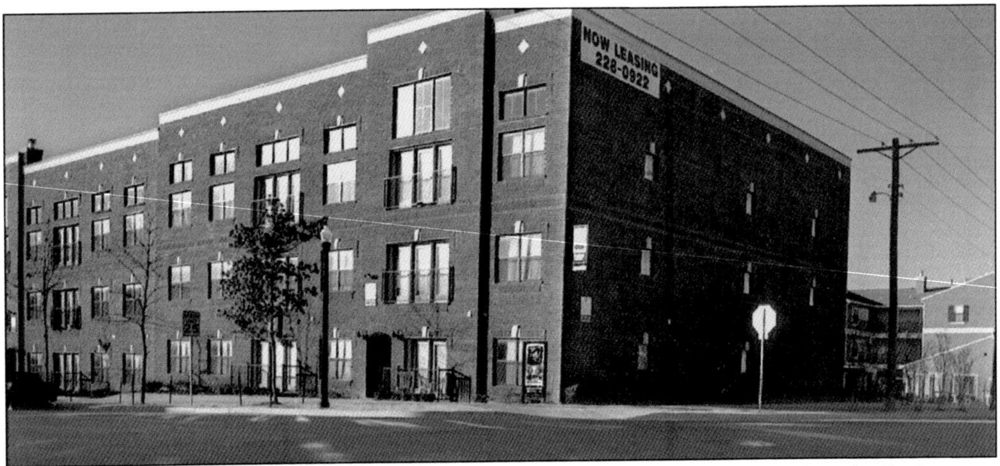

Since the late 1990s the area known as Deep Deuce has been actively redeveloped. The historic structures listed on the National Register of Historic Places still remain, but towering over them are modern upscale townhouses that occupy land once dominated by the African American community. From Walnut Avenue east to Stiles Avenue, the neighborhood has attracted individuals who want to live near downtown Oklahoma City, and it is within walking distance of Bricktown just to the south. This view is from Northeast Second Street and Stiles Avenue looking northwest. (Courtesy Black Liberated Arts Center, Inc.)

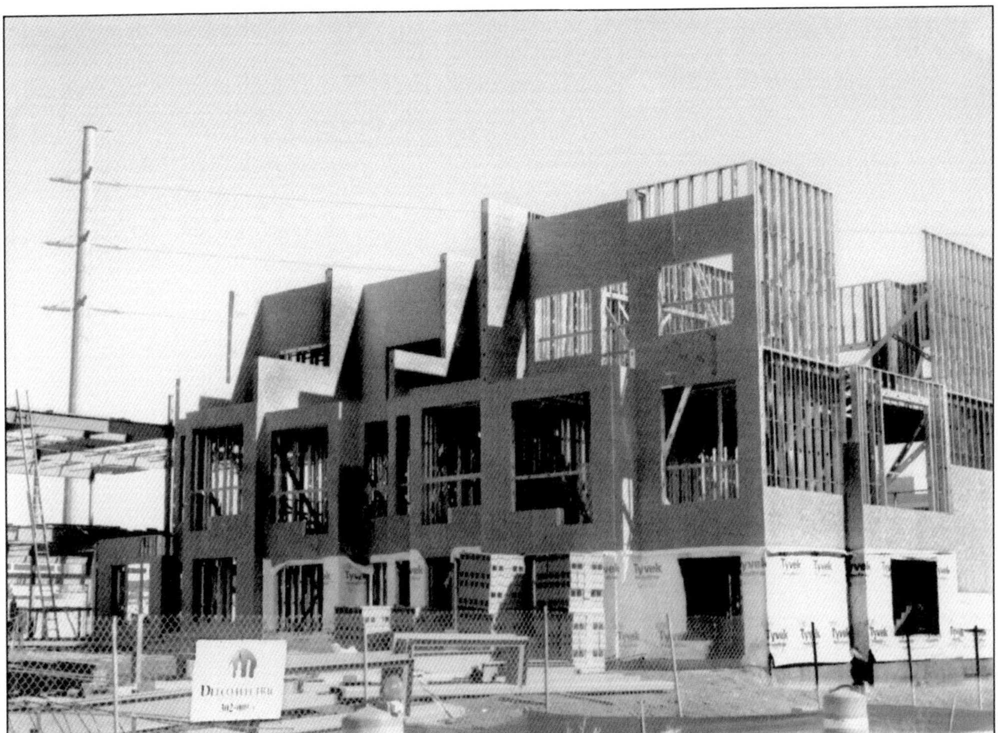

The redevelopment of Deep Deuce continues as additional buildings are being constructed along Northeast Fourth Street and Stiles Avenue. This new construction is for upscale condominiums called the Brownstones at Maywood Park. It was at this location that the Hotel Youngblood once stood. This image was taken in early 2007. (Courtesy W. D. Welge.)

Seven

Oklahoma City Post–World War II

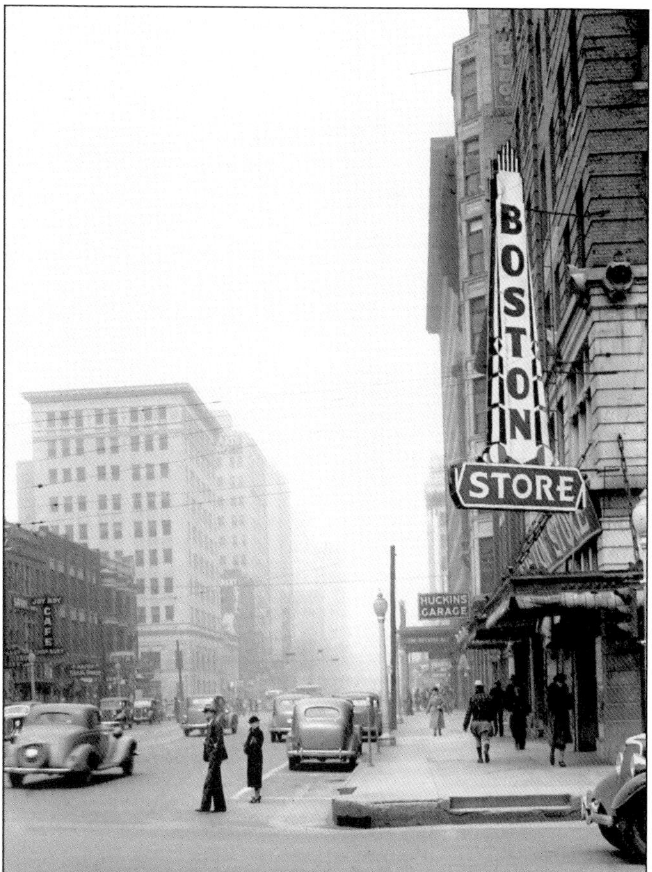

Oklahoma City in 1930 was a community in transition. Although the stock market crash a year earlier had plunged the United States into a major economic decline, Oklahoma City had not yet felt the devastating effects. In the mid-1930s, banks began to fail, a prolonged drought in the Midwest added to the misery of Oklahomans. Then if that was not enough, dust storms from eastern Colorado to the Texas panhandle raked the already crop-depleted land, pushing clouds of dirt eastward. For most Americans the perception of the "dust bowl" was only confined to the panhandle of Oklahoma. However, dust storms blew east, clear to the Atlantic Coast. Here in this Clayton Soule image is evidence of a storm in 1936 in downtown Oklahoma City along North Broadway. (Courtesy Oklahoma Historical Society.)

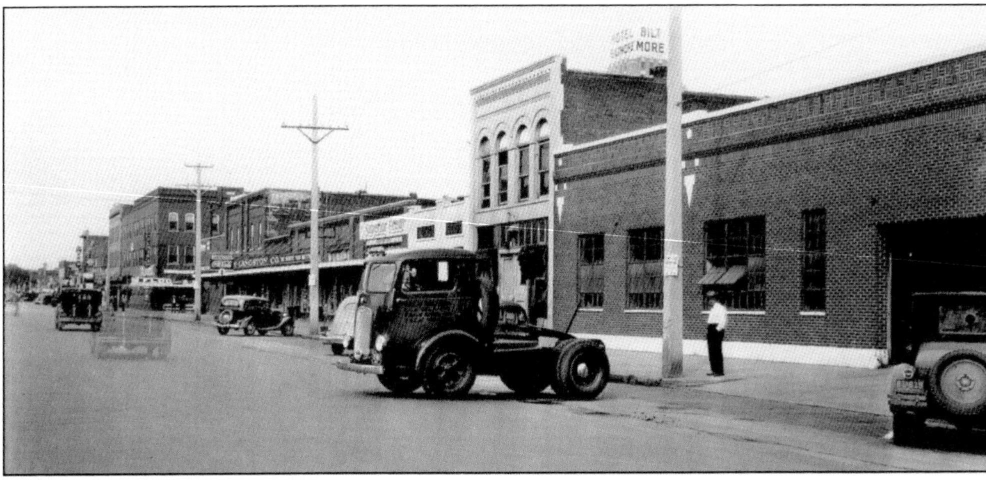

Economic conditions in Oklahoma City during the 1930s caused many businesses and industries to either scale back jobs and production or cease operations. Those that held on would not see actual relief until the country went to war in 1941. Commerce Street along Reno Avenue and Shields Boulevard, seen here, is sparse in this Z. P. Meyers photograph taken in 1937. (Courtesy Oklahoma Historical Society.)

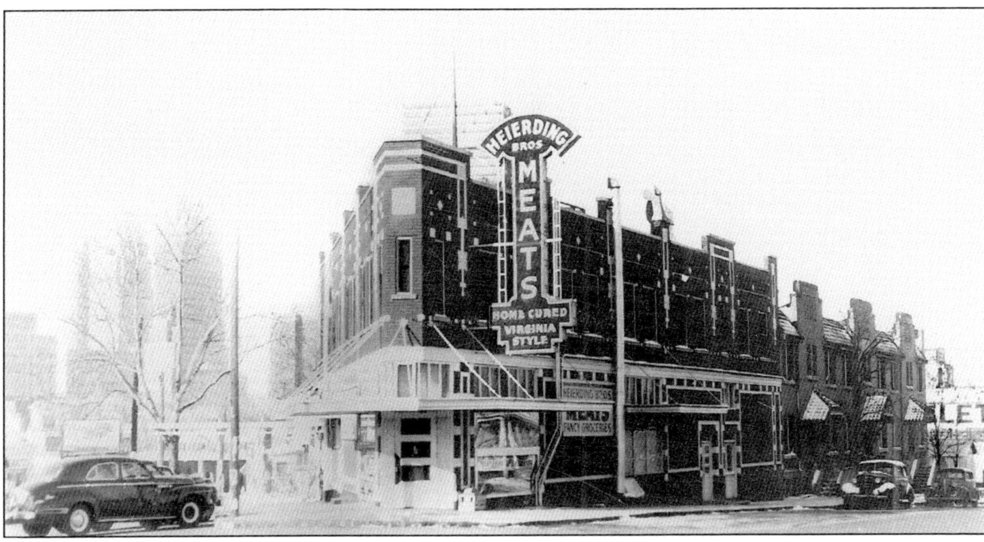

Just two blocks east of Broadway is a historic building of unique design that has served at one time as a meat market, lawyer's office, and now the offices of Rand Elliott and Associates. The Heierding Brothers Building, at Northeast Fifth Street and Harrison Avenue, was built in 1914 by August F. Heierding. A native of Germany, Heierding migrated to the United States in 1905. Arriving in Oklahoma City, he worked for a meat and produce store until 1907, when he and his brother Fred established their business. The design of the building has a "flat iron" look to it and has been referred to as the "flat iron building." The Heierdings' business was on the first floor with their residence being on the second story. After the business closed in the 1960s, it was heavily damaged by a fire in 1987. That is when Rand Elliott restored the building to serve as his corporate offices for his architectural firm. The photograph seen here is from around the 1940s period. The building has been listed on the National Register of Historic Places. (Courtesy Rand Elliott.)

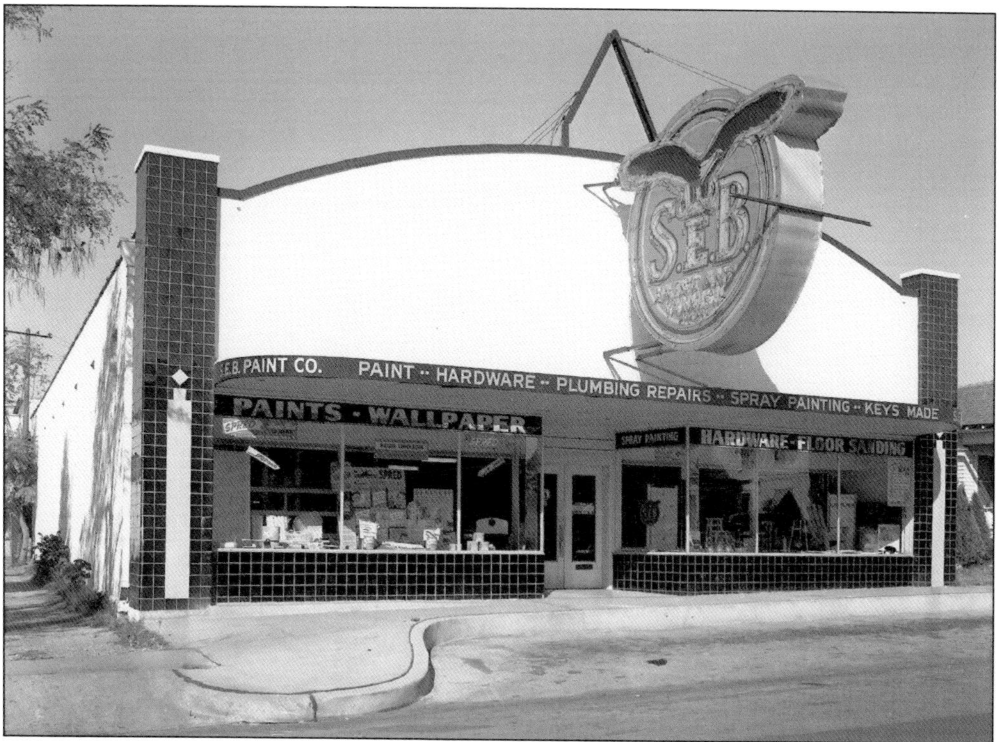

Another building one block east of Broadway is the S.E.B. Paint and Hardware building. Located at 115 Northeast Tenth Street, it served as a neighborhood hardware and supply store for several years. Photographed by the Meyer Photo Shop, this image was taken in 1942. (Courtesy Oklahoma Historical Society.)

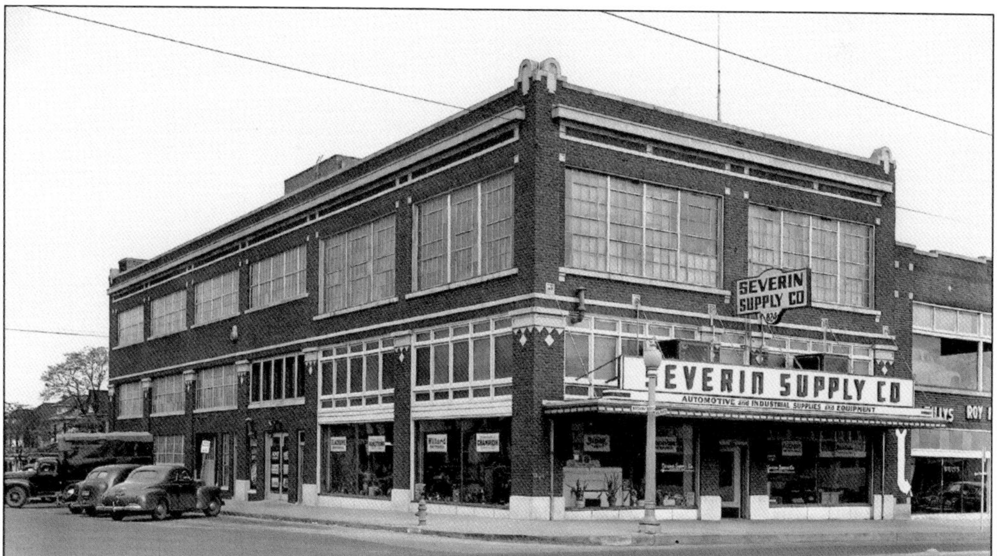

A mainstay on North Broadway was the Severin Supply Company. The business sold automotive and industrial supplies. Built around 1920, it is located at 712 North Broadway. The building is among the historic structures included in the Automobile Alley Historic District. Z. P. Meyers took this photograph in April 1946. (Courtesy Oklahoma Historical Society.)

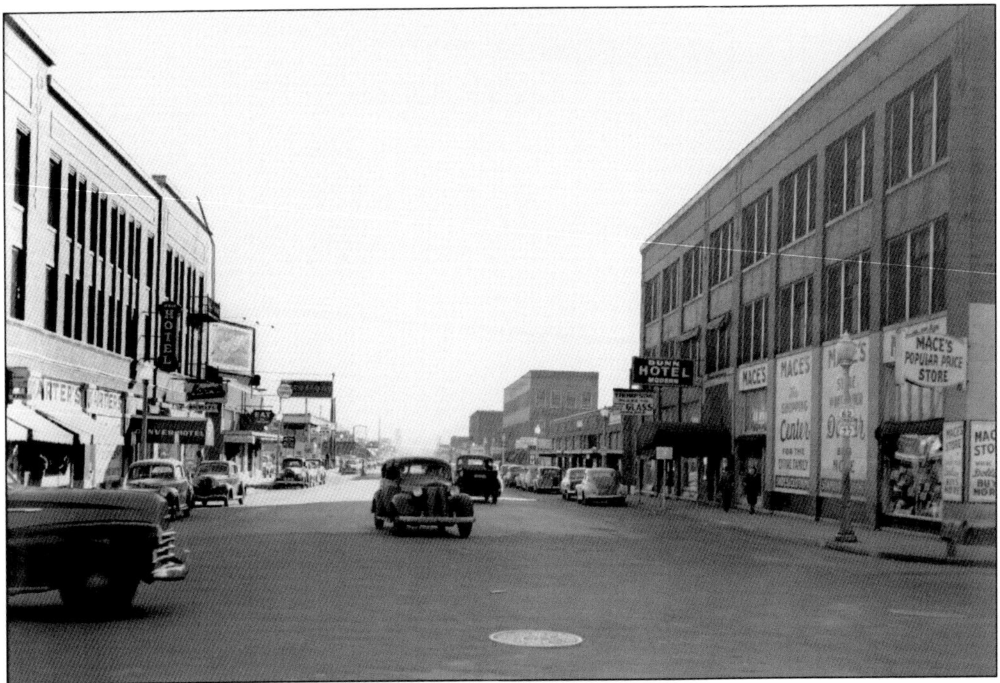

This image is of South Robinson Avenue, just south of Reno Avenue, and was taken after World War II by Meyers Photo Shop. The only structure still standing from this November 1948 view is one building on the right. It served for a number of years as the City Rescue Mission. (Courtesy Oklahoma Historical Society.)

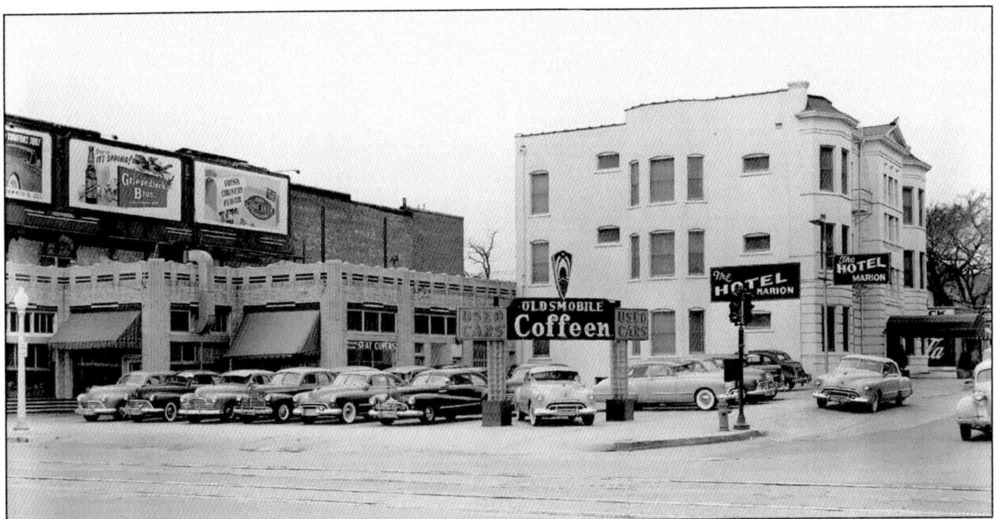

This image is an excellent example of the reason Broadway has been designated Automobile Alley. In this 1948 image is the Coffeen Oldsmobile dealership located at 901 North Broadway. In the background is the Hotel Marion. Built in 1904, it is one of the last buildings of the pre-statehood period left in Oklahoma City. Located at 110 Northwest Tenth Street, the hotel has been closed for a period of time. There has been an attempt to renovate the structure into possible office space. This image was photographed by Meyers Photo Shop. (Courtesy Oklahoma Historical Society.)

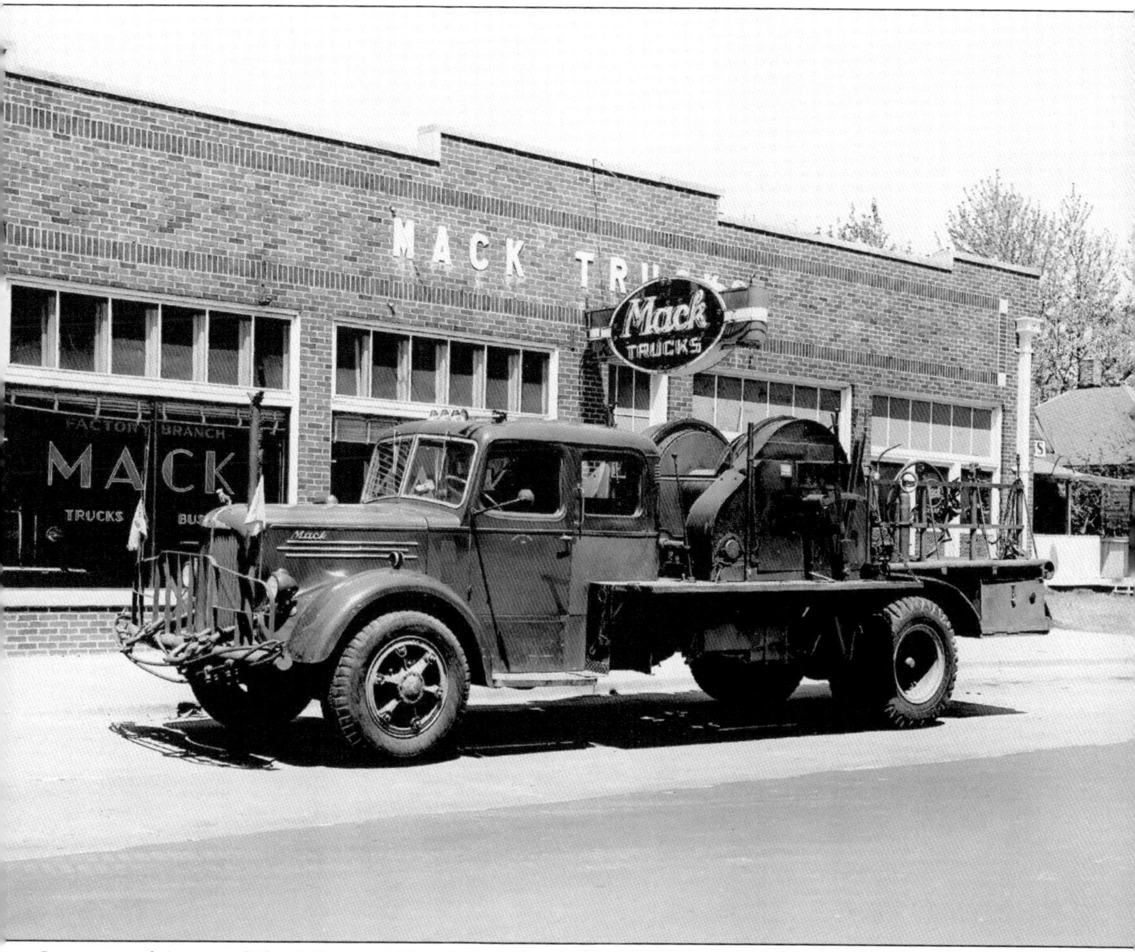

Just east of Automobile Alley at 1 Northeast Tenth Street was the Mack Truck Company. Here the latest model is being shown for the public. This photograph was taken in April 1949 by Meyers Photo Shop. (Courtesy Oklahoma Historical Society.)

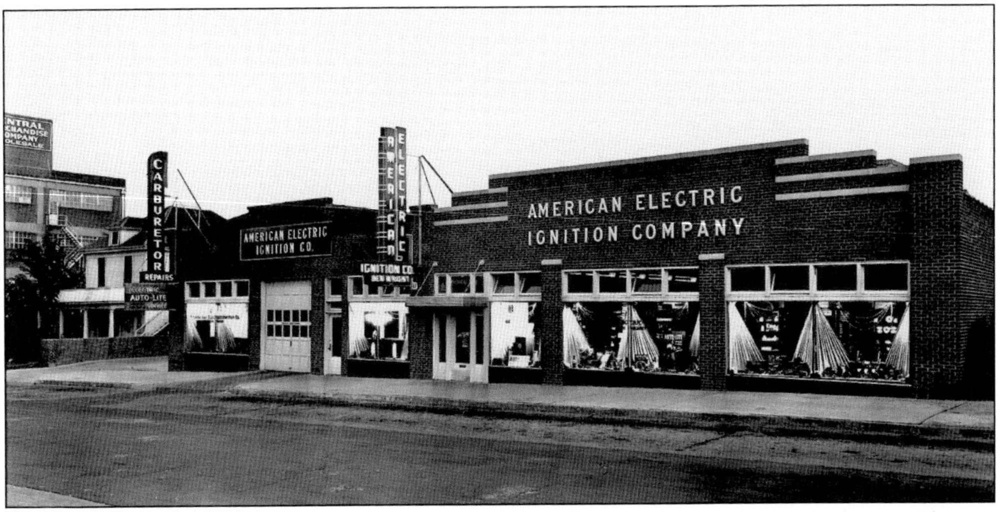

Another building included in the Automobile Alley Historic District is the American Electric Ignition Company of 725 North Broadway. Built in 1915, this one-story brick commercial-style building had large plate glass windows for easy viewing of products. Because of extensive changes to the exterior of the building, it is considered a noncontributing structure to the district. This image was taken by Meyers Photo Shop in the 1950s. (Courtesy Oklahoma Historical Society.)

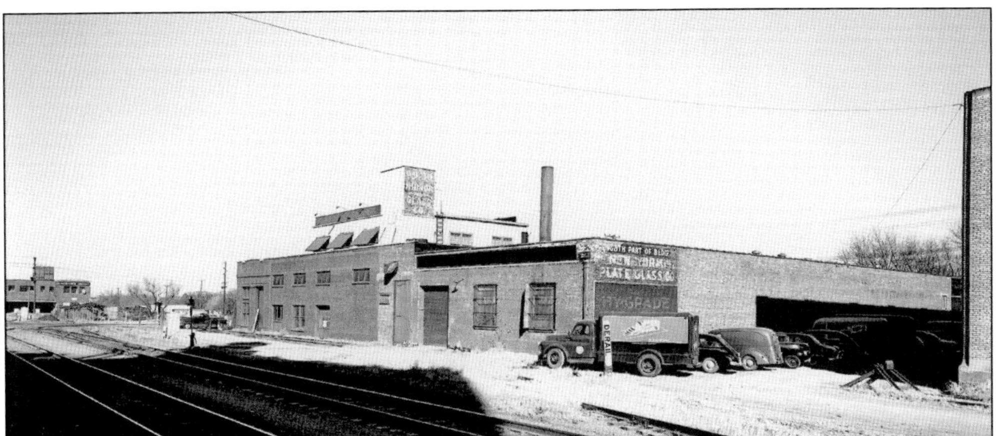

One block east of Broadway is the AAA Root Beer company offices. Just a few feet east of the Santa Fe railroad tracks, this image was taken in December 1950 by Z. P. Meyers. (Courtesy Oklahoma Historical Society.)

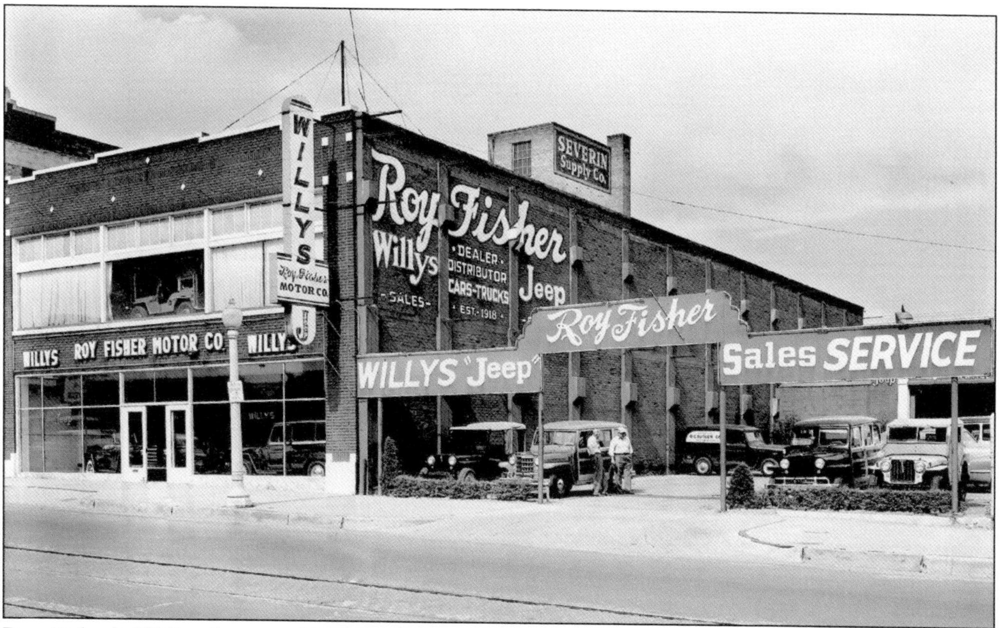

Roy Fisher's Willys Jeep, at 720 North Broadway next to Severin's Supply Company, sold the distinctive Willy and Jeep brand of automobiles. Note on the second floor of the dealership behind the window is a Jeep model on display. This image was taken by Meyers Photo Shop in May 1950. (Courtesy Oklahoma Historical Society.)

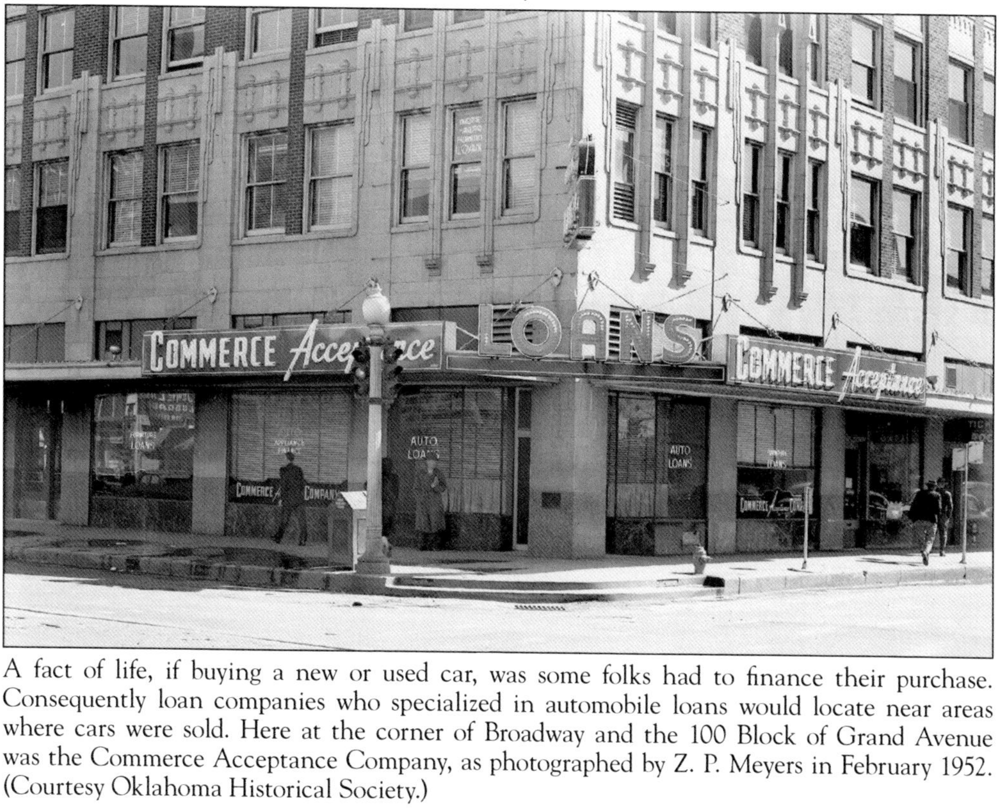

A fact of life, if buying a new or used car, was some folks had to finance their purchase. Consequently loan companies who specialized in automobile loans would locate near areas where cars were sold. Here at the corner of Broadway and the 100 Block of Grand Avenue was the Commerce Acceptance Company, as photographed by Z. P. Meyers in February 1952. (Courtesy Oklahoma Historical Society.)

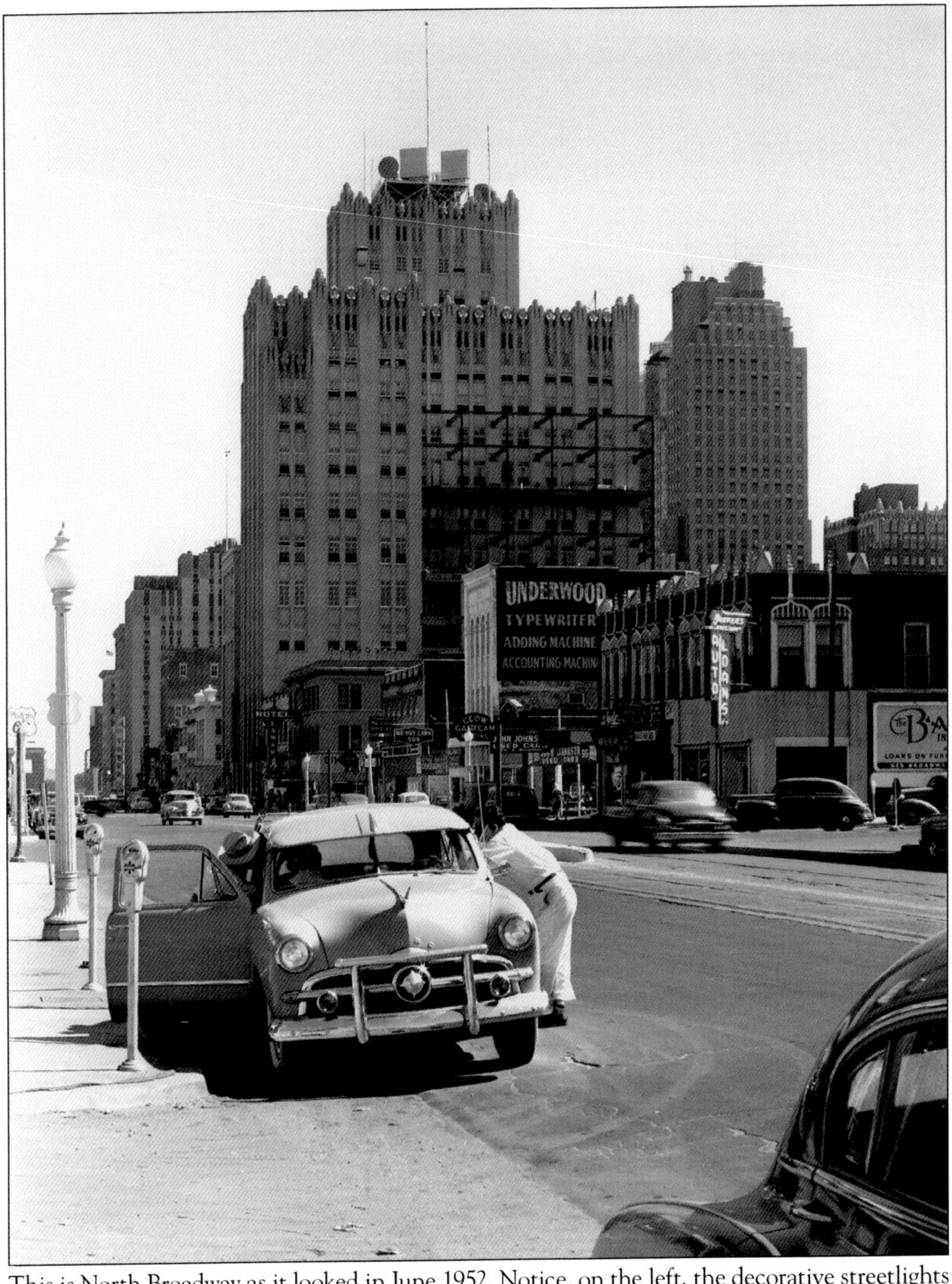

This is North Broadway as it looked in June 1952. Notice, on the left, the decorative streetlights that line the avenue. In the background is the Pioneer Telephone Company Building. This photograph was taken by Meyers Photo Shop. (Courtesy Oklahoma Historical Society.)

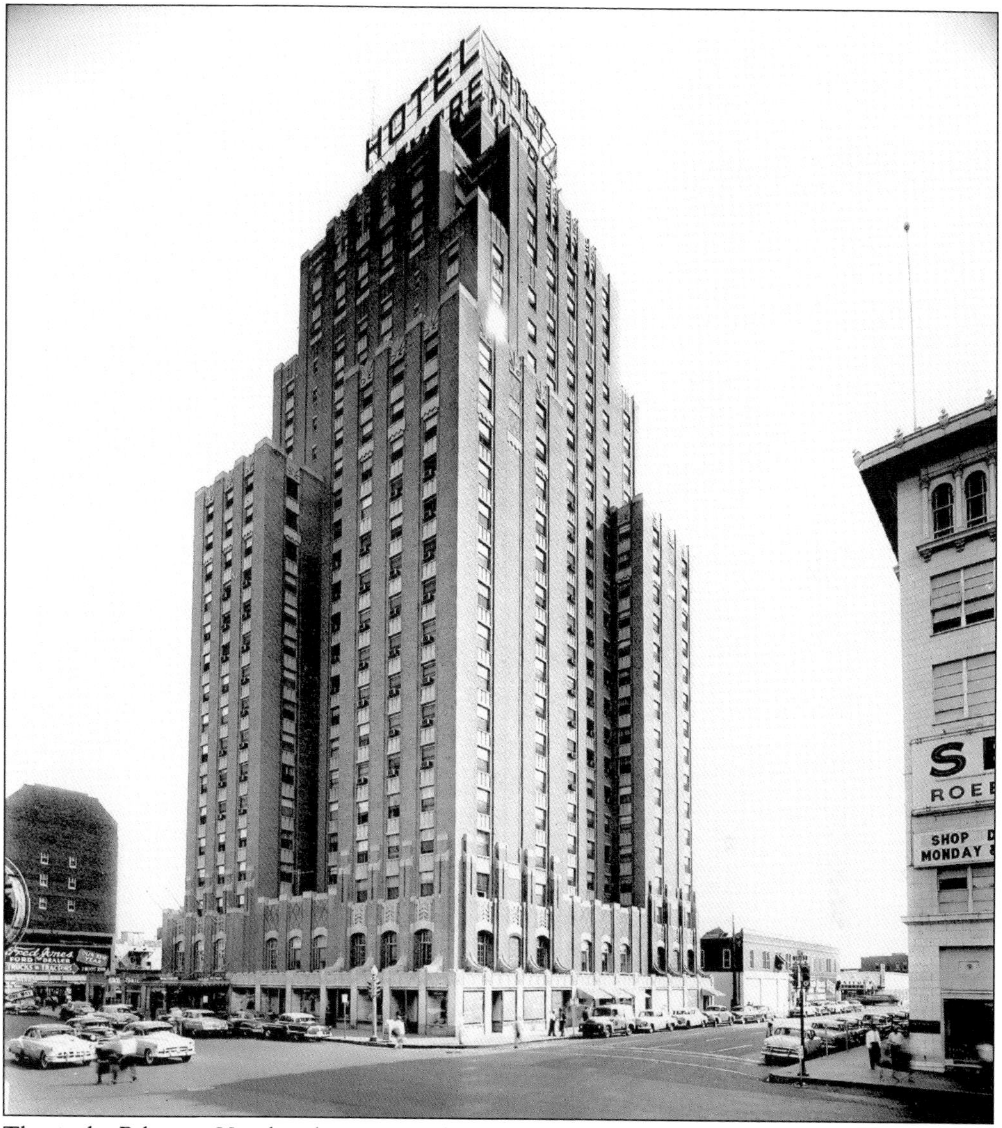

This is the Biltmore Hotel in downtown Oklahoma City at 228 West Grand Avenue as it looked in October 1952. The hotel was the meeting place of choice for politicians and lobbyists who cut many a deal in smoke-filled rooms. Under the Pei plan for urban renewal, the hotel was to be spared, but was brought down by explosives in the early 1970s. The Myriad Gardens has taken its place, where each April the Oklahoma City Arts Festival is held. (Courtesy Oklahoma Historical Society.)

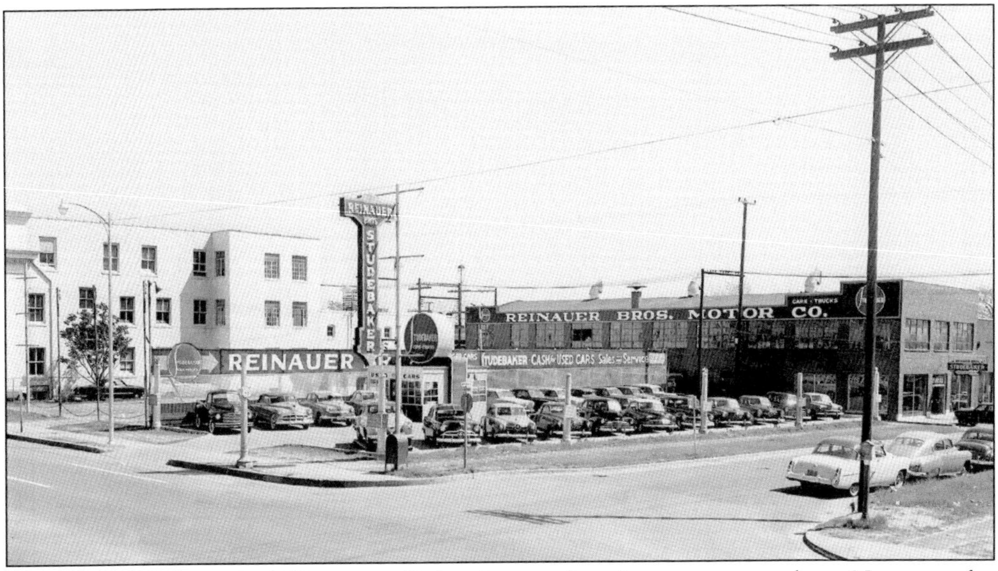

Downtown, by the early 1950s, was still the place to shop for a new or used car. New car sales increased especially after the war years (both World War II and Korean War). The Reinauer Brothers Motor Company at 25 Northwest Ninth Street had been selling cars since 1928. It was the main dealership for Studebaker for years. This image was taken in April 1953 by Meyers Photo Shop. (Courtesy Oklahoma Historical Society.)

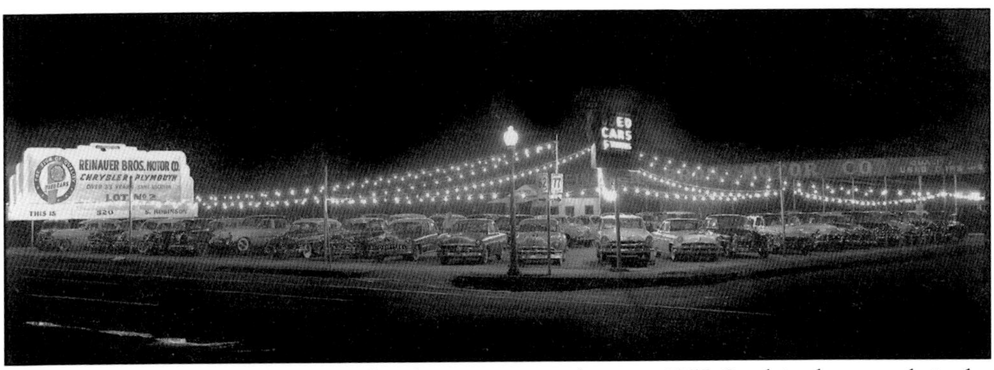

This is the same view taken at night about two years later in 1955. In this photograph is the Reinauer Brothers used car lot at 25 Northwest Ninth Street. The photograph was taken by Meyers Photo Shop. (Courtesy Oklahoma Historical Society.)

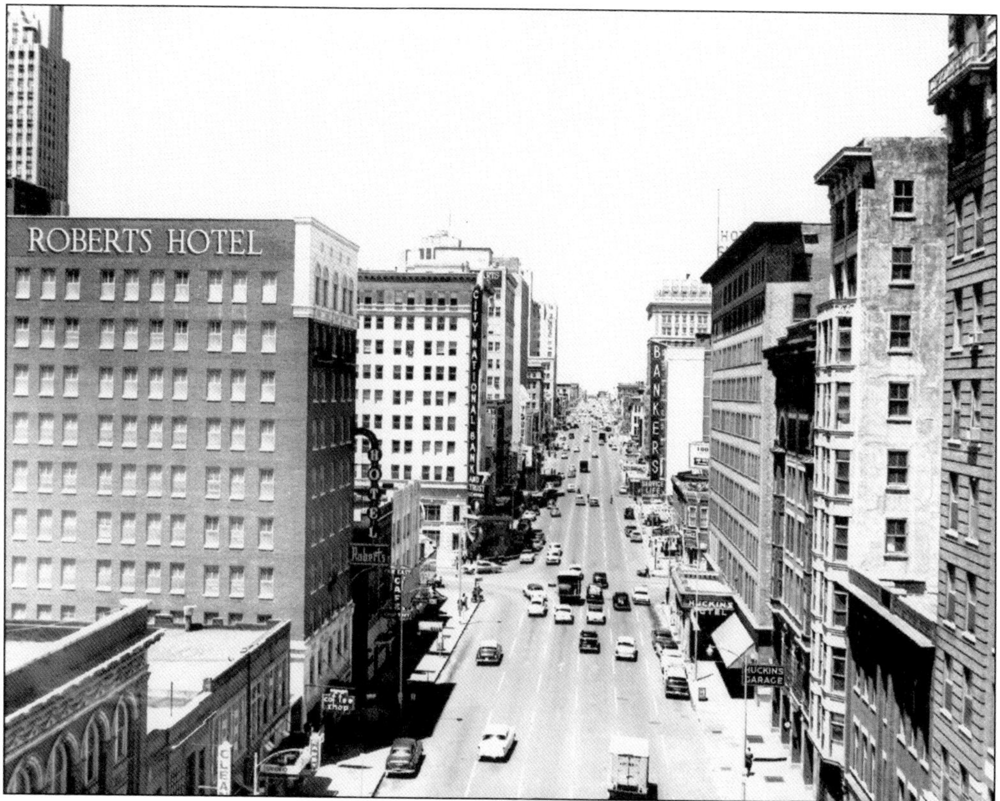

This view of Broadway, looking north, would change by the late 1960s. Urban renewal would eventually tear down nearly every building seen in this photograph. At the far upper right, the top of the Skirvin Hotel at 1 North Broadway can be seen. It survived demolition only to close in 1988. It reopened to the public on February 26, 2007, after more than $50 million in renovations. This photograph was taken by Barney Hillerman in 1956. (Courtesy Oklahoma Historical Society.)

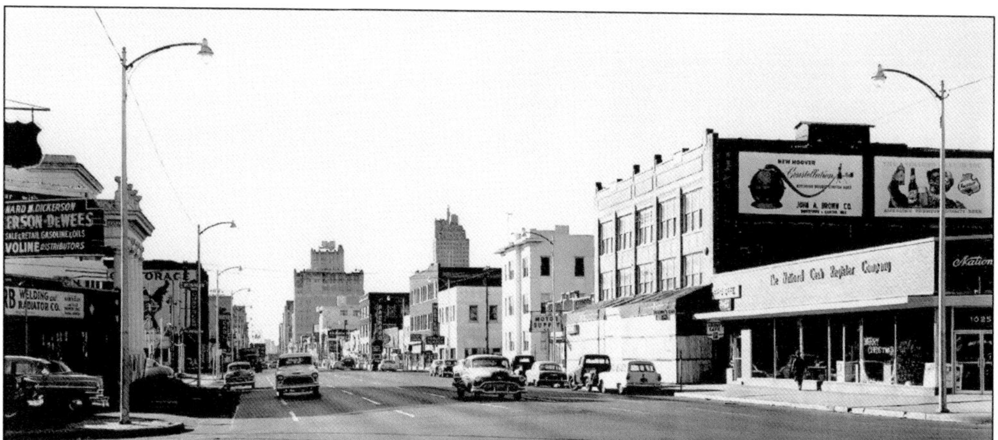

By the mid-1950s, a slow transition from automobile and truck dealerships to other types of businesses began to occur. As the population base shifted to the suburbs, so did the dealerships. This image, taken in 1956 by Meyers Photo Shop, is looking south on Broadway from Northwest Tenth Street. (Courtesy Oklahoma Historical Society.)

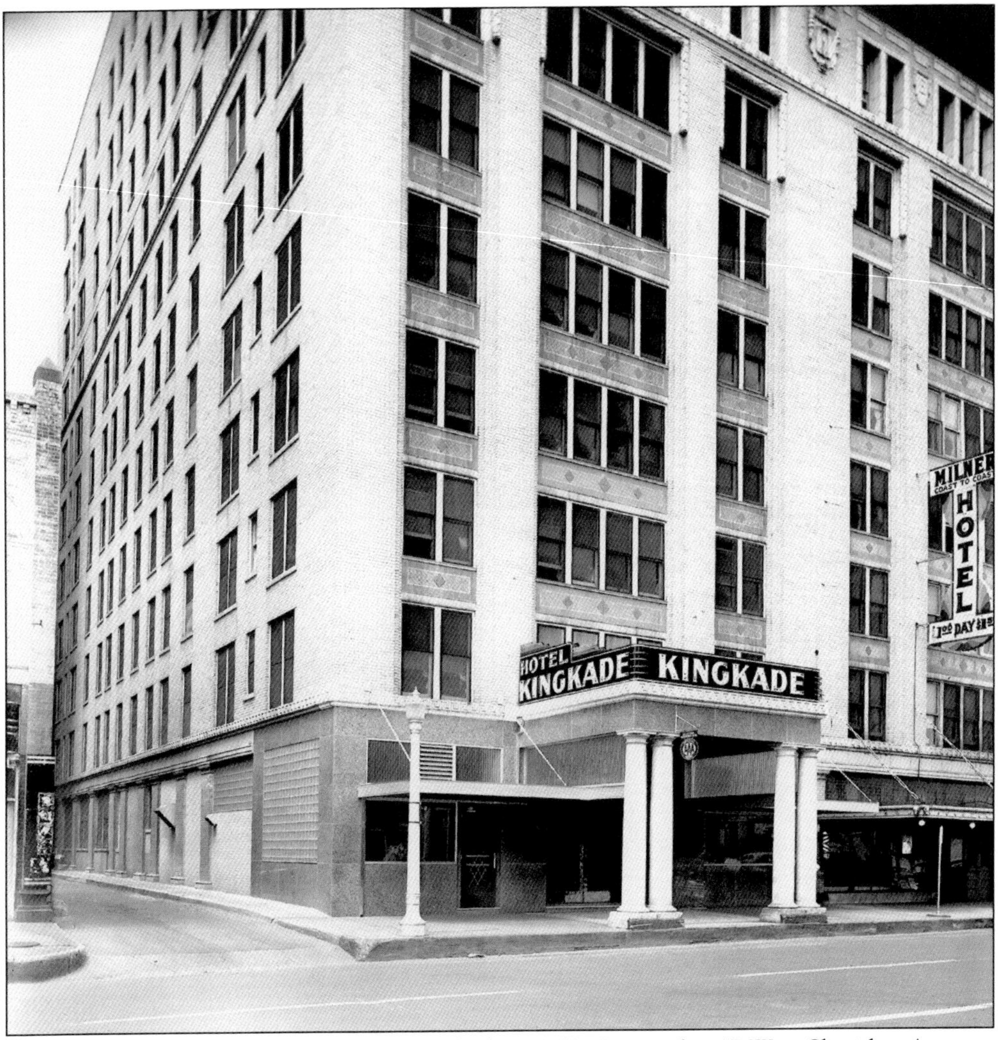

This is the Hotel Kingkade as it looked in the late 1950s. Located at 17 West Sheridan Avenue, the 11-story hotel is where the author first saw Oklahoma City in 1966. Martin Kingkade was president and general manager when this photograph was taken by Z. P. Meyers in 1958. (Courtesy Oklahoma Historical Society.)

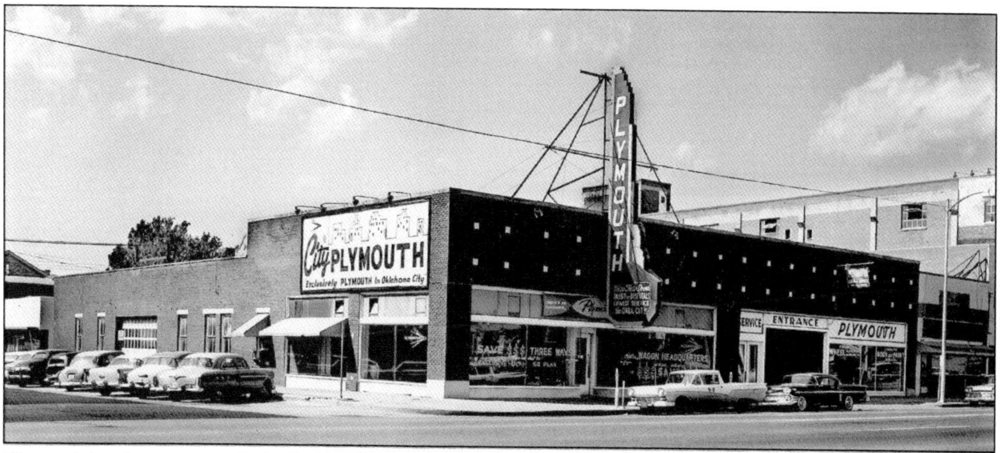

One of the last automobile dealerships on Broadway was City Plymouth at 901 North Broadway. This image was taken by Ray Jacoby in October 1958. (Courtesy Oklahoma Historical Society.)

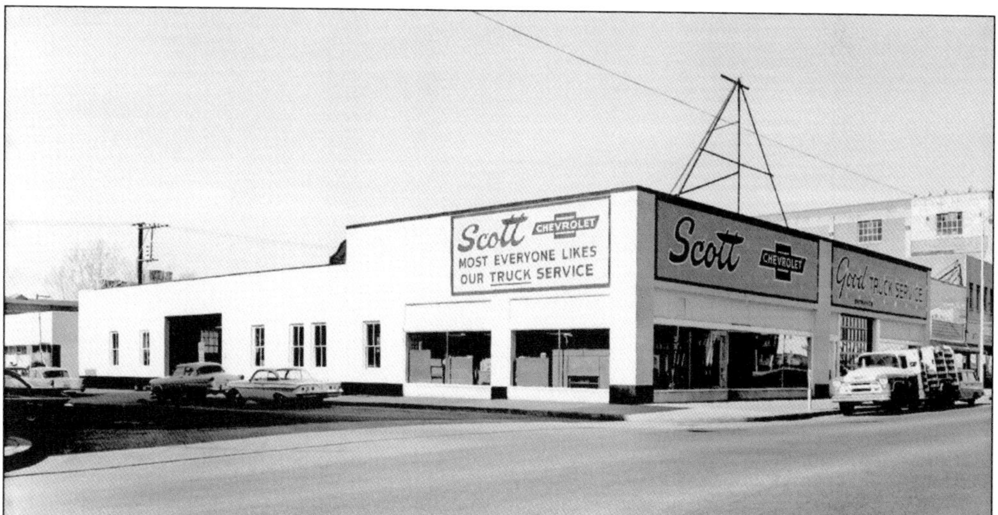

By the 1960s, only three dealers who sold automobiles remained on Broadway. The last left in 1983. Since the development of the historic district at least one car dealer, Mercedes Benz, has occupied a location at Northwest Thirteenth Street and Broadway from 2001 to the present. This photograph of Scott Chevrolet at 800 North Broadway was taken by Johnny Melton in the early 1960s. (Courtesy Oklahoma Historical Society.)

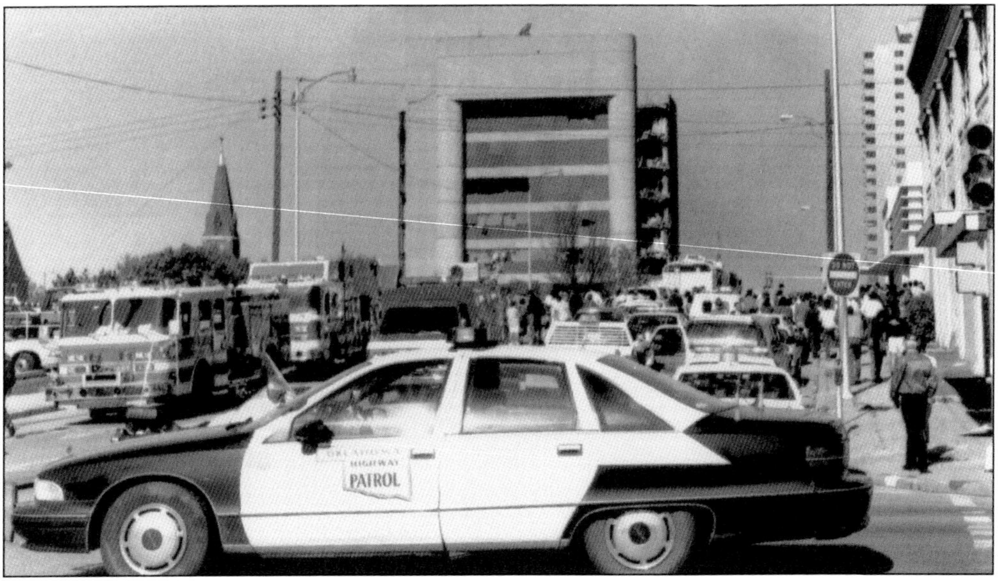

On April 19, 1995, the fabric of downtown Oklahoma City would be torn asunder by a domestic terrorist. On that misty Wednesday morning at 9:02 a.m., the Alfred P. Murrah Federal Building was blown up, killing 168 innocent men, women, and children in a matter of seconds. Over 900 persons were injured. The destruction on that fateful day was widespread, not only in the toll of humankind, but also of the buildings that radiated out from Northwest Fourth Street. This image, taken by photographic archivist Chester R. Cowen of the Oklahoma Historical Society, was taken within minutes of the tragedy. The view is looking west from Broadway on Northwest Fourth Street with the Murrah Federal Building in the center. (Courtesy Oklahoma Historical Society.)

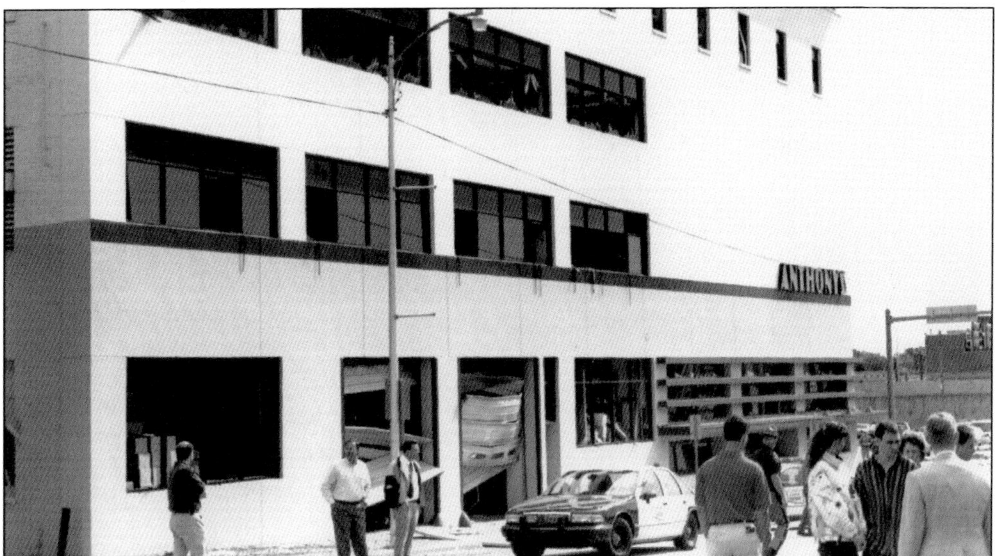

Damage from the Murrah bombing was extensive. Buildings several blocks away to the north received from severe to light damage. The C. R. Anthony Building, seen here at Northwest Sixth Street and Broadway, had almost all the windows blown in. The building is now Nichols Hills Bank. This photograph was taken by Chester R. Cowen. (Courtesy Oklahoma Historical Society.)

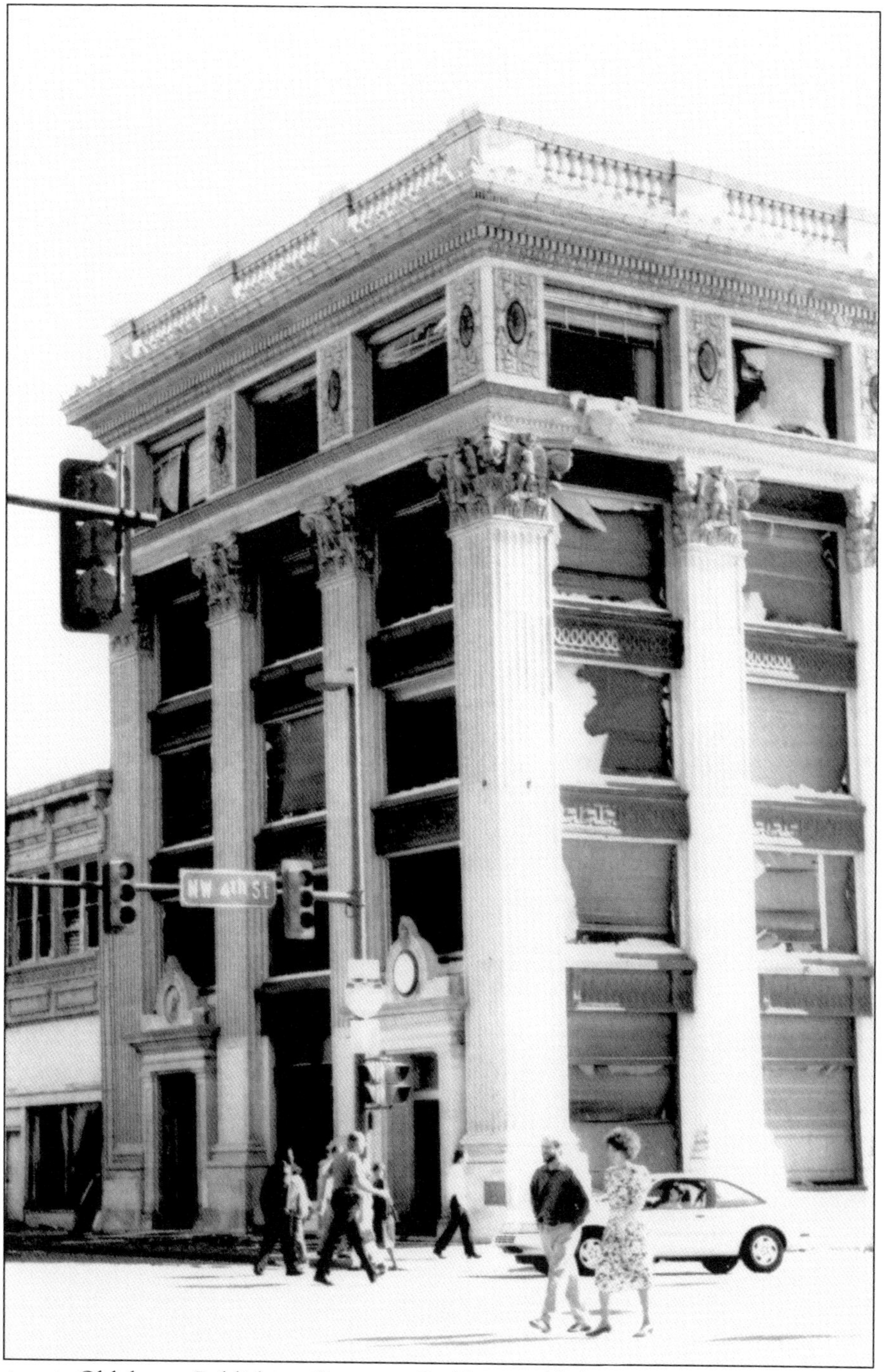

The historic Oklahoma Publishing Company Building, publisher of the largest newspaper in the state, was heavily damaged as it was only two blocks east and one block north of the Murrah Federal Building. Located at Northwest Fifth Street and Broadway, the building was constructed in 1909 and consists of five stories and is an excellent example of classical revival style. This photograph was taken by Chester R. Cowen on April 19, 1995, about 40 minutes after the blast. (Courtesy Oklahoma Historical Society.)

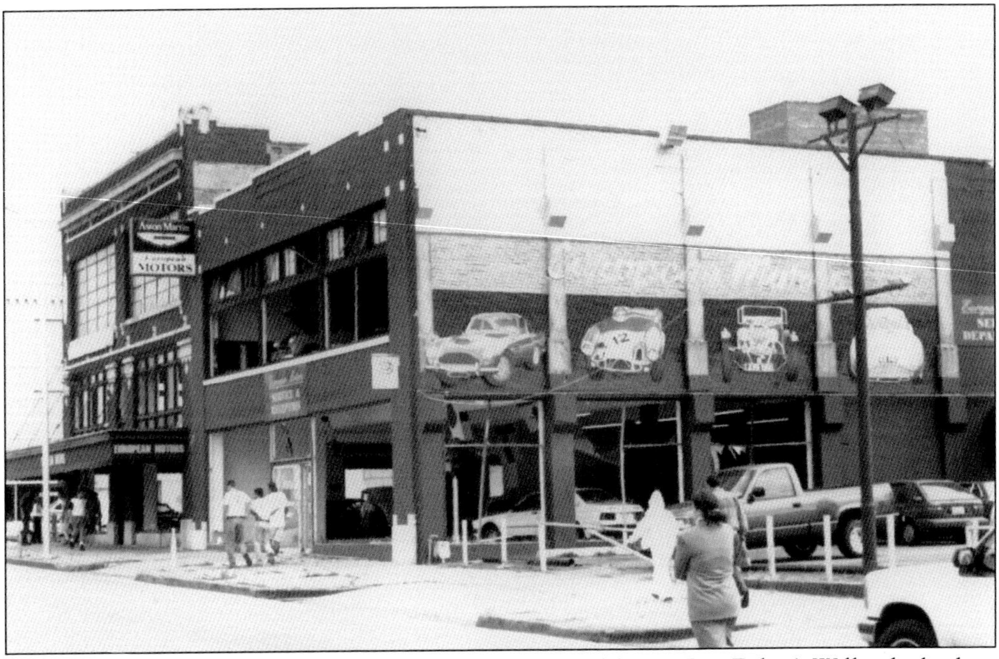

Extensive damage to the old Severin Supply Company and former Roy Fisher's Willys dealership, now European Motors at the 700 block of North Broadway, can be seen. This image was taken by Chester R. Cowen slightly more than an hour after the bombing on April 19, 1995. (Courtesy Oklahoma Historical Society.)

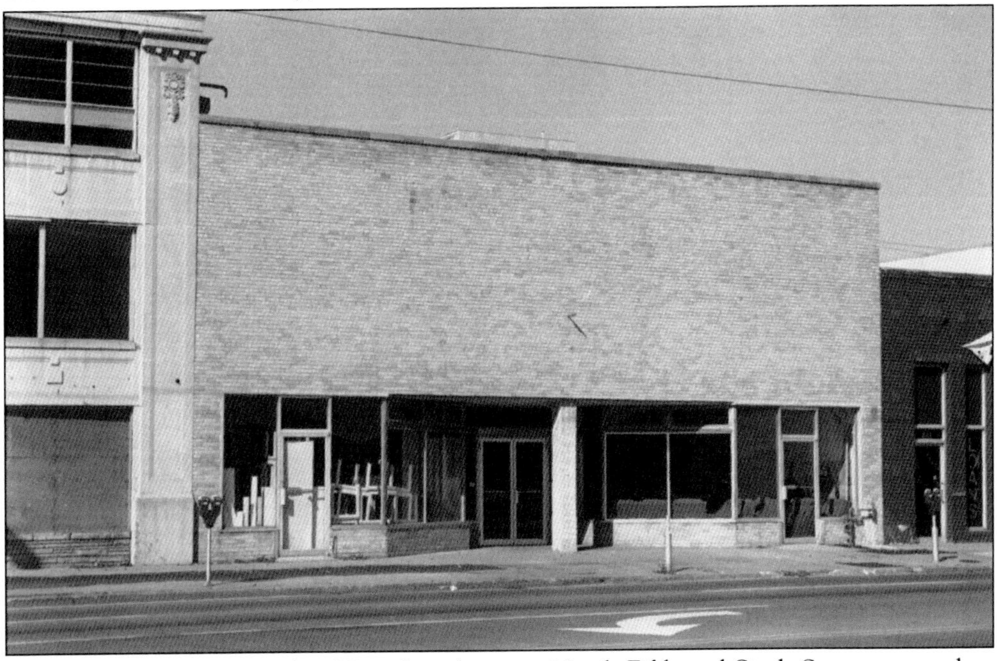

This image, on the west side of Broadway between North Fifth and Sixth Streets, was taken several months after the bombing. Evidence of the bomb damage lingered for several years prior to the creation of the Automobile Alley Historic District. This image was taken by Chester Cowen on October 18, 1995. (Courtesy Oklahoma Historical Society.)

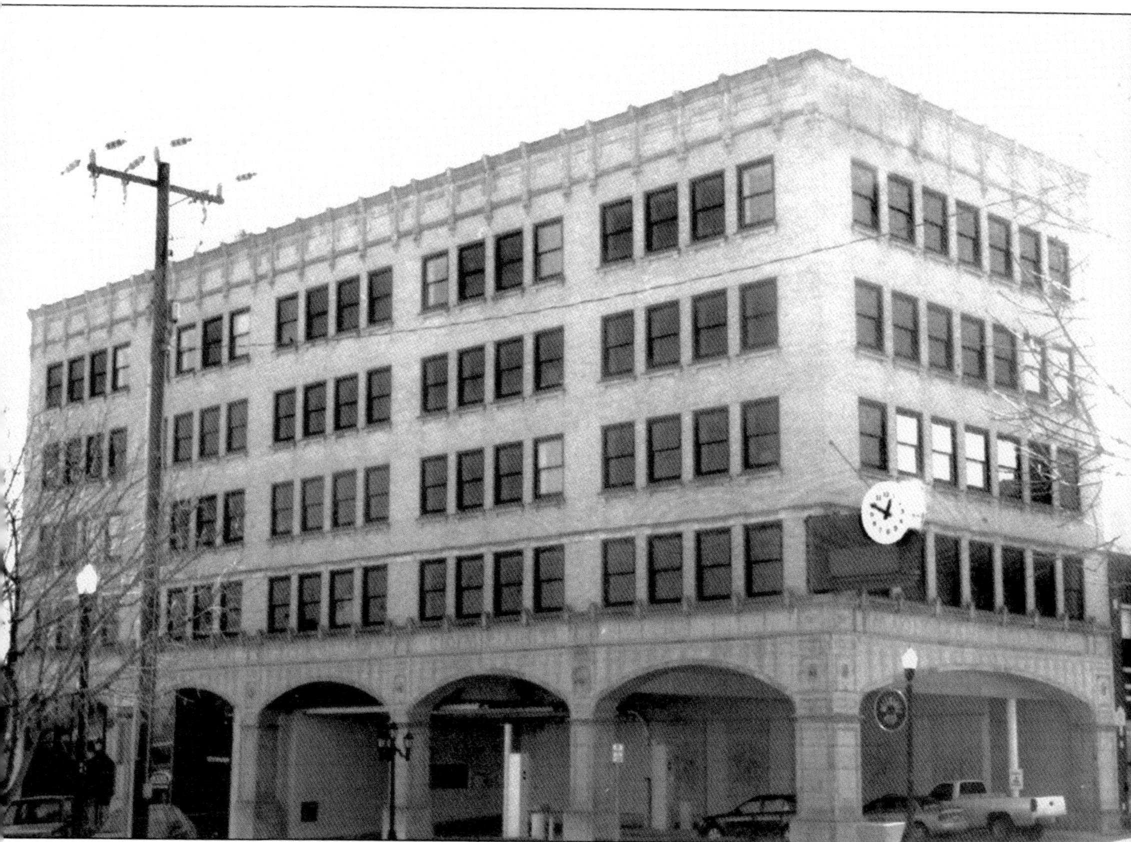

This is the Magnolia Petroleum Building as it appeared in January 2007. Photographed by W. D. Welge, it has held its historic significance for nearly 90 years. (Courtesy W. D. Welge)

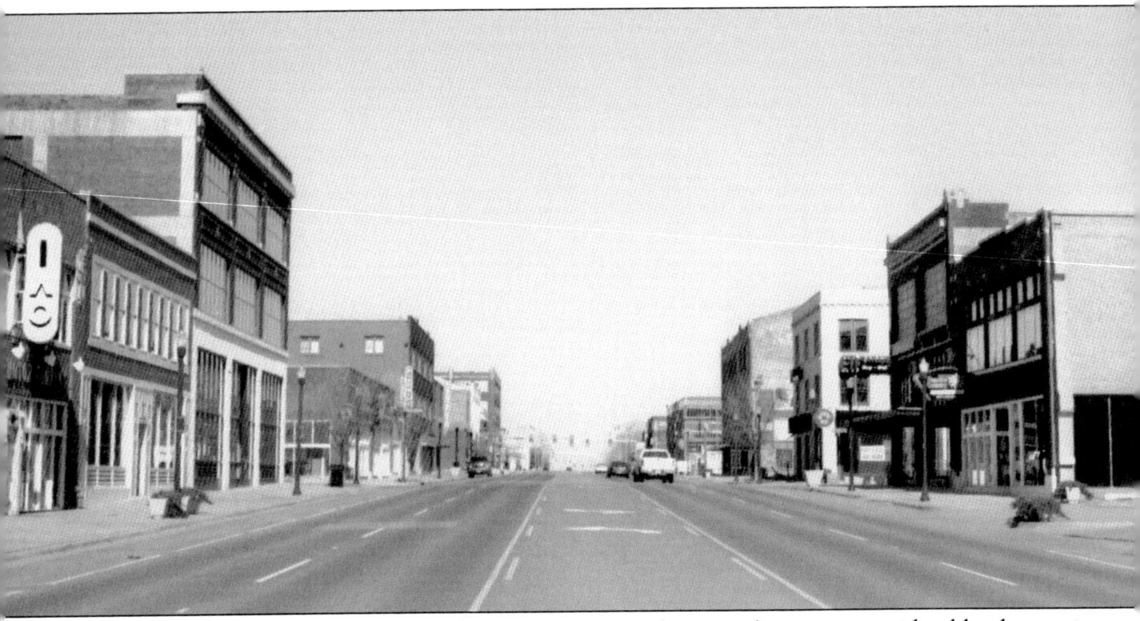

Oklahoma City, like any metropolitan community of its size, has seen considerable change in its 118-year history. From a refueling point for the Santa Fe railroad prior to settlement to a city with a population approaching 600,000 within the corporate city limits (over a million if satellite communities are included), the city has weathered many cyclical economic events that determined growth and prosperity. City leaders focused on redevelopment of downtown in the mid-1960s and 1970s to hopefully reenergize the flagging infrastructure of the city. With urban renewal, this was somewhat successful but failed in its effort to draw people back downtown after business hours. The redevelopment of Bricktown was highly successful in achieving that goal. The Metropolitan Area Projects of the 1990s generated enormous success in adding new venues for recreation for the general public. Since the tragedy of the bombing of the Alfred P. Murrah Federal Building on April 19, 1995, Oklahoma's image was changed forever. Prior to that tragic day, Oklahoma City was considered a pass-through community, meaning travelers driving through the city did not stop, they did not spend their money on sites and other attractions. After April 19 that changed, and with the MAPS projects of the ballpark and arena, plus a higher number of hotel and motel rooms added to the mix, Oklahoma City has become a place to visit and has aspirations of becoming a second-tier city for larger attractions to locate to this area. This is North Broadway in January 2007, looking north from Northwest Seventh Street. Many of the buildings are occupied and fulfilling new roles as law offices, civic organizations, and other types of businesses in this historic district north of downtown Oklahoma City. This scene was photographed by W. D. Welge. (Courtesy W. D. Welge.)

Eight

A Final Glimpse of Oklahoma City

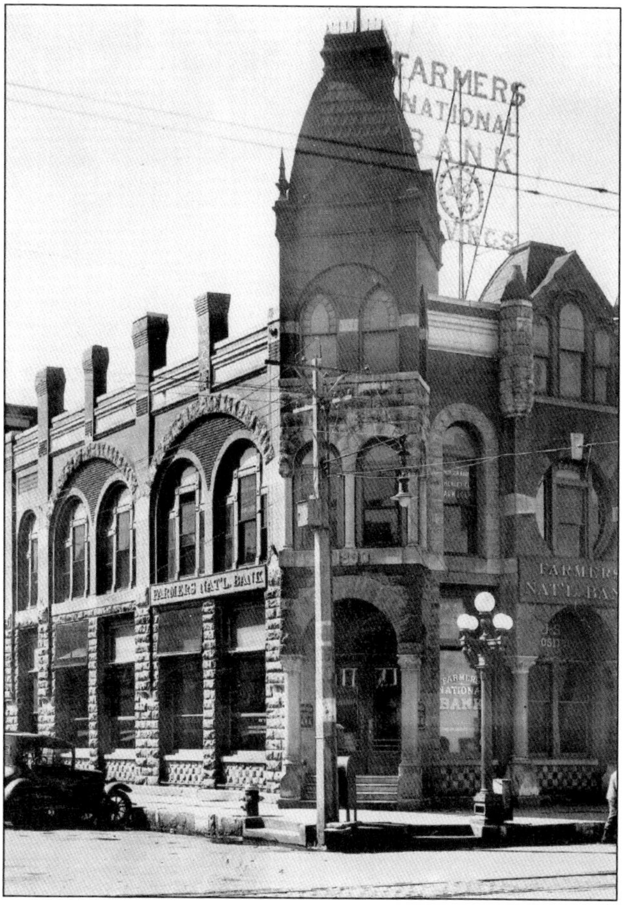

Although little of Oklahoma City's early heritage remains, such as the Farmers National Bank that was located at 200 West Grand Avenue, seen here, it has taken five generations of residents to finally understand historic preservation of the architectural heritage downtown. For most of the city, it has come far too late. But with efforts in Automobile Alley, Bricktown, the memory of Deep Deuce, and Capitol Hill, at least some vestiges of the city's past will be preserved for future generations. (Courtesy Oklahoma Historical Society.)

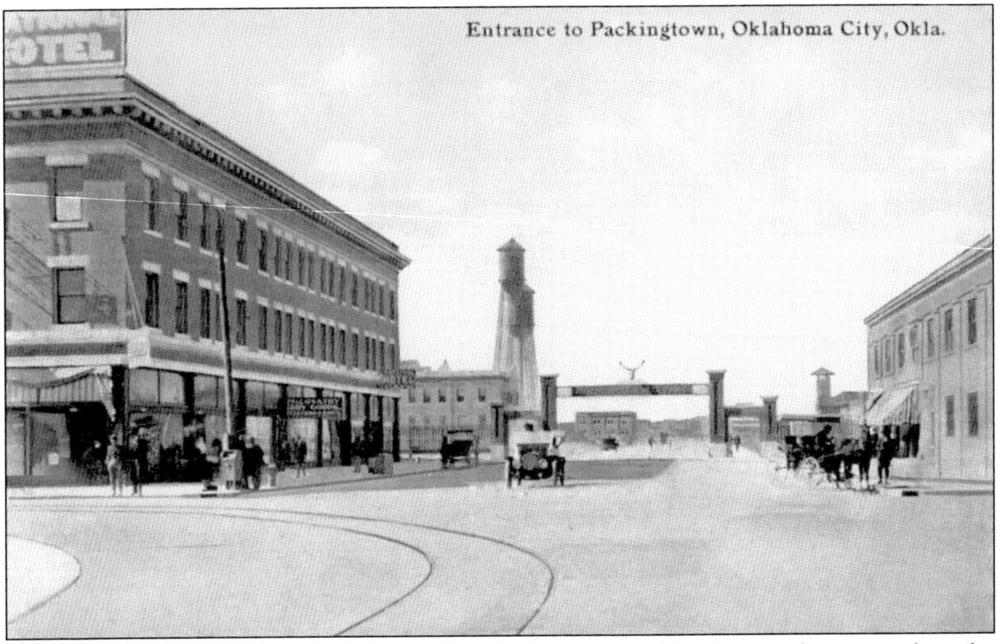

This historic picture postcard of the stockyards shows several businesses that catered to the farmer and rancher who brought their livestock to market. It was a gathering place for families as well. This image of the entrance to the stockyards was taken in 1914, five years after the packing plants were founded. This image was published by Sadler and Pennington of Oklahoma City. (Courtesy Oklahoma Historical Society.)

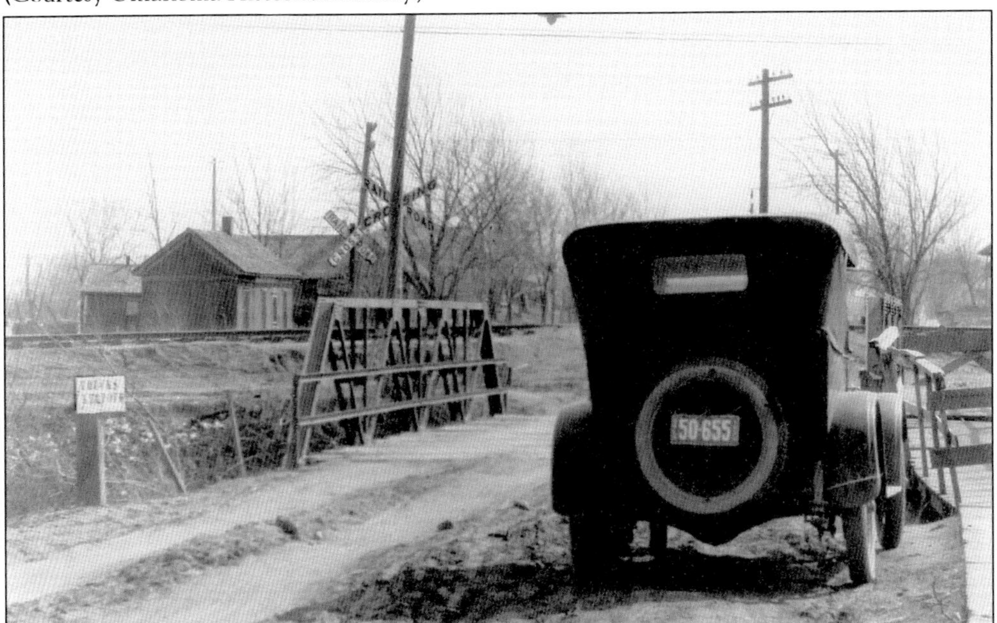

In the early years before and after statehood, Oklahoma City, and in particular Capitol Hill, had very few paved roads. This one-lane iron bridge with a dirt road leading to and from the bridge is an excellent example of the poor system of roads that beset the traveler. This image is probably from around 1920. (Courtesy Capitol Hill Beacon.)

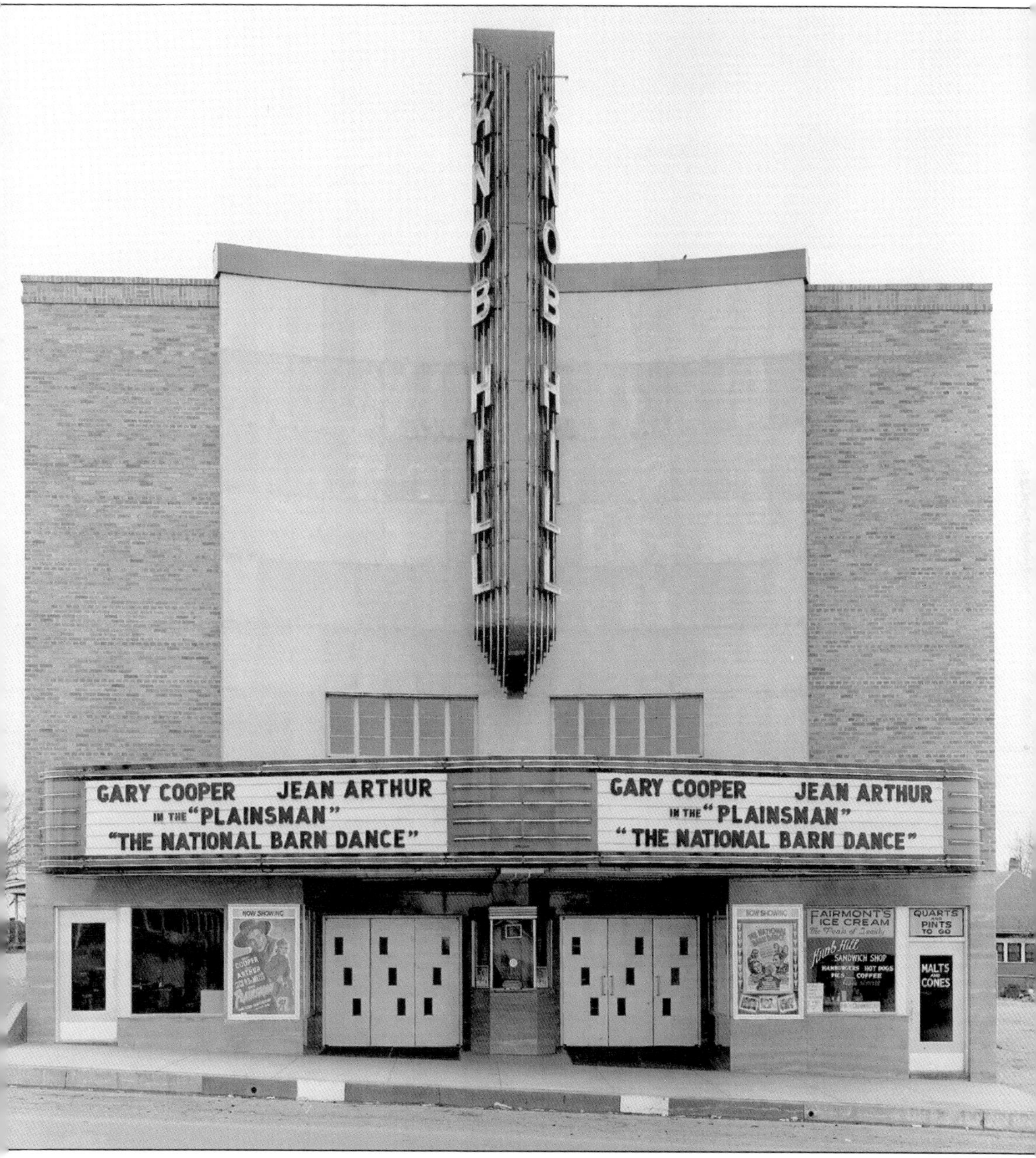

By the 1950s, Capitol Hill had at least three motion picture theaters. One building that still stands, but no longer serves as a venue for entertainment, is the Knob Hill Theater located at 404 West Commerce Street. When this photograph was taken, Phyllis Clancy was the theater manager. This photograph was taken by Barney Hillerman in the 1950s. (Courtesy Oklahoma Historical Society.)

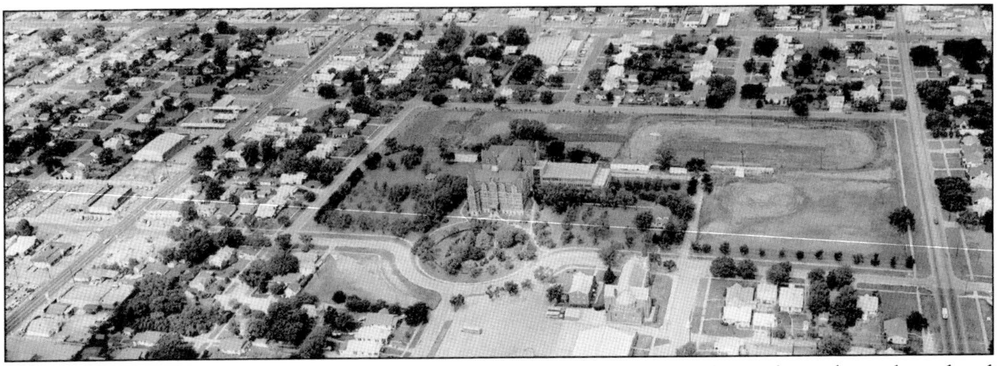

This aerial view of the grounds surrounding Mount St. Mary's Academy shows how the school has expended over the last 70-plus years. The original building can be seen in the center of the image, with new additions that have been constructed as the school has grown over the years. The photograph also documents how the neighborhood along Southwest Twenty-eighth Street and Shartel Avenue has grown as well. This image was photographed by Barney Hillerman in the 1970s. (Courtesy Oklahoma Historical Society.)

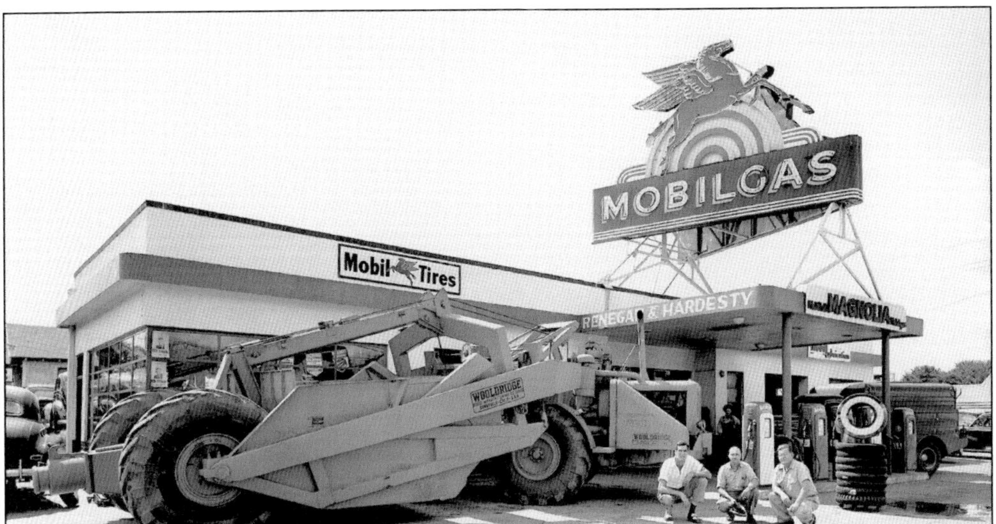

This image depicts the transition from Magnolia Petroleum Company to Mobil Oil. The flying monarch was still the symbol of the company and is as ornate as company logos come. This service station was located at Southwest Twenty-ninth Street and South Robinson Avenue. The photograph was taken by noted commercial photographer Ray Jacoby on June 29, 1948. (Courtesy Oklahoma Historical Society.)

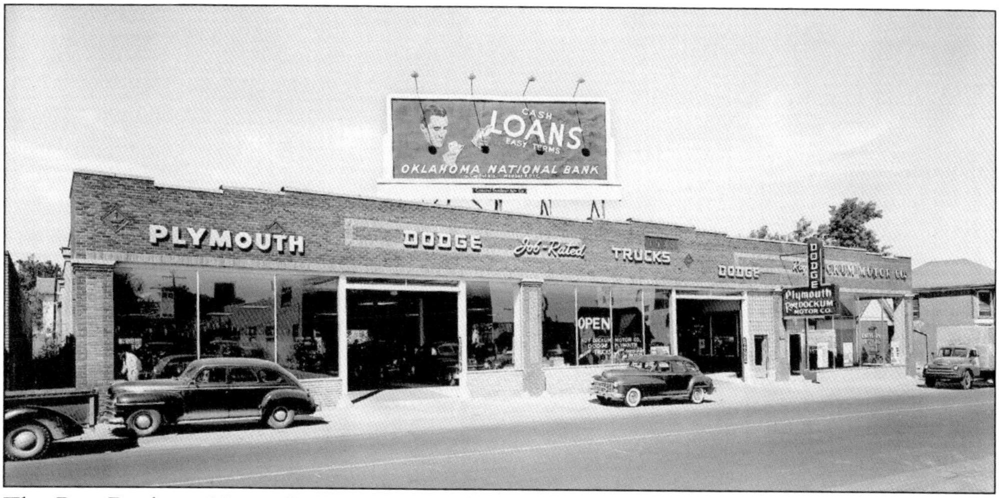

The Roy Dockum Motor Company was a fixture in Capitol Hill for many years. Located at 2205 South Robinson Avenue, Dockum sold Plymouth and Dodge products. In later years, he switched to Pontiac models and continued in car sales until the 1980s. This image was taken by Ray Jacoby in September 1948. (Courtesy Oklahoma Historical Society.)

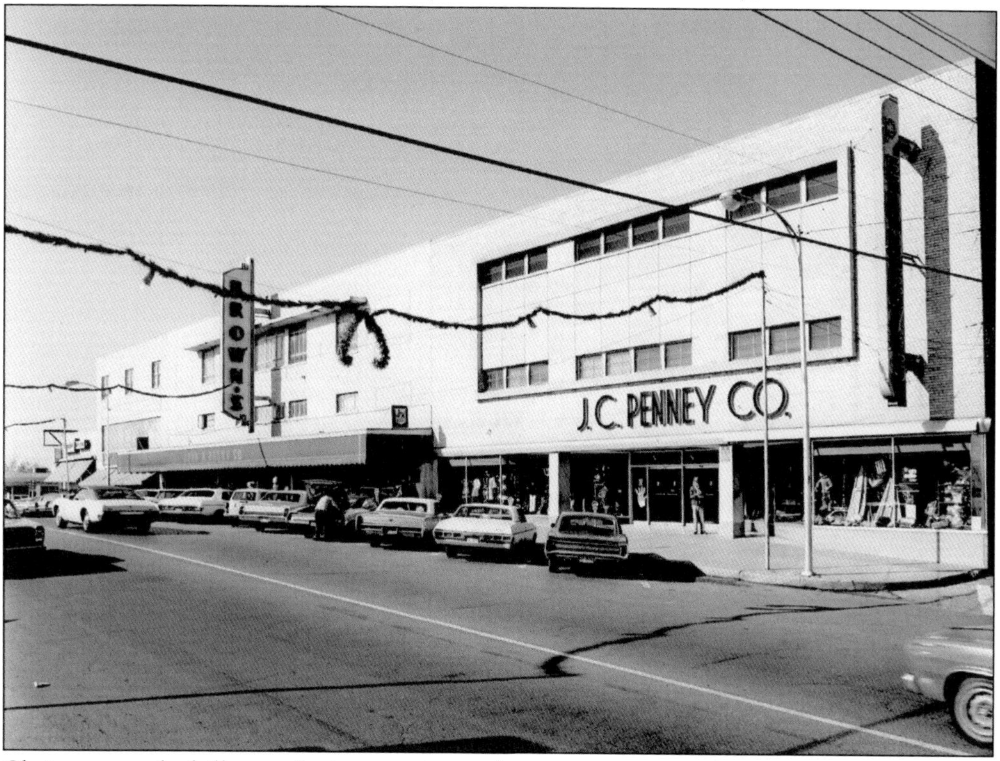

Christmas on the hill was a festive occasion as department stores such as J. C. Penney Company and local merchant John A. Brown served customers for miles around until the first shopping mall to be constructed, at Interstates 35 and 240, siphoned off business to the point that each store relocated in the 1980s. From that point on, Capitol Hill has struggled to maintain a presence as a business district. This photograph was taken sometime in the 1970s before Crossroads Mall had a major impact on the retail businesses on the hill. (Courtesy Oklahoma Historical Society.)

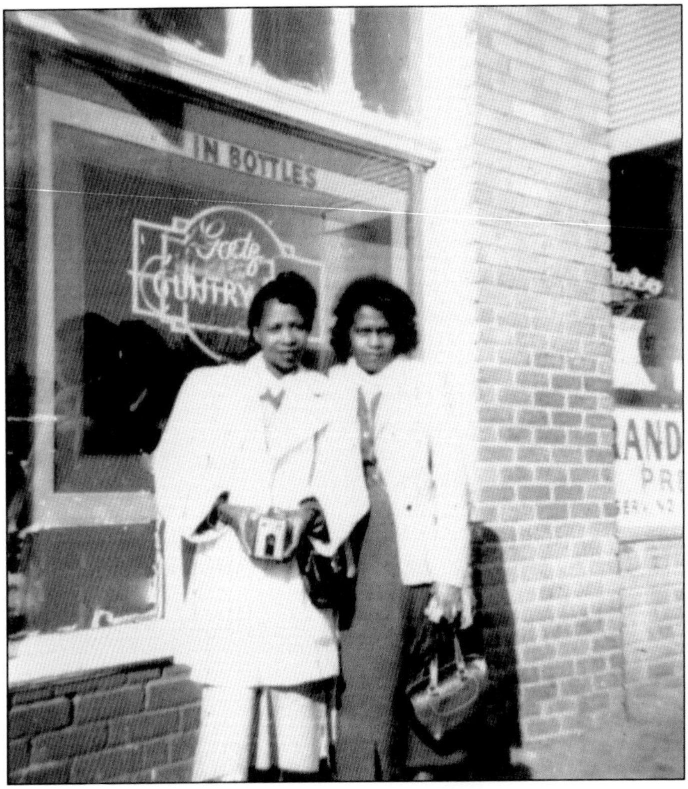

Seen here are two young African American ladies on Second Street in front of Randolph Drug Company as they appear to be going to a social event. The photographer and ladies are unknown; however, the photograph is from August 1952. (Courtesy Oklahoma Historical Society.)

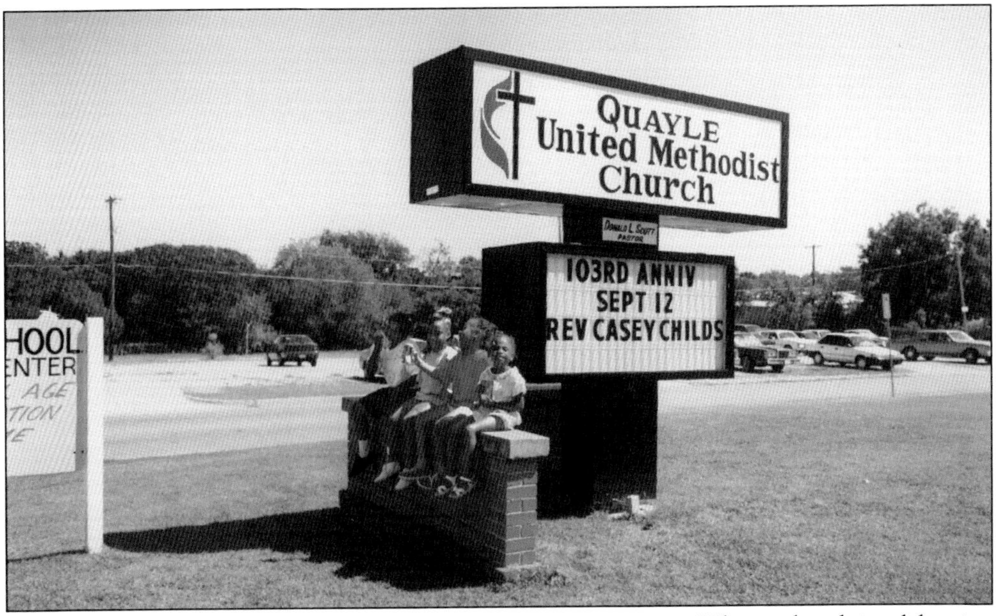

Anniversaries are special events for people, groups, or organizations. When a church is celebrating more than a century of ministry to the community it is a very special event. Here are several young people attending the 103rd anniversary of the Quayle United Methodist Church located at 5001 North Everest Avenue. The special event took place on September 12, 1994, and was photographed by James C. Gatewood. (Courtesy Oklahoma Historical Society.)

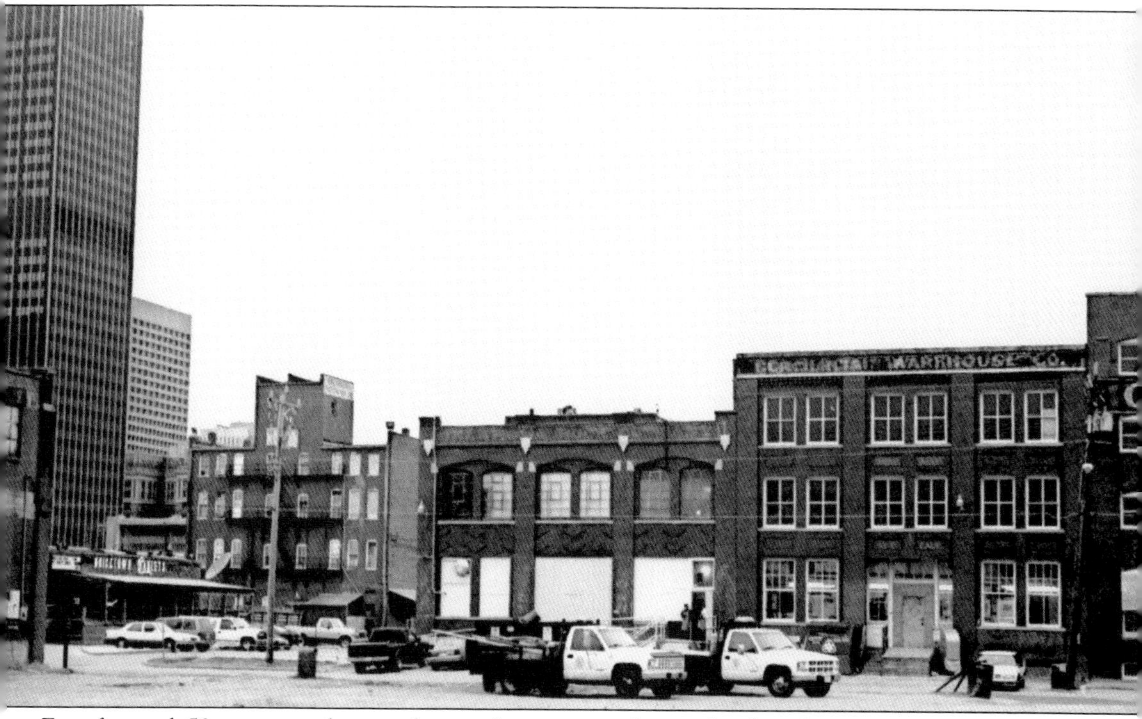

Fast forward 50 years to the warehouse district, now being developed at Bricktown. Here, looking toward California Avenue from Reno Avenue, are several buildings destined to be renovated for business enterprises. Bricktown has been and continues to be, in 2007, a success story. On the southern edge of the district, new structures have been built to accommodate a growing customer base. Business interests such as Bass Pro Shop, Harkins Theatre, Toby Keith's restaurant, and the latest hotel, a Marriott Residence that has opened at the beginning of 2007, have Bricktown brimming with energy. This photograph was taken by W. D. Welge in 1995. (Courtesy Oklahoma Historical Society.)

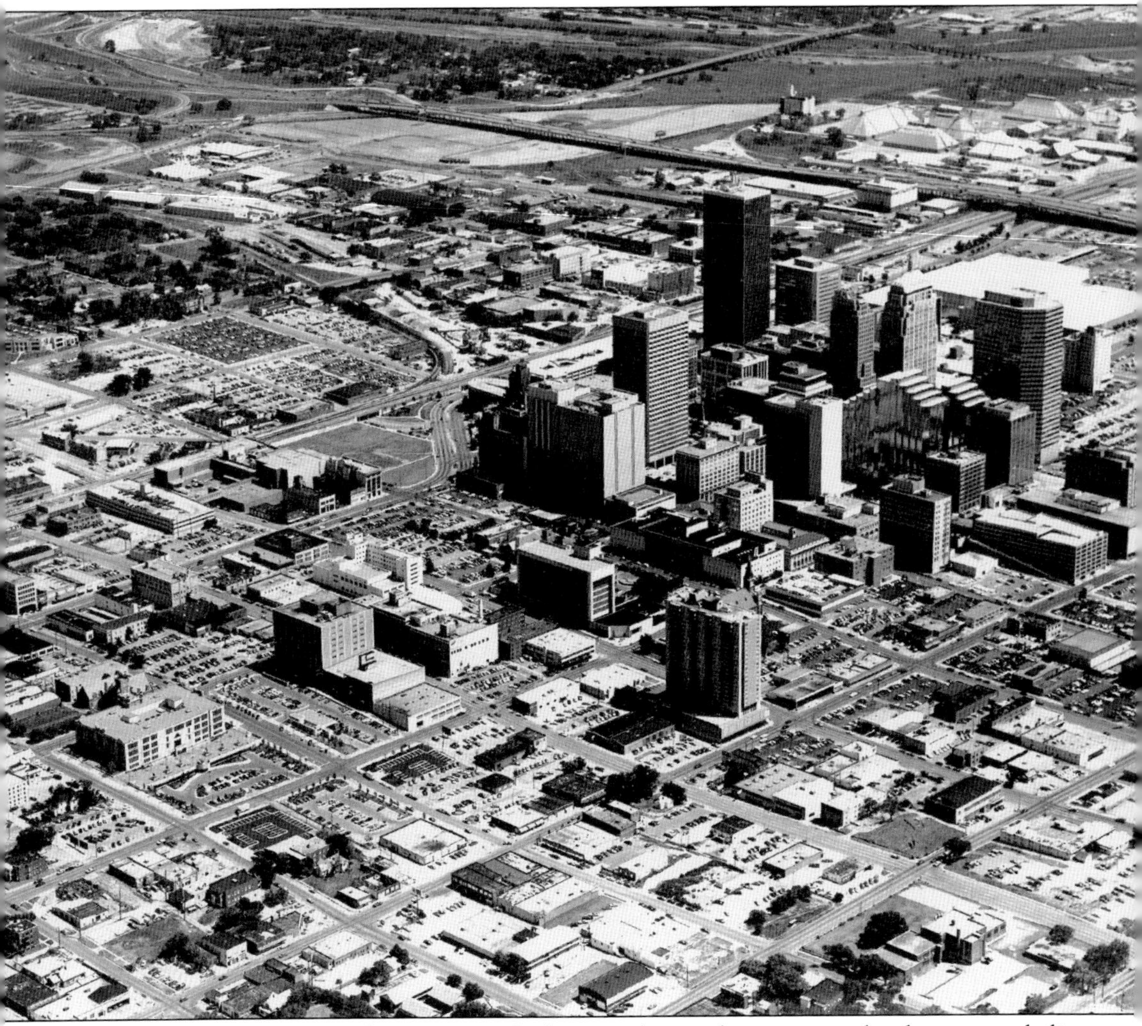

This aerial view of Oklahoma City is looking to the southeast across the downtown skyline. Seen here is the Murrah Federal Building near the very center of the photograph, just two blocks east (to the left) is Broadway, from Northwest Fifth to Eighth Streets. The Oklahoma Publishing Company Building is visible just left of the curved roadway, renamed E. K. Gaylord Boulevard, that runs into Broadway. One can also see in the upper left-hand corner a portion of Second Street or Deep Deuce. And lastly, in the upper center of the photograph is an excellent view of the warehouse district before its reincarnation as Bricktown in the mid-1980s. Urban renewal was nearing completion, with the MAPS some 20 years yet to come. But downtown Oklahoma City had changed dramatically. With MAPS and MAPS for Kids, much has been achieved to create a more vibrant city that all residents can be proud of. This image was shot by commercial photographer Ray Jacoby in the late 1970s. (Courtesy Oklahoma Historical Society.)

BIBLIOGRAPHY

Blackburn, Bob L., Arn Henderson, and Melvina Thurman. *The Physical Legacy: Buildings of Oklahoma County 1889 to 1931*. Oklahoma City, OK: Southwestern Heritage Press, 1980.

Blackburn, Bob L. "Red Brick Warehouses." National Register of Historic Places listing. Oklahoma State Historic Preservation Office, Oklahoma City, 1983.

Calhoon, John R., R. Brett James, Jerry Hunter, and Todd Scott. "Automobile Alley Historic District." National Register of Historic Places listing. Oklahoma State Historic Preservation Office, Oklahoma City, 1999.

Faulk, Odie B., and William D. Welge. *Oklahoma: A Rich Heritage*. Sun Valley, CA: American Historical Press, 2004.

Geran, Monica. "Fiat Lux." *Interior Design*, 1997.

Kerr, W. F., and Ina Gainer. *The Story of Oklahoma City Oklahoma*. Chicago: S. J. Clarke Publishing Company, 1922.

Meacham, Maryjo, Kerri Robinett, and John R. Calhoon. "Littlepage Building." National Register of Historic Places listing. Oklahoma State Historic Preservation Office, Oklahoma City, 1995.

Meredith, Howard L., Kent Ruth, Melvena K. Thurman, and Bill E. Peavler. "Stockyards City Historic District." National Register of Historic Places listing. Oklahoma State Historic Preservation Office, Oklahoma City, 1979.

Moore, Kendrick. *Oklahoma City African-American Discovery Guide*. Oklahoma City, OK: African American Trail of Tears, Tours, 2000.

Morris, John W., ed. *Geography of Oklahoma*. Vol. 6. Oklahoma City, OK: Oklahoma Historical Society, 1977.

———. *Cities of Oklahoma*. Vol. 11. Oklahoma City, OK: Oklahoma Historical Society, 1979.

The Negro City Directory. Oklahoma City, OK: Oklahoma City Negro Chamber of Commerce, Sponsors, 1941.

Polk, R. L. and Company, Dallas, TX: R. L. Polk and Company Publishers.

Robinett, Kerri, Maryjo Meacham, and John R. Calhoon. "Elks Victory Lodge-Ruby's Grill Building." National Register of Historic Places listing. Oklahoma State Historic Preservation Office, Oklahoma City, 1995.

Robinett, Kerri, Maryjo Meacham, and John R. Calhoon. "Haywood Building." National Register of Historic Places listing. Oklahoma State Historic Preservation Office, Oklahoma City, 1995.

Royal, Gary. "Melvin Luster Home." National Register of Historic Places listing. Oklahoma State Historic Preservation Office, Oklahoma City, 1982.

Warden's Official Oklahoma City Directory. Oklahoma City, OK: Warden Printing Company, 1912.

Worley-Friss Directory of Oklahoma City. Oklahoma City, OK: Press of Oklahoma Engraving and Printing Company, 1911.

Discover Thousands of Local History Books Featuring Millions of Vintage Images

Arcadia Publishing, the leading local history publisher in the United States, is committed to making history accessible and meaningful through publishing books that celebrate and preserve the heritage of America's people and places.

Find more books like this at
www.arcadiapublishing.com

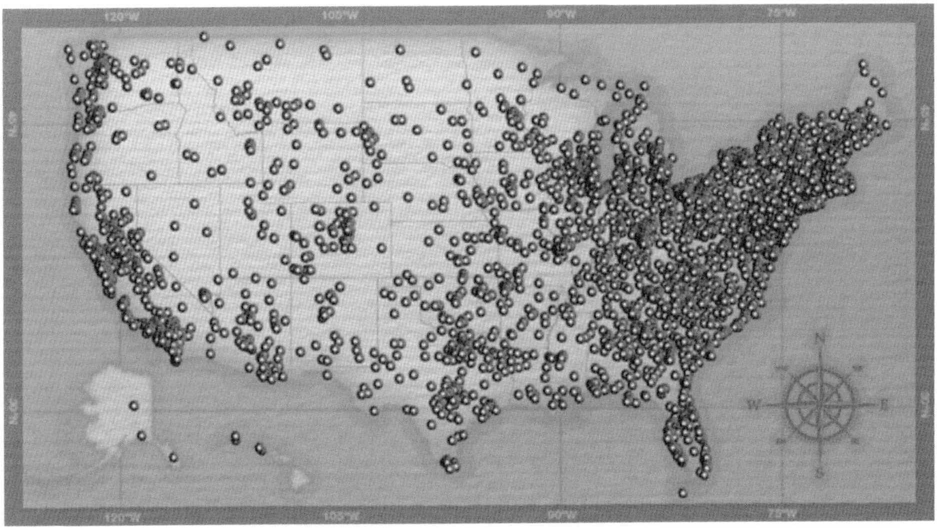

Search for your hometown history, your old stomping grounds, and even your favorite sports team.

Consistent with our mission to preserve history on a local level, this book was printed in South Carolina on American-made paper and manufactured entirely in the United States. Products carrying the accredited Forest Stewardship Council (FSC) label are printed on 100 percent FSC-certified paper.

MADE IN THE USA